Feeding the People in Wartime Britain

Food in Modern History: Traditions and Innovations

Series Editors:
Peter Scholliers
Amy Bentley

This new monograph series pays serious attention to food as a focal point in historical events from the late 18th century to present day. Employing the lens of technology broadly construed, the series highlights the nutritional, social, political, cultural, and economic transformations of food around the globe. It features new scholarship that considers ever-intensifying and accelerating tensions between tradition and innovation that characterize the modern era. The editors are particularly committed to publishing manuscripts featuring geographical areas currently underrepresented in English-language academic publications, including the Global South, particularly Africa and Asia, as well as monographs featuring indigenous and under-represented groups, and non-western societies.

Published:
Rebellious Cooks and Recipe Writing in Communist Bulgaria, Albena Shkodrova (2021)
Food and Aviation in the Twentieth Century: The Pan American Ideal, Bryce Evans (2021)
Champagne in Britain, 1800-1914: How the British Transformed a French Luxury, Graham Harding (2021)

Feeding the People in Wartime Britain

Bryce Evans

BLOOMSBURY ACADEMIC
LONDON • NEW YORK • OXFORD • NEW DELHI • SYDNEY

BLOOMSBURY ACADEMIC
Bloomsbury Publishing Plc
50 Bedford Square, London, WC1B 3DP, UK
1385 Broadway, New York, NY 10018, USA
29 Earlsfort Terrace, Dublin 2, Ireland

BLOOMSBURY, BLOOMSBURY ACADEMIC and the Diana logo are
trademarks of Bloomsbury Publishing Plc

First published in Great Britain 2022
This paperback edition published 2023

Copyright © Bryce Evans, 2022

Bryce Evans has asserted his right under the Copyright, Designs and
Patents Act, 1988, to be identified as Author of this work.

For legal purposes the Acknowledgements on p. viii constitute an extension
of this copyright page.

Cover image: American Lease and Lend Food being eaten by workers in
Liverpool, UK, 1941. Photo by Ministry of Food Official Photographer/Imperial
War Museums via Getty Images.

All rights reserved. No part of this publication may be reproduced or transmitted
in any form or by any means, electronic or mechanical, including photocopying,
recording, or any information storage or retrieval system, without
prior permission in writing from the publishers.

Bloomsbury Publishing Plc does not have any control over, or responsibility for, any
third-party websites referred to or in this book. All internet addresses given in this
book were correct at the time of going to press. The author and publisher regret
any inconvenience caused if addresses have changed or sites have ceased
to exist, but can accept no responsibility for any such changes.

A catalogue record for this book is available from the British Library.

Library of Congress Cataloging-in-Publication Data
Names: Evans, Bryce, author.
Title: Feeding the people in wartime Britain / Bryce Evans.
Identifiers: LCCN 2021054364 | ISBN 9781350259713 (hardback) | ISBN
9781350259720 (pdf) | ISBN 9781350259737 (epub)
Subjects: LCSH: Emergency mass feeding–Great Britain–History–20th
century. | World War, 1939–1945–Food supply–Great Britain. | World
War, 1914–1918–Food supply–Great Britain.
Classification: LCC TX946 .E93 2022 | DDC
363.8/2094109044–dc23/eng/20211129
LC record available at https://lccn.loc.gov/2021054364

ISBN:	HB:	978-1-3502-5971-3
	PB:	978-1-3502-5975-1
	ePDF:	978-1-3502-5972-0
	eBook:	978-1-3502-5973-7

Series: Food in Modern History: Traditions and Innovations

Typeset by Integra Software Services Pvt. Ltd.

To find out more about our authors and books visit www.bloomsbury.com
and sign up for our newsletters.

Contents

List of figures	vii
Acknowledgements	viii
Introduction: Emergency public feeding in twentieth- and twenty-first-century Britain	1
The 'National Kitchen'	2
The 'British Restaurant'	3
Public feeding	4
The state's role	5
Eating out	7
Emergency measures	8
1 British food and feeding up to the First World War	11
Introduction	11
Faith and consumption	11
Female voluntarism, class and gender	13
Scientific advance, class and nutritional reform	16
Humanitarianism, socialism and the New Liberalism	18
Conclusion	20
2 The birth of emergency public feeding in the First World War	21
Introduction	21
From soup kitchens to communal kitchens	23
The radical threat of communal dining	29
Avoiding the taint of charity and establishing the female role: the organization of the new National Kitchens	34
Conclusion	39
3 The development of emergency public feeding in the First World War	41
Introduction	41
Food Control Committees and the forward march of public feeding	41
The Peripatetic Piewoman: A case study in female leadership in public feeding	46

	Food reformers: Nutritional instruction and egalitarian eating	50
	'Civilizational Value'? Arnold Bennett versus GK Chesterton	56
	Resistance grows	60
	Conclusion	66
4	British food and feeding in the interwar period	71
	Introduction	71
	Public-feeding limps on as British society changes	71
	Nutrition, the body and national health	73
	Communal feeding as communism and the female call for 'permanent relief'	75
	International comparisons	77
	Conclusion	81
5	The birth of emergency public feeding in the Second World War	83
	Introduction	83
	The British Restaurant is born	85
	Nutritional reform	90
	British Restaurants: How they looked and how they worked	94
	Left/Right political divisions	103
	Conclusion	110
6	The development of emergency public feeding in the Second World War	111
	Introduction	111
	Nutritional reformers versus the sausage roll	112
	A plethora of schemes	118
	Eating out with Tommy Trinder (and Barbara Cartland)	122
	Utility – 'marginal' to the war effort, or more significant?	127
	Conclusion	130
	Conclusion: Emergency feeding in historical perspective	135
	Notes	142
	Bibliography	169
	Index	177

Figures

2.1	David Alfred Thomas, 1st Viscount Rhondda, Minister of Food Control 19 June 1917–3 July 1918	25
2.2	Halifax National Kitchen, 1917	32
2.3	National Kitchen, London, 1918	34
3.1	Florence Horsburgh (1889–1969)	48
3.2	Daily Mirror, 15 March 1918	48
3.3	Eustace Miles (1868–1948)	53
3.4	A bustling National Kitchen in Bow, London, 1918	60
3.5	A cheery Lord Rhondda (left) opens the shutters of a new National Kitchen in January 1918. Within six months Rhondda was dead and his National Kitchens in terminal decline.	68
5.1	Flora Solomon (1895–1984)	84
5.2	Public feeding on Clydeside following a bombing raid, 1942	89
5.3	A British Restaurant in Ilford is decorated with a painting from the royal collection, Buckingham Palace	95
5.4	Queue at a London Citizens' Kitchen, 1940	103
6.1	Eating out in Whitehall, London, 1943	112
6.2	London tube shelter canteen, 1942	117
6.3	Frederick James Marquis, 1st Earl of Woolton (1883–1964)	128

Acknowledgements

I wish to gratefully acknowledge the generous financial support for this research from the following organizations:

The Wellcome Trust, The Arts and Humanities Research Council, the Pasold Trust, the Scouloudi Trust, the Royal Historical Society and Liverpool Hope University.

I am grateful to Professor Deborah Sugg-Ryan for her advice on the copyright and provenance of certain images which she sourced for an online article on British Restaurants.

Thanks also to the many archivists and librarians who assisted this research. Particular thanks for extraordinary generosity in terms of access and advice are due to the staff of:

The National Archives; Churchill Archives Centre, Churchill College Cambridge; Marks and Spencer Archive, Leeds; Glasgow Caledonian University Archives; Liverpool John Moores University Archives; People's History Museum Archives, Manchester.

At Bloomsbury Academic, I wish to thank all who assisted me with this work; I am particularly indebted to my long-suffering editor, Maddie Holder, to Abigail Lane, and to the series editors Peter Scholliers and Amy Bentley for their faith in the project.

Thanks to my fellow Churchill Fellow and constant supporter, Lindsay Graham, and to Marsha Smith and Lisa Pine. I am grateful to the *Journal of War and Culture Studies*, published by Taylor and Francis, for permission to reproduce small sections of this book which originally appeared in a 2017 article.

Lastly, in love and gratitude to my family, in particular Peter Evans and Ros Evans for his work on the images.

And to Eileen Evans, to whom this book is dedicated.

Introduction

Emergency public feeding in twentieth- and twenty-first-century Britain

This book is about feeding the British public in time of national emergency. The Coronavirus pandemic of 2020, a national crisis popularly dubbed 'the greatest emergency since the Second World War', saw the unexpected re-emergence of a form of emergency national public food provision in Britain, with central and local government, the voluntary sector, the private retail trade and the armed forces collaborating to provide 'emergency food parcels' to the doorsteps of millions of people deemed 'most vulnerable' according to National Health Service records. This initiative was followed by the 'Eat Out to Help Out' scheme, which operated in August 2020, through which the state subsidized dining out in private restaurants. Yet despite the frequent mention of how 'unprecedented' the Coronavirus emergency was, the 2020 measures were preceded in the twentieth century by the two most significant instances of emergency public feeding in modern British history, which were witnessed during the First and Second World Wars (1914–18 and 1939–45).

The public-feeding schemes of the two world wars were rolled out, similarly, on a national scale. They excited great political and cultural debate: welcomed by some as symbolic of a Brave New World of communal consumption, they were derided by others for the very same reason. Whether loved or loathed, the experience of public feeding, or communal dining, or social eating was something shared by tens of millions of British people in both the First World War and the Second World War. And yet this major episode in British social history has all but disappeared from both the popular and written memory of the wars. When it comes to food and the wartime 'Home Front', the story of public feeding has largely been nudged aside and forgotten, overshadowed by queues and ration books. This book seeks to fill a major gap in historical knowledge surrounding these measures by providing the first in-depth comparative study of these wartime schemes.

In doing so, it is indebted to the pioneer work of the semi-official historian William Beveridge and the official war historian Richard J. Hammond, who both briefly considered emergency public feeding in comparative perspective.[1] Like these authors, this book confines its focus to the life of public-feeding schemes during the time of the conflicts themselves, or the emergencies 'proper' of wartime, rather than their peacetime afterlives. It is therefore divided into two sections, one examining emergency public feeding in the First World War (1914–1918) and the other examining emergency public feeding in the Second World War (1939–1945). This study begins by introducing and defining the term public feeding, distinguishing it from rationing and 'eating out' more broadly. It goes on to consider public feeding as a policy issue at the turn of the twentieth century, before outlining the first sustained attempt by the British state to undertake emergency feeding, which occurred during the First World War.

The 'National Kitchen'

The National Kitchen of the First World War was the state's attempt to break with Victorian feeding models. The food supply disruption and price inflation caused by the war demanded something more than the old voluntary stereotype of the 'Lady Bountiful' doling out soup to the 'deserving poor'. Civil servants at the newly formed Ministry of Food thought that they had seen the future, and it was one in which private dining might die out altogether in favour of public feeding; the experiments in emergency feeding that they oversaw took the form of both seated communal eating and the mobile distribution of food. The proponents and practitioners of the new public feeding were diverse, including an eccentric upper-class woman who fed the East End while riding a donkey and blowing a tin trumpet, but the role of such 'Ladies of the Ladel' gradually became subsumed by a more professionalized and statist management of mass feeding.

This process was riven by tensions between the Ministry of Food's director of the newly developed 'National Kitchens' – self-made-man and Yorkshire tramway magnate Charles Spencer – and food control bodies. Nutritional reformers, too, were recruited by the government; their titular leader was the acclaimed outdoorsman Eustace Miles, who sought to turn a British populace reluctant to embrace the greater consumption of vegetables towards a diet regarded as healthier. Meanwhile, the great literary figures of the age considered how emergency public feeding might become a feature of everyday life and agonized over whether it threatened civilizational decline. They need not have fretted: in contrast to the Second World War, when retail guru Frederick Marquis (Lord Woolton) was appointed Minister of Food, the failure of the government to properly incorporate the private retail trade in the emergency feeding schemes of the First World War would contribute to their abrupt demise, a death hastened by the extension of rationing and the influenza pandemic of 1918.

The 'British Restaurant'

Emergency feeding was, however, to reappear a short time later. In 1936 William Beveridge, Director of the London School of Economics and Political Science (LSE), composed a landmark memorandum, grim yet accurate in its prediction of the coming aerial destruction of war and calling for the re-establishment of emergency feeding schemes. During the Second World War, the British state duly funded both mass canteen dining and emergency public-feeding ventures in air raid shelters and schools. Prime Minister Winston Churchill famously re-christened communal dining centres 'British Restaurants', arguing that the Ministry of Food's proposed title 'communal feeding centre' was suggestive of communism and the workhouse. Although it's hard to disagree with Churchill in this instance, disagreements between Churchill and his Minister of Food Woolton – aggravated by the Prime Minister's penchant for fine dining – would shape emergency wartime feeding. Once again, the Ministry's nutritionists were eager to get the Great British public eating more vegetables; once again, public resistance to healthier fare was pronounced. The reintroduction of emergency feeding was accompanied by similar anxieties over its civilizational and cultural value and many British Restaurants therefore incorporated specially commissioned artwork and attractive decoration. While it might be assumed that the political left would champion communal feeding and the political right dismiss it, the political reception was more nuanced and examples of its proponents – from the writer Barbara Cartland to Margaret Thatcher's father, grocer Alf Roberts – demonstrate this.

Alongside sit-down dining, the emergency mobile distribution of food was undertaken by the women of the glamourized 'Queen's Messenger Convoys'. Like in the First World War, emergency feeding featured colourful champions, most notably the redoubtable Flora Solomon of Marks and Spencer. The expanded bureaucracy of the Second World War allowed for an often confusing network of public-feeding schemes – from British Restaurants to Air Raid Shelter Canteens, yet the slick propaganda of Britain's Ministry of Food played a leading role in the relative success of public feeding during Britain's second great national emergency of the twentieth century.

Public feeding

The re-emergence of the term 'emergency feeding' in Britain would not occur again until the early twenty-first century, when many of the poorest people in society started to receive sustenance via charitable 'food banks', a system revolving around what was referred to as the 'emergency food parcel'. In early twenty-first-century Britain, the most basic and common form of emergency food parcel, or food bank, system operated as follows: food donations from supermarkets were distributed locally by volunteers for private charities; these volunteers provided free non-perishable foods to members of the public who presented themselves at the food bank; in return, such recipients were usually required to provide evidence of their neediness via a referral letter from a medical professional or a state official; the food was then taken home for private preparation and consumption.[2] In the popular imagination the food bank, a North American import, seemed to have arrived on the British social scene 'overnight', to quote one observer, and although it elicited plenty of discussion, such debate was frequently marked by an obliviousness about its historical precedents. The notion of an emergency food parcel prompted debates about how best to ensure the general public was adequately and nutritiously fed. What, for example, was the proper role of the public and the private sector? Should government provide greater nutritional and administrative oversight of these charitable schemes? Did the emergence of the food bank represent the return of 'Victorian' notions of the 'deserving' and 'undeserving' poor? Or was the food bank an example of voluntary action filling a gap in state welfare provision that had been widening since the end of the Second World War?[3]

This book does not concern itself specifically with these contemporary policy debates, but it does seek to address a notable and recurrent tendency in the broader discussion around both food banks and the emergency feeding of the 2020 Coronavirus crisis: the amnesia around the most significant form of public feeding in Britain's recent history – the wartime schemes of the twentieth century.

To do so, the term 'public feeding' first demands explanation. In this work, it is taken to be broadly analogous to alternative descriptions such as social eating, communal dining or, to employ an anthropological term, commensality. These terms are occasionally used in this book because, at the most basic level, all refer to the act of people eating food together and that is what, at heart, this study concerns itself with. And yet public feeding is here defined as something distinct from the family meal because it is *public and not private.* Similarly, it is considered more *organized* than, for example, a private restaurant meal with friends while – at the same time – more *social* than the basic food bank model as outlined above. Reflecting the Christian ethic underlying the 'common table' of medieval and early modern Europe, in the Victorian period public feeding tended to be a voluntary preserve targeted at the poor, with faith-based groups operating soup kitchens in Britain's expanding urban centres. Normally, such ventures were preoccupied with the moralizing goal of 'improving' the character of the impoverished.[4] At the same time, the new nutritional sciences emerging in the nineteenth century were changing the ways in which medical professionals and the public viewed the consumption of food. Nutritional chemistry, which expanded as a discipline in the late Victorian period, presented empirical rules and standards for the population at large, displacing the emphasis on an individual's constitution found in earlier dietetic theories.[5]

The state's role

A similar merging of the moral and the scientific emerged following the shock of Britain's relatively poor performance in the Anglo-Boer war of 1899–1902. The shadow of the Boer war loomed across the Edwardian period; a major enquiry into physical deterioration in 1904 highlighted the extent to which poor nutrition and overcrowding in Britain's towns and cities explained the disproportionate number of recruits deemed unfit for military service in the conflict.[6] In a subsequent House of Lords debate, anxieties about national deterioration echoed some of the older demands for 'improvement', with concerns voiced that Britain was home to 'a race which is slowly slackening in its speed and diminishing its output of power'.[7] The attendant moral panic did, however, result in a significant form of action from central government on public health, and public feeding specifically, when, as part of a number of measures brought in by the Liberal government elected in 1906, schools were given permission to offer meals to their pupils.

As discussed subsequently, the total war contexts of the First World War (1914–1918) and the Second World War (1939–1945) represented a decisive shift and expansion in what constituted public feeding, with central government for the first time taking a significant role in sustaining its people. These were times of national emergency and therefore public feeding took on emergency dimensions. In Britain during the Second World War the high streets of most big towns and cities featured at least one state-subsidized 'British Restaurant', the inspiration for which came from their First World War predecessors, 'National Kitchens', both of which are discussed extensively in this work. However, in British popular memory of the world wars, particularly the Second, food rationing has tended to dominate the historiography of food on the Home Front, overshadowing these major communal dining schemes and the other forms of emergency social feeding that took place.[8] Although rationing was less extensive than popularly imagined, its roll-out would help to determine the fate of public-feeding schemes, as is outlined later. In both world wars, rationing functioned alongside price controls, central purchasing and subsidies as part of an overarching statist approach aligning consumption with total war imperatives.[9] Although a more comprehensive form of rationing was not introduced until the latter stages of the First World War, in both conflicts it would prove the central plank in the state's efforts to regulate and control the public's consumption of food. Despite rationing assuming many historical forms,[10] it is here defined – in its classic twentieth-century wartime application – as a paper-based state-run system of vouchers redeemable for food at retail venues. It is therefore considered as a separate phenomenon to public feeding, although their inter-relationship is outlined in the pages that follow.

The early- to mid-twentieth-century turn towards public feeding/communal dining/social eating/commensality was not restricted to Britain's shores. During the world wars of the twentieth century and the interwar crisis in between many national governments endorsed and supported major feeding programs to combat supply disruption and price inflation. For many European governments, the idea behind such schemes was a better nourished, physically fitter populace: one which dovetailed neatly with martial priorities. Therefore mass public feeding was a feature not only of democratic countries such as Britain, but authoritarian polities such as Nazi Germany, Fascist Italy and the Soviet Union, all of which endorsed communal dining, whether politically justified – in the Soviet case – to liberate women from 'kitchen slavery' and challenge capitalist privatized individualism or – in the fascist case – to act as a symbol of a more traditionalist and völkisch national idiom.[11] As these examples suggest, although public feeding was often reduced to its nutritional aims, it was an inherently social and political act, attracting attendant social and political anxieties and ideologies. Britain, as outlined in this book, was no exception to this rule.

Eating out

Whether the twenty-first-century food bank model or the emergency food parcel scheme of the Coronavirus crisis can be said to constitute public feeding in a similar way to the above examples is highly questionable. Essentially, both were based around the 'emergency food parcel', handed over to recipients in the form of tins and boxes of food in a plastic bag or box. The provision of the food may appear public, but the preparation and consumption of the food generally occur later – in private, at home – and consumed by the recipient and his or her immediate family. Some early twenty-first-century food banks, however, did incorporate cafes where meals were offered at economical prices and the re-emergence of food charity in twenty-first-century Britain was accompanied by a number of social enterprises operating not as food banks but as 'community kitchens' in which food, often donated by businesses, was prepared and served in the form of cut-price meals. Although such schemes were the preserve of *private* initiative, what gave the communal kitchen or the food bank cafe a *public* veneer is the fact that the feeding and eating were done collectively, cheaply and, crucially, outside the home.

This relates to the very notion of 'eating out' itself which, in Britain, has quite a lineage. It was chronicled by the historian John Burnett who, in 2004, published the seminal *England Eats Out*, a social history of food consumed outside the household in England from 1830 onwards. Burnett detailed how the idea of the restaurant soared in popularity in the nineteenth and early twentieth century. Associated with the great French gastronome Georges Auguste Escoffier, *haute cuisine* had a cultural impact beyond just those who could afford it, establishing the restaurant meal as a grand, and expensive, occasion.[12] Imperial Britain's leading role in the global market ensured that by the turn of the century 'the masses' could avail of cheaper and more diverse foodstuffs while wealthier sections of the population enjoyed the purchasing power to consume luxury foodstuffs. As the middle class expanded, its members developed richer and more varied dietary patterns and new types of eating venues started to emerge, most notably the Lyons chain of tea houses. Lyons provided a non-alcoholic middle way between decidedly working-class spaces of consumption like fish and chip shops, street eateries or public houses, on the one hand, and the extravagance of the upper class luxury restaurant, on the other.[13] Nonetheless, as in previous centuries, the food intake disparity between income groups persisted. Importantly, on the eve of the First World War, 'eating out' was still regarded by many as something reserved for the wealthier echelons of society.

To later policymakers devising ways in which the government might aspire to feed the population at large in hard times, the notion that to eat out was a luxury pursuit would prove both obstacle and inspiration. Could eating out become the new norm for the mass of people, not just those who could afford it? This idea, as this book details, would inspire many to look to a Brave New World of public feeding which, trialled in wartime, would in the future replace the private consumption of food forever.

Arguably, this dream became a partial reality from the 1950s onwards, when 'eating out' in an exotic venue would become accessible as never before, with Chinese and Italian restaurants becoming a fixture of British life.[14] Nonetheless, the return of forms of public feeding in twenty-first Britain exposed not only the inability of many people to afford a private restaurant meal, but also a huge gap in knowledge about twentieth-century examples of *communal eating* in Britain: the other form of 'eating out' previously consigned to posterity. Perhaps unsurprisingly, public feeding in Britain underwent its peak amidst the unequivocally 'emergency' conditions of the First and Second World Wars, which explains the focus of this study.

Emergency measures

This book argues that these wartime measures should not be written off as mere aberrations or extraordinary measures: the public-feeding schemes of wartime Britain not only carried on into peacetime, they also provide the essence of the age-old argument about whose responsibility it is to keep people fed, and how. Nonetheless, it confines itself to the wartime experience because, despite the ideals attached to public feeding, it remains largely a wartime experience, regarded as exceptional – an 'emergency' measure resorted to in times of national emergency.

This study is based upon a range of primary sources including private and corporate records, contemporary surveys of opinion, newspapers, parliamentary proceedings, ministerial records, periodicals, pamphlets and propaganda material. Feeding the public in wartime might appear at first glance a somewhat drab subject, suggestive of food queues and unpalatable substitute foodstuffs, with Prime Minister Winston Churchill famously deriding the term 'communal feeding centre' as suggestive of 'communism and the workhouse'[15]; ultimately, however, Churchill backed the idea of emergency public feeding, and the history of such schemes is anything but dull. This history is character-rich, exploring how eating out as a public endeavour was advocated by such politically diverse figures as J.B. Priestley and Barbara Cartland, to name but two. To quote another of its colourful proponents, Flora Solomon – the daughter of a multi-millionaire Russian Jewish émigré, who was instrumental in the flourishing of British communal restaurants during the Second World War – 'don't greet [the term] with a yawn. Restaurants existed, and so did communities; but put the two together and you were introducing a practice so alien to the mentality of the British people it could be likened to replacing the brick walls of the Albert Hall with glass and turning the place into a nudist colony.'[16] Solomon's reflection hints at the persistent collective amnesia that seems to distinguish public feeding in Britain whenever it is revived: the schemes she described were taking off less than twenty years after the national roll-out of public dining during the First World War.

Unlike John Burnett's study, this book concerns not just England but Britain as a whole. Like Burnett's work, however, it does not discuss 'eating out' in general. Instead, its sole focus is *emergency public feeding*: in other words, attempts by the state to feed the country's population en masse during national emergency. In line with Burnett's history, by dint of its definition of *public* this book excludes the history of feeding in institutions (such as hospitals, prisons, schools, factories, industrial sites or the armed forces) as well as the private consumption of food in the home.[17] As mentioned, state-supported feeding experiments were also witnessed in other nations during the war, but the international history surrounding wartime public-feeding schemes remains as similarly underdeveloped as in the British case; accordingly, this book restricts itself to a national focus in the hope that in the future it will form a contributory part of a more comparative and extensive international historiography of public feeding in modern history.

1

British food and feeding up to the First World War

Introduction

The wartime public-eating schemes discussed in this book stemmed from a variety of policy and ethical impulses that can be traced back to the late nineteenth and early twentieth century: female voluntarism, faith-based and humanitarian initiatives, nutritional science and the new wave of municipal liberalism in Victorian and Edwardian England. There were flashes of patriotic conservatism too, and pangs of socialism. As this book goes on to explain, wartime public feeding presents a pronounced break with these earlier trends in a number of ways; however, in order to properly assess the phenomenon, it is necessary to contextualize British food and feeding prior to the First World War and in the early stages of the conflict.

Faith and consumption

Although distinct from its Victorian antecedents, wartime public feeding owed a debt to the pioneer faith-based efforts of the nineteenth century. The Salvation Army is of particular relevance. The organization was founded in London's East End in 1865 by William Booth, a former Methodist minister who argued that the Anglican church, and his own Methodist congregation, ought to intensify their mission to the poor in urban Britain. As will become evident, traces of the Salvation Army's approach are visible in First World War feeding: from the communal feeding model of the 'soup kitchen', to the emphasis on discipline and organization, the absence of alcohol and the central role of women.[1] Female initiative was conspicuous in the Salvation Army, with Catherine Booth

(William's well-educated, articulate and radical wife) doing much to define the interventionist ideals which her daughter, Evangeline, would carry on in practice.

The influence of that nineteenth-century Christian yearning for authenticity of experience and the purposeful public life can be seen in wartime society, too. Alongside the statist measures of the First World War, voluntary and philanthropic effort, which was often led by faith groups, was mobilized beyond state boundaries with 18,000 new charities founded during the conflict.[2] Many of these charitable endeavours centred around food, whether in the form of food parcels for soldiers or soup kitchens for the poor. The volunteers of the Salvation Army in the Edwardian era continued to follow the idea that the organization's founder Booth had established: Jesus had called on the faithful to redeem public life; this redemption would be achieved first through soup, then later salvation. Soup, as the first step, meant addressing material needs and Salvationists viewed taking care of people through feeding as a basic expression of faith in public life.

As the next chapter makes clear, amongst the civil servants of the wartime Ministry of Food there was a disdain for any feeding models considered out of date and Victorian, and this included any suggestion of food as an instrument of proselytization. Many would have concurred with the spirit of Liberal Prime Minister Herbert Henry Asquith when he told the Commons, at the introduction of the Licensing Bill in 1908, that in the new century 'paramount supremacy' lay in 'public over private', in 'general over particular interests'.[3] Although Asquith was referring to big business and the established social order, here was the essence of the 'New Liberalism': the state, not the private individual or charitable concern (however well meaning), ought to function as the ultimate guarantor of the public good.

At the same time, questions of consumption in wartime retained some of the tinges of late nineteenth-century faith-based radicalism. The millennial optimism of the Edwardian period, even if expressed in secular terms, often struck the tone of the physician, campaigning for a healthier body politic and linking better nutrition with abstinence from alcohol: an established trope of religious radicals. Moreover, much discussion around consumption habits still focused on the supposedly wayward and feckless working man.[4] This was emphasized in the early stages of the war when teetotal government minister David Lloyd George, who was of a Welsh nonconformist background described as 'excessively puritan' by the contemporary press, told a crowd in Bangor, North Wales, that intemperate working men were to blame for poor productivity.[5]

Although Lloyd George's concern was armaments, and although he was subsequently pilloried by large sections of the press, the Bangor speech was a signal of the greater government controls over everyday life that would typify Lloyd George's ministry from 1916 onwards. Of relevance to this study is the subsequent growth of the Central Control Board, a government body which tightened wartime controls over industry and which was responsible for establishing 'industrial canteens'. These were large facilities within factory sites across the country where hot food was served as an alternative to a 'liquid lunch' in the pub.[6] Industrial canteens are not specifically addressed in this book because they were institutional (that is, based in factories) rather than public, and as such targeted directly towards improving British industrial output. Nonetheless, in scrutinizing wartime feeding, the legacy of the nineteenth-century temperance movement is of note here; even if historians disagree over the extent to which Lloyd George's Baptist upbringing shaped him, there is consensus over the longer term influence of the broader temperance movement on early twentieth-century policy and policymakers.[7] It is also of interest that industrial canteens occasionally served weak beer in moderate quantities whereas National Kitchens, as discussed below, were completely 'dry' sites.

Female voluntarism, class and gender

Social eating, or public feeding, represents the mixing of a normally private activity with a public act. For this reason, it chimes with the historiographical layers of complexity that have been added to the well-worn Victorian gendered dichotomy between public sphere (male) and the domestic, or private sphere (female).[8] As well as female involvement in wage labour, which implicitly challenged this 'separate spheres' ideology, studies have shown how women of all classes battled against these restrictions and into the public arena.[9] Yet women's emergence into the public sphere was accompanied by sexist assumptions. It has been argued, for example, that the relationship between thought and action that emerged in the early twentieth century was itself gendered, with the pursuit of academic knowledge considered male, and the pursuit of social work female.[10] Despite social work's supposedly female emotional traits such as empathy and care, feminists were integral to the development of social work as a profession in the early twentieth century.[11] Female visibility in turn-of-the-century feeding ventures thus constituted a potentially subversive act: one in which women, unusually, were visible in the public sphere. Viewed in this way, it represented a radical challenge to established notions of a 'woman's place', echoing currents of thought from Owenism to suffragism which critiqued the nuclear family and urged for greater female participation in public life. Even when stripped of any radical or revolutionary connotations, female philanthropy represents a critical site for the development of women's agency within the public sphere, with influential legacies in both the wartime feeding discussed in this book and the later development of the welfare state.[12]

On the other hand, late Victorian and Edwardian public feeding was often championed by upper class, and upper middle class, women and as such sometimes adhered to the domestic ideology of anti-suffragism. Women of a more conservative political bent felt that females ought to operate within the realm of parochial charity. Feeding the poor and needy of the community and the locale, they considered, was a more appropriate – if no less valuable – function for a woman than that of active participant in the masculinist affairs of state and empire.[13] Although the popular image of what may be termed the 'Lady Bountiful' has undergone revision, this type of female figure was a fixture of pre-war voluntary feeding, whether administered from a soup kitchen or door to door.[14]

Historians of female philanthropy have rightly cautioned that the condescending stereotype of the 'Lady Bountiful' – sympathetic to the poor while benefiting from the separatist social structures that kept her at the top of the pile – has haunted both scholarship and popular parlance, to the detriment of a fuller and fairer understanding of the phenomenon.[15] Accordingly, this book seeks to consider such women in the wartime context. In doing so, it is first important to acknowledge their predecessors. One such was the aristocrat and later acclaimed humanitarian Muriel Paget. Paget was a patron and organizer of the Southwark 'Invalid Kitchen', a charitable feeding centre in the London borough which provided cheap and nutritious food to young mothers, the sick and the convalescent. Paget's 'invalid kitchens' were a form of targeted feeding (which is outlined in greater depth below); with the target of this charitable relief loosely defined as the 'invalid', potential recipients were assessed according to their income or professional medical referral. The number of 'invalid kitchens' in the capital expanded in the years prior to war and attracted the royal patronage of Queen Mary.[16] Paget's war work would take her to Eastern Europe, where she used her London experience to organize emergency feeding centres[17]; significantly, these were feeding centres 'for all': as in many national contexts, the wartime necessity of mass feeding had trumped the targeted approach and Britain, as we shall see, was no exception.

A contemporary of Paget, the acclaimed Suffragette and socialist Sylvia Pankhurst was also highly influential in early wartime feeding initiatives. Sylvia Pankhurst's left-wing political trajectory had caused a rift with her mother Emmeline and sister Christabel and prompted her to found the socialist East London Federation of Suffragettes (ELFS) in 1914. Sylvia, who was opposed to the war but alert to its effects, established a milk distribution centre in London's East End and a medical clinic where patients were treated without charge. In the early stages of the conflict, in the autumn of 1914, Sylvia lobbied Walter Runciman, the President of the Board of Trade, to introduce food price controls to combat the price inflation and panic buying ushered in by the war. Importantly, in a striking pre-echo of the government's National Kitchens scheme, the ELFS also opened a small chain of cost-price restaurants. By 1915, Sylvia Pankhurst's cost-price restaurants were serving around 400 meals a day.[18]

Describing her motivation for public-feeding efforts in the East End, Sylvia Pankhurst recalled 'we had good families of people coming to my house without a penny and with six or seven children, and I opened two penny restaurants where you could get two penny meals… But I know it is all palliatives; it will not do any good really; I want to change the system.'[19] As the quote suggests, as well as her militant direct-action Suffragettism, she was a revolutionary socialist and conceived of public feeding as a radical act.[20] A founder member of the Communist Party in Britain, Sylvia's pioneer social work was of the radical or 'popular' type, and as such was distinct from the reformist early professional social work of the English Settlement Movement, in which middle-class 'settlement workers', often attached to universities, situated themselves within poorer communities.[21] When it came to state action versus voluntarism, Pankhurst was unequivocal, agonizing about the risk to 'affectionate comradeship' if her feeding scheme was perceived as an exercise in 'patronage or condescension' and insisting that such measures did not signal a preference for 'private effort' over collective action. Rather than a smugly charitable hobby for affluent women, her desire to transform the state itself was clear: 'our main duty was to bring pressure to bear on the government to secure the needs of the people'.[22]

Female voluntarism around food in the late nineteenth and early twentieth centuries contributed to the gradual erosion of gendered notions of public and private, albeit often within an 'acceptable borderland area'.[23] During the First World War, the middle-/upper-class woman would remain influential in public feeding and historians like Peter Grant are right to caution against the corrosive spirit of condescension towards voluntary and philanthropic contributions to the war effort, many of which were run by middle-and upper-class women.

However, as the war ground on, working-class women themselves would prove the real pioneers of emergency commensality and the 'National Kitchen', providing a clear break with earlier patterns of elite benevolence by bureaucratizing, professionalizing and universalizing the notion of public feeding. On the one hand, then, state-supported emergency feeding was more in keeping with the feeding efforts of Pankhurst – who was always at pains to avoid the taint of charity and to maintain focus on the greater goal of systemic change – than the aristocratically endorsed activity of Paget. On the other, the patriotic rebranding of communal feeding as the 'National Kitchen', which is discussed subsequently, would frustrate what Pankhurst viewed as the radical potential of commensality. But whatever the political implications of the state assuming a public-feeding role, the National Kitchen provides a striking example of what Derek Oddy memorably termed 'the failure of voluntary restraint' in food consumption in Britain between 1916 and 1917, examples of which included King George V and his household solemnly pledging, in May 1917, to reduce their consumption of bread by a quarter. By the end of the war wider ranging statist measures – price-capped public feeding followed by full rationing – had supplanted the voluntary when it came to food control. As Pankhurst hoped, the 'pressure' on government had been brought to bear.

Scientific advance, class and nutritional reform

The technological improvements of the nineteenth century transformed the British people's relationship with food. Imperial trade was enhanced through quicker and more extensive rail and sea routes, while mechanization led to the mass production of food and new products. As Britain's share of overseas trade grew, sugar became an everyday commodity and new sugar-based foodstuffs became increasingly popular; chocolate, for example, went from an expensive drink to an affordable solid bar.[24] Britain's pre-eminent global trading position, coupled with advances in food preservation techniques such as canning and refrigeration, ensured that by the turn of the century the British consumer was able to avail of a greater range of meats, fish, fruit and vegetables than ever before and, most significantly, Britons of all classes were now able to avail of food at *cheaper* prices. For those towards the top of the nation's class hierarchy this meant a greater variety of luxury foodstuffs; for those towards the opposite end it translated as the cheap white loaf of bread: a tangible symbol of national pride illustrating how the nation, through its empire, was delivering affordable food to its people.

On the wave of the scientific progress of the late century came the development of food science and better understanding of nutrition and bacteria and, as a corollary, educational institutions dedicated to food science began to appear. The growth of cookery schools in nineteenth-century Britain provides another example of how late Victorian trends underlay First World War feeding. The National Training School of Cookery in London, which opened in 1873, established cookery education as a science, and cookery schools subsequently sprung up in other British cities. For the first time, the preparation of food was recognized as impacting public health and occupying a role in preventive medicine and medical care. Communicating advances in the understanding of hygiene and nutrition to a wider audience, the nation's new cookery schools helped to establish diet as a public, rather than a private, concern; this scientific approach to consumption would be replicated in hospitals and the armed services.[25]

Yet the greater scientific knowledge around food would serve to illustrate the nagging nutritional class gap. Surveys into the working-class diet conducted in the early Edwardian period put the average energy intake for a member of this class bracket at between 2,300 and 2,500 kcal a day; however, the last two major surveys into labourers' diet of the pre-war period estimated that this figure was between 1,900 and 2,100 kcal. Meanwhile, other urban studies had identified serious nutrient deficiency in pockets of urban Britain, with figures as low as 1,200 kcal in the poorest parts of London.[26] Although class boundaries were porous, the British working-class diet tended to include more starchy food than its middle-class equivalent, especially bread, and not nearly as much fat and protein. The diet of the lower orders, in summary, was typically more sugary and less nutritious than that of their middle-class equivalents: bread, jam and tea was something of a staple meal. The cheap white loaf may have been celebrated, then, but its dubious nutritional value was increasingly raising eyebrows. The discovery of vitamins in the 1910s provided the link to deficiency diseases such as rickets, and in the years before the First World War the notion of dietetics emerged as a policy issue. Food reformers, who were largely drawn from the ranks of the concerned middle class, pointed to the need to improve the living conditions of the poor through healthier consumption, nutritional education and scientific housekeeping.[27] These individuals would play an important role in the development of Britain's National Kitchens.

Humanitarianism, socialism and the New Liberalism

It was the previously mentioned Second Boer War, Britain's great fin de siècle flop, which illuminated a significant gap in the municipal interventionism of the late nineteenth century. Both Conservative and Liberal administrations of the late Victorian period presided over an expansion in public services such as baths, parks, museums and libraries; primary education became compulsory in England and Wales in 1880, and public health regulations were tightened considerably. Yet despite the decidedly more statist ethic of the 'New Liberalism' of the last two decades of the nineteenth century, the period did not witness the introduction of any wide-ranging measures to feed the British people.[28] This situation changed in 1906 with the Provision of School Meals Act. Margaret McMillan, the American-born social reformer who lobbied for the legislation, argued that if it was compulsory for children to receive an education then the state ought to provide a hot meal for them. McMillan was a member of the newly formed Labour Party, and her campaign was telling of both the growing political influence of the labour movement and the coalescence of Labour and Liberal agendas on questions of progressive social change.

The introduction of school meals remains distinct from the wartime public feeding 'for all' described in this book in one important respect: it was targeted towards a specific group. As historian Nadia Durbach has argued, in providing food only to certain subsections of the population rather than 'the people' at large, the British state's provision of food remained within the ideological parameters of political economy forged in the nineteenth century. In this way, the challenge of humanitarianism – which, for some Conservatives and Liberals alike, smacked of excessive generosity or, worse still, socialism – was checked by the *targeted* nature of feeding interventions, which were justified as delivering improvement to the recipient as a means of enriching state and empire. This can be seen in the manner in which institutional feeding was applied in Britain's workhouses and prisons, where the utility of labour formed the central dietary criteria. In British India, too, echoing the experience of the Great Irish Famine, government-run feeding stations – or 'kitchens' – sifted 'the needy' (the emaciated who qualified for free food) from the 'able bodied', who were enlisted in public works projects and ought to be self-reliant when it came to feeding themselves.[29] The term 'kitchen', though, would prove an abiding one. It is telling that this Victorian nomenclature was applied to First World War emergency feeding which, in breaking with the previous targeted approach, aroused great anxieties amongst political conservatives. In the same way, the introduction of school meals can be viewed as a measure by which the British state cynically ensured it had better fed and thus fitter fighting bodies for its future imperial conflicts.[30]

It is perhaps too indulgent of hindsight, however, to point to the coincidence of free school meals and the many members of the 'lost generation' lost to the violence of 1914–1918, as later observers of British social policy asserted, most notably Eleanor Rathbone in the 1930s. The introduction of school meals was a highly significant step forward for government feeding and was an important challenge to the lingering notion of the 'deserving poor' enshrined in the Poor Law Amendment Act of 1834. It also established a precedent for the wartime interventions discussed later in this book. While the state's self-interest and the lingering orthodoxy of political economy cannot be discounted as motivations for the measure, analogies with Victorian institutional or colonial targeted feeding must be counterweighed against a genuine spirit of social reform and universalism, one heavily influenced by socialist thought and demonstrated by the New Liberals' pre-war introduction of unemployment and medical insurance and the old-age pension (1909–1911). Even if the term 'Kitchen' belonged to an era of political economy rather than welfare statism, wartime public feeding announced a march towards the latter.

In Britain on the cusp of war, it has been argued, workers were increasingly turning away from voluntarism and placing greater faith in the state and its services. Under New Liberalism the British state was taking on the aspect of 'an all-powerful but benevolent force with, for all practical purposes, unending resources at its command'.[31] Although the experience of war would strain these resources, demonstrating that they were far from 'unending', it would also illustrate the force of the state. Although British civilians never suffered food shortages comparable to those in central Europe at the end of the conflict, there were significant episodes of social discontent around matters of wartime food supply. There was significant mob violence against German pork shops in Liverpool, London and elsewhere following the sinking of *The Lusitania* in 1915, for example.[32] These disturbances were neither classic food riot nor outright pogrom, but their bigoted and nationalistic character does not remove the fact that they were, at least in part, based on perceptions around food pricing. Likewise, people's experience of price inflation and queues for food roused popular ire.

Conclusion

Critically, given the wartime intensification of the state's interventionist role, such disaffection around food was increasingly coupled with the expectation and mounting consensus that it was now the state – above all other actors – whose responsibility it was to address the problem. This was the direction in which the century-spanning trends of humanitarianism, New Liberalism and socialism were heading: away from the notion that it was the role of private faith-based charity to feed the poor and needy and towards the notion of fairer shares for all with the state as guarantor. Scientific advance and nutritional understanding, too, were on the side of the social reformers. Yet it would be the overriding wartime imperative of economic efficiency and social cohesion that jolted the British government into action when it came to food and feeding.

2

The birth of emergency public feeding in the First World War

Introduction

According to John Burnett's history of eating out in England, 'before the Second World War few people in England visited a restaurant at all frequently'.[1] Burnett's reflection holds true for private restaurants and captures how eating out at a restaurant was considered alien to British working-class culture. At the same time, however, it ignores the national roll-out of public restaurants between 1917 and 1919. Their title is deceptive – known as National Kitchens, these were in fact large long-bench dining rooms, part of a major nationwide government-sponsored programme to alleviate the effects of food shortages. Yet these 'kitchens' were more than mere greasy canteens, possessing many features typical of restaurant dining: music, artwork, tablecloths, flowers. As outlined below, National Kitchens grew out of female-run efforts in working-class communities to combat supply disruption and price inflation but morphed into vehicles for national and civilizational improvement. First sponsored by the state in May 1917, by mid-1918 there were over 1,000 National Kitchens in Britain, but a year later the movement had all but disappeared.[2] This section of the book explains why. It outlines the history of the National Kitchens of the First World War, which existed between 1917 and 1919, and argues that as one of several techniques for feeding Britain National Kitchens formed a popular arm of British wartime food supply policy hitherto underappreciated by historians.

Between 1914 and 1918 the nation's food policy encompassed centralized purchasing, food rationing and price controls: a mixture of controls which historians have deemed generally successful. This verdict, however, ignores the extent to which National Kitchens were part of the national picture.[3] In terms of popularity, the harmony between organized labour, consumers and government in the British acceptance of a comprehensive rationing system was relatively pronounced, particularly in comparison with Germany in the latter stages of the war. But the success of rationing in Britain has overshadowed the National Kitchen. Whether termed communal, municipal or national, public-feeding schemes preceded the roll-out of rationing by book, which arrived later on in the conflict (summer 1918). Despite this, they are mentioned only in passing in works discussing British wartime food policy.[4]

When the National Kitchen has appeared in histories of the First World War it has not been looked upon favourably by historians. To Margaret Barnett, who assessed the overall operation of food policy during the conflict, National Kitchens failed to move beyond the old pre-war soup kitchen model, remaining 'stolidly lower class institutions located in a dingy back street or public baths and presided over by the familiar Lady Bountiful'. The image of the patronising largesse of the nobility is an abidingly stuffy one, redolent of Victorian models of charitable relief. According to Barnett, despite (and maybe because of) support from prominent women such as Sylvia Pankhurst and Queen Mary, egalitarianism in public dining held no appeal for the British public because the unexotic air of 'social levelling, communism and fair shares' hung over the venture.[5] Barnett's appraisal echoes Winston Churchill's, and in invoking the figure of the 'Lady Bountiful' (to which we will return) she raises the persistent theme of noble patronage of public feeding. However, her explanation for what she sees as the failure of the National Kitchen differs from the verdict of Derek Oddy, another historian of British food policy and foodways in the twentieth century, who cites the Food Controller of North West England describing the British working man's dining tastes: 'the fried fish shop he knew, the cold supper bar where he could by his tripe of "trotters" he was acquainted with, but a restaurant was not in his line'.[6] Oddy's assessment is therefore the opposite of Barnett's. He holds that National Kitchens were unappealing not because they were unexotic, but precisely because they were considered *too* exotic by the average working man, who liked to eat meals prepared by his wife at home and considered 'eating out' to be above his class station.

This section of the book weighs these contradictory judgements against the available evidence. Social class was certainly a factor in the British public's receptiveness to public feeding in both world wars, but although a male working-class disdain for the idea of eating out at a restaurant is certainly significant – as highlighted by Oddy and Burnett – it should not be taken to indicate wider unpopularity. Neither should male working-class dismissiveness drown out the activities of the working-class women who pioneered and popularized wartime communal eating, or the urban middle class amongst whom they seem to have been most popular. Rather, like other aspects of wartime food policy, the fate of National Kitchens had much more to do with an absence of *political will* following the coming of peace than public indifference. As late as mid-1918 the Ministry of Food was boasting of National Kitchens becoming a 'permanent national institution'.[7] This was not to be, but they did reappear as British Restaurants just twenty years later. As explained in this part of the book, National Kitchens had, in fact, proved popular, especially among lower middle-class workers and many – contrary to Barnett's view – were attractive venues at which to eat. Their demise can be attributed to a number of factors: the introduction of full rationing in 1918 played its part, as did the expectation of a return to 'normality' following the Armistice and 1918's public health crisis, but so too did the vocal opposition of the food retail trade to the idea of public feeding. First, though, the Victorian hangover of the 'Lady Bountiful' is discussed.

From soup kitchens to communal kitchens

When Churchill dismissed public feeding as redolent of the workhouse, the image of the Dickensian soup kitchen was doubtless in his mind. Run by charities like the Salvation Army, public soup kitchens had become a fixture of Edwardian Britain, as mentioned previously. With the arrival of war in 1914, these charitable ventures would become more important in offering cheap but nutritious food to people caught out by the price inflation accompanying war.[8] The rising price and falling availability of food indeed increased in Britain from July 1914,[9] but for the first two years of the First World War shortages tended to be localized.[10] The need was greatest in Britain's urban centres, in which women's voluntary groups such as the Patriotic Food League provided cookery and food economy classes for working-class women.[11] Other female-run charitable schemes sought to deliver nutritious food to the urban poor, for example, London's 'invalid kitchens', which were organized, as mentioned, by the humanitarian aristocrat Muriel Paget.[12]

As the war dragged on, however, it became clear that many facets of the British home front required reorganization. With the intensification of the British war effort came a change of Prime Minister in December 1916 and an attendant shift in tempo from Herbert Henry Asquith's 'Wait and See' administration to David Lloyd George's 'Push and Go' approach. Lloyd George had been appointed Secretary of State for War in July 1916, at a time when the sinking of shipping was compromising food supplies. Britain's empire was founded on its maritime prowess and, as population increased across the nineteenth century, the modern nation found itself ever more reliant on shipped imports of food from abroad. Faced with food scarcity at home, the British press eyed the enemy's situation, reporting the great communal feeding schemes organized in Berlin and other German cities to cope with shortages on the German home front.[13] Against the backdrop of a more potent U-boat campaign in spring 1917, a commission of enquiry into industrial unrest linked labour agitation to food price inflation and recommended the opening of more industrial canteens.[14]

The prospect of labour unrest was naturally daunting to a nation engaged in large-scale modern industrial warfare. Yet the commissioners' recommendation of government-run industrial canteens implied a greater realization: that charitable feeding ventures were increasingly inadequate in meeting public demand. The political turmoil experienced by Britain's ally Russia in 1917, starting with the February Revolution and culminating in the Bolshevik seizure of power in October, jolted the British establishment. It also meant the arrival in Britain of wealthy Russian émigrés like Flora Benenson (later Solomon), then a young heiress, who would go on to become one of the great champions of public feeding in Britain. The voluntary work Solomon undertook in First World War Britain, however, was, in her own words, 'a cosy niche for women who refrained from "doing their bit" in the factories', reserved for women of her class 'who customarily opened charity bazaars, rode to the hounds, and revealed in their dress, accent and politics that the egalitarian society was as far away as in the days of Henry the Eighth'.[15] Here indeed, then, was the image of the entitled weekend philanthropist so despised by Sylvia Pankhurst, doling out soup to the grateful poor before returning to a life of affluent comfort. But when it came to public feeding, this model was rapidly becoming an anachronism, as the role of the interventionist state grew. There was a growing feeling within government, too, that the state's role in feeding people would have to extend beyond the industrial canteens chiefly targeted at factory workers.

In May 1917 Lloyd George appointed fellow Welshman and millionaire businessman D.A. Thomas (Lord Rhondda) as his Food Controller.[16] Rhondda's predecessor Hudson Kearley (Viscount Devonport) was not a popular figure with the British wartime public.[17] Devonport, who preferred voluntary action to state-imposed measures and urged personal abstinence rather than government 'push and go' had, however, introduced the 'meatless days' control in early 1917, which had done much to secure his unpopularity in the public mindset.[18] Urged on by Devonport, there were tens of thousands of voluntary campaigns to save food witnessed across Britain, ranging from children's essay competitions to cinema screenings devoted to food economy. Yet as queues for staples like bread soon developed, it was becoming increasingly clear that voluntary action had its limitations.[19] Rhondda, by contrast to Devonport, had an air of dynamism to him, and soon responded to price inflation by announcing the full rationing of sugar, and later meat, followed by a succession of maximum price orders.

The popular juxtaposition of Devonport and Rhondda tends to ignore the fact that it was Devonport who introduced the first restrictions on private restaurants via the Public Meals Order of December 1916, limiting day meals to two courses and evening meals to three courses.[20] Viewed in hindsight, such controls on private feeding were nudging Britain towards public feeding. This was underlined when Rhondda followed Devonport's measures by further restrictions on private restaurants. He introduced the rationing of food by weight in restaurants in April 1917 and introduced restrictions on the serving of afternoon tea. Initially, though, Rhondda also favoured voluntary initiative over statist action when it came to the prospect of communal feeding. Rhondda's

Figure 2.1 David Alfred Thomas, 1st Viscount Rhondda, Minister of Food Control 19 June 1917–3 July 1918 (Wikimedia Commons).

early preference for voluntarism over statism was reflected in the language of the Ministry of Food's early endorsement of communal feeding schemes: in May 1917, the department publicly encouraged the opening of more of what it called *voluntary* communal kitchens.[21]

But despite Rhondda's professed admiration for voluntarism over statism, it was clear that the tide was moving in the opposite direction. One of Rhondda's men at the Ministry, Kennedy Jones, was duly instructed to find an example of communal dining which could be used as a template if the state were to seriously consider endorsing and financing the feeding of the people. The plan was that Jones's example could then be used by local authorities wanting to open public restaurants. Local government would, in turn, receive financial support from central government.

Kennedy Jones was no left-leaning civil servant. He had the sort of dynamic business-like image favoured by Rhondda and had made his name as a journalist and Unionist politician who had contested the 1916 Wimbledon election on the radical right-wing ticket of the 'Do-it-now party'.[22] Yet the model which the Ministry considered most closely and would prove the initial inspiration for National Kitchens came from the left: the Croydon communal kitchen. A growing town, the south London borough of Croydon would become something of a beacon in both the First and Second World War when it came to pioneering schemes to control civilian consumption. The Croydon 'project', which is discussed below, was first endorsed and pushed by the War Emergency Workers National Committee. The War Emergency Workers National Committee (hereafter WNC) was an umbrella body formed at the outbreak of war to protect workers' interests. Its leader was the economist, social reformer and leading member of the Fabian Society, Sidney Webb; its secretary, J.M. Middleton, was also assistant secretary of the Labour Party. The Fabian and Labour influence on public feeding would prove durable, as the later involvement of William Beveridge demonstrates. Looking out of his office window on London's Victoria Street in April 1917, Middleton reported 'long queues of women waiting for potatoes' and noted scathingly that 'none of the restaurants or hotels in the West End have noted to refuse potatoes to their customers'.[23] Among the WNC's suggested remedies were harsher penalties for food profiteers and a comprehensive rationing system.[24]

Significantly, another of the WNC's recommendations was the extension of communal kitchens. After the government endorsed National Kitchens in May 1917, Middleton pointed to its long-standing backing of the communal kitchen in Croydon as evidence that the government had stolen a march on working-class initiative.²⁵ Established by the local borough council, the Croydon Communal Kitchen was staffed by a paid cook and a team of voluntary helpers. This wartime discount dining venture was located on two sites (both kitchens attached to local schools), operated on a ticketed take-away basis and opened only at lunchtime. Patrons queued and were admitted in groups of twelve. Once inside, they were met by a ticket distributor who handed out tickets for the various food prices (1 penny, 2 pence, 3 pence and 4 pence) in return for cash. They then proceeded to the counter where various foodstuffs were arranged separately and by their price.²⁶

The experiment in Croydon was trumpeted by the WNC as a communal *kitchen* rather than a communal *restaurant* because dining did not take place on-site. Significantly, there was a strict rule that no meals could be eaten on the premises. People in need of cheap and nutritious food brought their own dishes and filled them up with the various foods. These included items such as rice, maize, flour, beans, peas and dried fruit. There was fish on offer but no meat. The Croydon kitchen was subsidized by the local council but it was not a charitable institution; it did not have to turn over a profit but it had to cover its costs and support itself. The average user spent between 6 and 8 pence and the weekly takings were around £40. In a trend which would repeat itself as National Kitchens took off, users were not confined to the very poor.²⁷ The WNC's records contain many letters from parish councils and voluntary bodies seeking guidance on how to establish communal kitchens. The usual response was to send back a short pamphlet outlining the operation of the Croydon scheme.²⁸

The Croydon kitchen, then, was a bottom-up beacon for the upsurge in communal dining witnessed towards the end of the First World War. And yet it did not fully provide the government with its sought-after blueprint for how public feeding would work. The association of the project with the left-wing WNC was too much for a man of Kennedy Jones's political leanings to stomach. Although the Ministry of Food was certainly aware of the Croydon scheme, Jones instead settled on a group of prominent middle-class food reformers – R. Hippisley Cox, H.J. Bradley and Eustace Miles – to spearhead the new state-backed 'Kitchens For All'. Eustace Miles, the most famous of this trio, was a vegetarian who ran a well-known health-food shop and restaurant in Charing Cross, London.

In the considerable cast of public figures who backed public feeding in wartime Britain, Eustace Miles stands out. Born in 1868, his contribution to the culture of the day was his fusion of physical manliness with vegetarianism. A graduate of King's College Cambridge, Miles was an intelligent, handsome and athletic man who combined brains and brawn. A champion on the tennis court,

Miles also published widely off it, writing works not only on diet, exercise and self-help, but also on the classics. In 1908, just shy of forty, he won the Olympic silver medal for real tennis in the London Olympics; this was no mean feat since many of his opponents – including the gold medallist – were twenty years younger than him. He was also a successful businessman and the pricey but popular Eustace Miles Restaurant Company Ltd opened in 1906. Partly due to his relentless self-publicity, Miles seemed to embody the masculinist confidence of the British Empire in its Edwardian twilight. Yet his dietary choices ensured that Miles stood apart from the thrusting macho jingoism of the day. His favourite theory was that the meaty, heavy Edwardian diet was detrimental to health and explained various health problems from poor physical fitness to mental health problems.[29] Challenging the dominant red-meat masculinity with vegetarianism ensured that Miles, despite his achievements, was also something of a figure of fun.

On the other hand, Miles's muscular, manly and outdoorsy image would do much to combat the prevailing stereotype of the vegetarian man as sandal-wearing, wrong-headed and politically suspect.[30] True, the intellectual set were fond of his restaurants and he could count the great Irish writer and socialist George Bernard Shaw as a shareholder; he also indulged in non-mainstream cultural and religious beliefs such as reincarnation; and – the gravest insult to the 'common sense' masculinity of the age – he proclaimed himself a follower of the suffragette movement. But he was simultaneously a national treasure when it came to health as a patriotic virtue: former real tennis champion of England and the world, an Olympic medallist, a philanthropic champion of free food for the poor, virile, active, a popular man of commerce, an all-round 'good chap'. In part, Miles's acceptance can be seen as the product of his situation in the 'second wave' of popular vegetarianism. Whereas the first Vegetarian Society (founded in Manchester in 1847) possessed a strong political bent, advocating 'a many-sided liberalism', by contrast later vegetarian projects – such as the London Vegetarian Society (1888) – emphasized the personal health benefits of a non-carnivorous diet.[31] By the outbreak of the First World War, Miles was the poster boy of this 'second wave' of vegetarianism in which the emphasis would be on the body first and politics second.

In contrast to the Croydon scheme, which looked to provide simple calories to take away, the nutritional reformers selected by Kennedy Jones took a greater interest in lifestyle choices around health, diet, dining habits and nutrition (as discussed later). Therefore, instead of the WNC's pamphlet on the Croydon scheme, the new *Public Kitchens Handbook* written by Cox, Bradley and Miles was published in time for the opening of Britain's first government-backed National Kitchen on London's Westminster Bridge on 21 May 1917. The involvement of Miles, in particular, lent the whole venture a celebrity air, one heightened by the ministry's choice of Queen Mary to open the first site. By the end of the year National Kitchens were popping up in almost every British town and city and, like that in Westminster, they operated as large spaces where people could sit in and dine.[32] Viewing this expanding network of public cafeteria, J. M. Middleton bitterly boasted that, in its early advocacy of Croydon's municipal kitchen, the WNC had been 'eighteen months ahead of government policy'.[33]

Middleton, representing the War Emergency Workers National Committee, was right. Populist political agendas were at work in the state's adoption of communal kitchens and the conversion of them into National Kitchens. Effectively, the state would steal a working-class venture and relabel it. At a June 1917 meeting Rhondda told representatives of the WNC that he was 'in economics an anti-Socialist' but that 'under the abnormal conditions of war the principle of individualism must go by the board'.[34] The WNC – which had had long concentrated on the food trade, pointing to the increase in ship owners' and farmers' profits yet the decrease in the purchasing power of the consumer – were pleased to hear this.[35] However, there were clear limits to Rhondda's spirit of wartime anti-individualism. This would become evident in the rebranding process to which communal feeding and eating were soon subjected. Despite the movement away from the Croydon model and towards mass eating on-site, the WNC continued to regard community kitchens as *its* policy, one which the state later claimed as its own and rebranded without proper acknowledgement.[36] At the same time, the government's sponsorship of the National Kitchen was driven by patriotic priorities in which class divisions were, naturally enough, downplayed. Crucially, in order to achieve national popularity, the Ministry of Food were determined that communal dining would not be confined to just the poor or the working class, but would achieve cross-class appeal. Despite the deployment of Queen Mary, something much more far-reaching than an aristocrat ladling out soup was taking hold.

The radical threat of communal dining

Probably at some future time it will be difficult to believe that each household in the country did its own separate marketing, buying small amounts of food from retail dealers a hundred per cent above cost price, that every hundred houses in a street had each its own fire for cooking, and that at least a hundred human beings were engaged in serving meals that could have been prepared by half a dozen trained assistants

This was the vision of Kennedy Jones's hand-picked group of food reformers – Cox, Bradley and Miles – in their *Public Kitchens* handbook, prepared as an instructional manual at the behest of the Ministry of Food.[37] The term 'public kitchens' was significant in itself. The grass-roots origins of 'communal kitchens' like that in Croydon, which inspired 'public kitchens', would soon be obscured by their patriotic rebranding. The large communal dining centre opened by Queen Mary on London's Westminster Bridge on 21 May 1917 was described as a 'Kitchen for All', not a 'Public Kitchen', and would soon become a 'National Kitchen'. These were more than mere linguistic idiosyncrasies: the brave new world of communal dining would be riddled with the political anxieties echoed a generation later by Winston Churchill in his fears of its communist undertones. Once again, the government's desire to ensure that National Kitchens were broad-ranging in their cross-class appeal was paramount, accompanied by a tangible anxiety about the prospect of hundreds and thousands of working-class people gathering together at once.

In November 1917 Rhondda appointed a business friend of his, Charles Spencer, to head up the National Kitchens division of the Ministry of Food.[38] Spencer was typical of the go-getter types flooding into the department under Rhondda. He was, as he put it to Rhondda, 'not used to being chained up' [by bureaucracy]. A self-styled man of action who adhered to the 'do it now' attitude of Kennedy Jones, he took on the project on the condition that National Kitchens be 'untrammelled by red tape' and run as a 'business proposition'. Determined to circumvent 'municipal obstacles' to the efficient running of National Kitchens, Spencer declared himself in favour of employing 'real hustlers', if necessary, to make 'quick work' of the extensive surveying, building and engineering needed to establish a national public-feeding network. Spencer was all about 'economy with efficiency', promising Rhondda that 'wasters or inefficients' would be 'fired out immediately'.[39]

Spencer's driven entrepreneurship imbued his National Kitchens division with a near-evangelical zeal, but his approach was also to attract criticism. His hard-headed business mind, it seems, was responsible for the name change. Spencer confessed to Rhondda that he did 'not feel quite happy' with 'the word *communal*'. 'Its association with Socialism is too well known, and I am afraid it is rather a handicap', he confided in the peer. He suggested the following alternatives: 'War Emergency Food Kitchens', 'War Food Depots', 'War Catering

Depots', 'National Food Kitchens', 'Local Catering Centres', 'National Catering Centres', 'People's Food Supply Depots', 'Local Food Kitchens' and 'Food Supply Depots'. From this unwieldy-sounding list, the 'National Kitchen' emerged.[40] In a newspaper interview a week later Rhondda confirmed the name change, repeating the anti-socialist political prejudices of Spencer. 'I do not like the term communal' Rhondda told the *Manchester Guardian*; 'I should much rather talk of central or National Kitchens'. According to Rhondda, pre-echoing Churchill, 'community kitchens' implied, on the one hand, charity, on the other, communism.[41]

Somewhat paradoxically, the anti-socialism of Rhondda and Spencer was expressed amidst increasingly statist measures in food control that meant that Britain was moving further towards a system of war socialism. Under the extended powers of the Defence of the Realm Act, Rhondda had overseen the central takeover of food supply, control, pricing and distribution in September 1917.[42] With the state taking on ever greater powers, Spencer worried about the potential of home-grown radicalism to subvert these controls. 'The working classes are near breaking strain' he wrote to Rhondda, a situation which, he claimed, had materialized since 'June 1917'. This provided another compelling reason for the name change. When he considered the prospect of hundreds of the great unwashed collecting together under one roof, Spencer worried about the potential for dissent.[43] Therefore, the WNC's Croydon kitchen, with its take-away method of distributing cheap food, was originally favoured by Spencer when he was appointed head of the National Kitchens division in November 1917 rather than the public kitchens advocated by Eustace Miles and his ilk. Customers, he envisaged, would visit central depots, have their flasks or buckets filled with food, and return home to consume it.[44] Reading between the lines of Spencer's papers, it was as if he felt that a working-class uprising along the lines of the Russian October Revolution would be less likely if provision was done publicly but consumption occurred in private. In some ways, therefore, Spencer was envisaging an early version of the twenty-first-century food bank.

Spencer himself was something of a maverick, a technocratic Yorkshireman who stayed in post until January 1919, when he resigned citing the demands of his many other business interests.[45] Significantly, these interests included his chairmanship of the Halifax Tramways Committee. His nervousness about the radical potential of working-class assemblies merged with his verve for technological progress (and business acumen) into an idea for a novel form of National Kitchen offering meals on wheels. He called this take-away form of communal feeding the 'travelling kitchen'. This was a tramcar fitted with ovens and powered by overhead electricity wires that 'not only distributes the cheapest of cheap dinners but cooks them on the way' as the *Yorkshire Post* put it.[46] As food supplies waned in 1917, the government experimented with the propaganda use of trams in the food economy campaign, flying flags bearing the words 'Don't Waste Bread'.[47] Mobile canteens, however, were a new phenomenon altogether.

Spencer's 'travelling kitchens' were another version of the Brave New World of public feeding. On its maiden voyage, Halifax's inaugural 'perambulating electric kitchen' was met by an enthusiastic crowd 'armed with dishes, jugs, basins, or other domestic receptacles', a hungry mob which had to be ordered into queues by police. One elderly recipient, interviewed by the newspaper, gave the scheme her seal of approval by declaring it 'just champion'.[48] The *Electrical Times* approved as well. It had glimpsed the way forward for British cultures of consumption and it came in the shape of the perambulating electric kitchen. These electric-powered tramcars were of 'permanent value, especially in industrial districts' and would soon replace 'individualistic methods' of cooking and eating.[49] In this sense, too, Spencer was a man before his time since mobile forms of emergency feeding would become a fixture of emergency food relief

Figure 2.2 Halifax National Kitchen, 1917.

during the Second World War. There were echoes, too, of the futuristic designs of Eustace Miles and his fellow food reformers, in which dining in private would become a thing of the past.

Under Spencer's directorship of the National Kitchens division of the Ministry of Food, travelling kitchens also came in the form of motorcars driven by members of the Women's Reserve Ambulance and financed by the Ministry. The travelling kitchen functioned as a mobile 'agitprop' which pulled up at halls and other public venues, where its driver and passengers would show the assembled crowd how to run a 'business-like' kitchen. Spencer envisaged the future conveyance of food via motor cars as a way to remove the subversive taint of communalism from communal dining. To cope with the problem of keeping the food hot he had even designed a 'special water-jacketed carrier' – in the course of manufacture. He was also working on 'a rail-less car with electrical apparatus'.[50]

However the Ministry of Food, in general, took a cooler attitude towards meals on wheels than the transport enthusiast head of its National Kitchens division, pointing out that private businesses transporting food via motor cars would aggravate fuel shortages. The Ministry recommended the use of 'motors', where available, in overcoming the difficulties of delivering cheap wholesale supplies to outlying villages,[51] but Spencer's suggestion that all new National Kitchens be situated on a tramway route 'where a siding could be put in' was not implemented.[52]

In practice, too, the take-away model of emergency public feeding – whether doled out from behind a kitchen counter or tram window – was overtaken by dining-in. Slowly, the model of taking one's vessel to be filled up and returning home to consume the food would be replaced by the canteen form of National Kitchen. The success of the Westminster Bridge canteen impelled Rhondda to press for the establishment of National Kitchens 'wherever possible'.[53] The Ministry's model kitchen therefore came to be that located in Poplar in east London. It had a restaurant attached from its inception in 1917 and by late that year was feeding around 2,500 people a day on site.[54] Spencer's anxiety over the working class assembling together to dine was assuaged by Rhondda. Once safely rebranded 'National Kitchens', Rhondda damped any fears of radicalism by promising that local businessmen would be invited to run these new public-feeding spaces as commercial enterprises; local authorities would lend support, but these would be businesses first and foremost. Commercial nous would prevail, Rhondda insisted, in bringing together not one, but 'all classes'.[55]

Figure 2.3 National Kitchen, London, 1918 (Imperial War Museum).

Avoiding the taint of charity and establishing the female role: The organization of the new National Kitchens

The excitement surrounding the opening of the first 'Kitchen for All' in May 1917 soon gave way to confusion. National Kitchens were announced as a nationwide public-feeding scheme but local government and local enterprise were also to have a role. In the early months there was a good deal of uncertainty over whether local authorities were legally entitled to fund these new entities or would have to wait for funds from central government.[56] There was also confusion over whether local food vigilance committees would have powers to enforce and administer rationing via communal kitchen sites.[57] Food vigilance committees were generally grass-roots bodies supported by the Labour movement in an effort to ensure the fair distribution of food among working-class communities.[58] In general, women typical of those who stood in the escalating food queues of the winter of 1917–18 were to be found on these bodies.[59] In the gendered world of food preparation, it was also becoming clear that the success of community kitchens, or National Kitchens, depended on local political backing and the social outlook of local politicians concerning a woman's proper place.

In Llanelli, Wales, aldermen worried about National Kitchens removing a woman's domestic role and thereby robbing girls of the culinary training that they would be expected to perform as wives.[60] Another good example was Liverpool, a big city with a large working-class population which might have been considered a natural venue for public feeding to take off. However, Lord Mayor of Liverpool, Max Muspratt, a Liberal, urged limitations on the spread of communal dining. Such sites should only provide supplementary foods such as porridge and soups and should not, he instructed, displace the woman from the home.[61] Although the city's local education committee provided food and cookery lessons for schoolchildren and parents, until 1918 Liverpool possessed only one municipal communal kitchen (described in the local press as an 'unqualified success').[62] Similarly, Newcastle's city councillors recorded their concern at the threat to the female domestic position presented by communal eating.[63]

These anxieties reflected perspectives on the family common at the turn of the century. As recent research has shown, cohabitation – as opposed to marriage – was much more common at this time than is conventionally presumed and was officially recognized as such. Pensions and separation allowances were paid to all 'dependents' of servicemen, including women who were 'unmarried wives', to cite government terminology, 'where there was evidence that a real home had been maintained'.[64] Rather, the emphasis on the female maintenance of a 'real home' was important. While the role of the state in combating juvenile delinquency and vulnerability had been established via the Children Act of 1908, there was still much concentration on the family unit and the male role model as the fundament of social order.[65] For many, male war service had proved the great disruptor. Cecil Leeson, who prepared a report for the penal reform charity the Howard League in 1917, argued that the rising crime rate was directly linked to newly absent father figure. Leeson claimed that many mothers were unable to raise their children properly as – with fathers at the Front – they were exhausted by the manifold demands of war work, queuing for food, and domestic duties.[66] Given this context, some considered the National Kitchen as yet another factor pulling women away from the maintenance of a real home and thus heightening social disorder.

The hostility towards National Kitchens in Newcastle and Liverpool and Llanelli, though, was exceptional and the majority of local government policymakers came to the opposite conclusion: however conservative their views on family and state in peace time, the National Kitchen was justified precisely because it was viewed as an emergency war measure designed to address the specific wartime problems identified above. Rather than destroying the female domestic role, the National Kitchen was considered a helping hand to women attempting to hold together a 'real home' in the absence of their male companions. In any case, as outlined below, the wartime state's patriotic rebranding of public feeding ensured that concerns about women being displaced from home and hearth to a new radical public space were dampened.

Rhondda's appointment of Spencer in November 1917 had given the initiative an infectious entrepreneurial thrust and new sites were starting to appear across the country. Spencer was also determined the public face of the public eatery would be an aristocrat, not a working woman. The dominance of Spencer meant that food vigilance committees were soon to be disappointed in their aspiration to gain greater control over communal feeding. Spencer was suspicious of these bodies and declared himself resolutely opposed to National Kitchens becoming 'class kitchens'.[67] Clearly, Spencer viewed food vigilance committees – with their female and working-class profile – as representative of creeping socialism. In an obsequious despatch to Rhondda, he argued instead that elite patronage would dispel any taint of radicalism and ensure popularity:

> There is no one the working woman looks up to like a Lord. I have found it so in electioneering times. A Lord on a platform will draw more working women to any hall than anyone else. We should have to get noble Lords and Ladies to patronise the communal kitchens and have the fact well press-campaigned.[68]

Men like Rhondda – Lords Bountiful – were Spencer's preferred public relations mechanism. Yet this desire for noble patronage was not shared across the Ministry. The most significant instruction from the Ministry of Food was that National Kitchens were 'not to be conducted as a charity'; rather, they had to function as a business, complete with a full set of accounts.[69] Queen Mary may have opened the first 'National Kitchen', then, but under the new scheme the philanthropic lady of the ladel was becoming very much a thing of the past. The Ministry of Food's National Kitchens Handbook, published in late 1917 as the number of state-subsidized kitchens grew, warned against any spirit of 'condescension or patronage' towards customers.[70] Its tone was undoubtedly inspired by Sylvia Pankhurst's views on communal feeding, which she expressed early in the war: [it should] 'be a slogan against profiteering... carry no stigma of charity... supply first-rate food at cost-price'.[71] The anonymously authored National Kitchens Handbook largely concurred. These sites would, on the one hand, avoid the taint of charity and, on the other, 'be conducted without loss to the ratepayer or taxpayer'.[72] These were to be popular ventures rather than schemes solely for the very poor. The message from Spencer's civil servants seemed to be that if he really wanted National Kitchens to operate along business lines, he would have to drop some of his penchant for aristocrats.

In practice, the early running of National Kitchens was undertaken by a mixture of central government, local government and private enterprise. In the first few months, most were run by local businessmen and overseen by local government, while the overarching administration was centralized. Beneath Spencer, the director of National Kitchens, there were assistant directors for each British county. Reflecting the standards of the age, each local director was assigned a woman inspector or supervisor, not to assist in planning but to ensure cleanliness: 'to see that the standard of kitchens in his district is well kept up'.[73] National Kitchens, as businesses, may have been managed locally but they were subject to direction by the Food Controller (Rhondda) and assisted by a Treasury grant. The grant initially covered a quarter of costs and a further grant was available once a kitchen had proved its financial viability. Kitchens were only deemed official National Kitchens after proving to the Ministry over a number of months that they were viable financial concerns. Local authorities were then able pay back the loan via ten yearly instalments.[74]

As noted in a Commons debate of early 1918, working-class women had performed the 'pioneer work in starting public kitchens' yet they increasingly found themselves marginalized by the new order.[75] Voluntary communal kitchens run by working-class women, from which National Kitchens had sprung, could be established or re-established in the future, contended Spencer, but only if they subjected themselves to local authority supervision. In the eyes of Spencer the businessman, professionalism was paramount and any non-affiliated communal ventures would not be Treasury funded.

On the other hand, although the National Kitchens Handbook provided specific models for urban and rural kitchens,[76] Spencer was keen to disassociate the National Kitchens division of the Ministry of Food from accusations of statist uniformity. He had no objection to setting up 'special' kitchens to target particular occupational groups such as city clerks; likewise 'special kitchens' would also have to be established for areas in which Jews formed a majority of the population, he reasoned, 'as their mode of living must be considered special'.[77]

Spencer was certainly not having it all his own way at the Ministry, though, as the National Kitchen took on a communal appeal which overtook Spencer's preference for take-away feeding. In towns and cities, National Kitchens soon evolved into cheap restaurants. The initial policy that no food could be consumed on-site soon gave way to pressure and National Kitchens evolved seamlessly into restaurants, first by adjacent buildings being donated to or acquired by the Ministry to serve as dining rooms, then by design. These were large canteens where one received a ticket upon entering and then exchanged it for cheap meals at the counter. At the flagship 'Kitchen for All' on Westminster Bridge a small staff – two cooks, two kitchen-maids, a superintendent and a cashier – proved sufficient to cater for between 1,200 to 2,000 people a day.[78] For speed, customers purchased coupons from a cashier upon entering the premises rather than handing over money after eating. Contact with 'shippers and important dealers in the great markets' meant that meat was procured at 25 per cent of retail price – savings which were in turn passed on to customers.[79] Most National Kitchens opened at lunch and dinner time (from 11.30 am to 2 pm and between 5 pm and 8 pm). Fish was the predominant dish for the evening meal. The sample lunch menu provided in the official National Kitchens handbook also provided a price structure.[80]

Sample Menu (lunch):

Item	Price
Half a pint of soup	1d
Joint of meat (with entrees)	4d (6d)
Scones	0.5d
Side vegetables	1d
Puddings and cakes	1d

Another aspect crucial in differentiating National Kitchens from soup kitchens was the need to keep up appearances. The Ministry instructed that each outlet 'must not resemble a soup kitchen for the poorest sections of society', but rather a place in which 'ordinary people in ordinary circumstances' could purchase an attractive yet cheap meal.[81] Staff had to be well dressed and cooks experienced and the decor was not to look cheap. Gramophones and pianos were recommended to add to the ambience.[82] A report in the *Scarborough Post* on Hull's central National Kitchen encapsulated this:

> The Hull people do not go into a back street. They avail of commanding premises in a good and busy thoroughfare, they fit their premises on modern lines, and there is no suspicion of shabby genteelness to be observed. On the contrary, were it not for the artistically painted signs you would never dream it was a National Kitchen. The place has the appearance of being a prosperous confectionary and café business. It is dainty and pleasing to the eye and the goods delivered are in appetising form. The business done is enormous. So far fourteen kitchens have been started in Hull … [83]

In a further move away from the charitable aspect of the soup kitchens of the past, Spencer was determined that employees be paid rather than work voluntarily. 'Anybody's work is nobody's work' he contended, 'and you cannot dismiss a voluntary worker, you have to appeal to him'; therefore 'well-meaning amateurs' would not be entertained.[84] In feeding the masses, professionalism was overtaking voluntarism.

Conclusion

The product of bottom-up female voluntarism, the British communal kitchen of the twentieth century was the result of local working-class initiative which soon came to be appropriated by national government as a plank of the war effort. Along the way, as outlined, it was bureaucratized, professionalized and deradicalized. State sponsorship brought with it a patriotic makeover and aristocratic patronage. But there would be no return to the days of the 'Lady Bountiful' as the functions of National Kitchens expanded and price structures, wages and formats were formalized. Regional differences continued, and anxieties about its political connotations nagged, but the National Kitchen represented a marked expansion of the central state in wartime Britain. The following chapter discusses how the situation developed.

3

The development of emergency public feeding in the First World War

Introduction

In December 1917, as food queues lengthened, sugar and butter were placed under local rationing schemes. As a prelude to the extension of rationing, which came in January 1918, Rhondda introduced flour and potato subsidies and empowered local councils to control food via locally appointed Food Control Committees.[1] The impact of these bodies on public feeding is discussed below, as the phenomenon moved further away from local bottom-up action towards substantial standardization and growth, in the process becoming a threat to private food retail. At the same time, as this chapter shows, there was still room for colourful local agency in the broader movement, the social implications of which were a cultural shift in British dining habits which excited food reformers and alarmed conservatives. This chapter concludes with the mounting resistance to the National Kitchen and documents its untimely end.

Food Control Committees and the forward march of public feeding

While Food Control Committees (hereafter FCCs) were mostly composed of trade professionals familiar with food supply and distribution, when it came to questions such as the future location of communal kitchens, the female working-class consumer was arguably best placed to advise. Although FCCs were required to contain at least one woman and one representative of labour, it has been claimed that working-class women were largely absent from these new bodies.[2] This was not always the case[3] but the coming of FCCs nevertheless represented a broader shift away from working-class leadership on food supply problems and towards government control.

This change was reflected in the standardization of National Kitchens. The government's 'National Kitchens Order' of 25 February 1918 instructed local authorities to establish National Kitchens 'as a matter of urgency and as a form of insurance against acute food shortage'. The Ministry of Food was in favour of National Kitchens for four main reasons, which it summarized in pamphlet form:

- Food and fuel economy
- Nutritious food at reasonable price
- Skilfully prepared and properly cooked wholesome meals
- Economy of labour by collective preparation of food[4]

The National Kitchens order clarified that it was up to local authorities as to whether FCCs should run National Kitchens or whether a new committee should be formed to do so. It also offered advice on location: buildings with steam, such as public baths, were recommended, but location was left up to local initiative. For every large town or city, Spencer envisaged central kitchens (where cooking would take place) supplying a number of outlying 'distribution centres'.[5] However, similarly, the Ministry's order left this to local discretion.

The Ministry of Food also encouraged local authorities to take over kitchens which local food vigilance committees had decided to shut down because they were financially unviable.[6] This move further removed kitchens from the hands of voluntary local food committees, tying them up in the purse strings of local government. These transitions did not wholly remove bottom-up action in communal feeding. There were cases where deputations of workers, despairing at high retail prices, successfully lobbied local FCCs to open communal kitchens. Such was the case in Sheffield in January 1918, where the local FCC resolved to introduce its own communal kitchens despite the refusal of the Ministry of Food to provide financial assistance.[7] Theoretically, too, communal kitchens could be run independently of the local FCC or the National Kitchens network. In Liverpool, for example, women workers filled the vacuum by establishing their own cafe, canteen and 'Rest Room' serving very cheap meals.[8] However, fluctuations in rationing and supplies, accompanied by national orders, meant – practically speaking – that any independent communal feeding venture had to dialogue with FCCs in order to guarantee supplies and, more often than not, this meant coming under the aegis of Spencer's National Kitchens division of the Ministry of Food.[9]

By mid-1918 the Ministry of Food was pressing local authorities to establish National Kitchens and offering generous financial incentives if they did so. The largest National Kitchen in London, in Hammersmith, could feed 50,000 people a day and the biggest in Manchester 3,000.[10] Even villages (of 1,000 people or less) were urged by the Ministry to turn their local kitchen into a village canteen. National Kitchens could only be established, it ordered, in areas where there was sufficient population density and transport facilities. But villages were permitted to open so-called village canteens. Village canteens were also subject to special Ministry instructions designed to enhance agricultural productivity: soup had to be accompanied by food items which could be easily 'taken into the field', for example, Cornish pasties.[11]

In July 1918 Glasgow Corporation appointed three of its civic officers to visit National Kitchens across Britain and report back on their workings. The deputation presented its findings two months later. They showed that National Kitchens were booming. In Birmingham there was one central kitchen and seven 'subsidiary' kitchens (which appear to have functioned as depots for the central venue as well as canteens in their own right); the largest Birmingham public feeding site seated seventy-two people and served 2,500 portions a day. Hammersmith's massive central kitchen was doing a roaring trade, the deputation noted, and the Ministry's flagship kitchen on New Bridge Street in London was turning over a 'substantial profit'. 'There can be no doubt as to the success and popularity of the restaurant and the value received for the prices charged' was the verdict on the main London site, with the Glaswegian civic officers reporting queues to gain admission composed of 'all classes of the community' and stretching 100 yards up the pavement outside. The kitchens at Poplar, Holborn and Wandsworth were located in public baths but also proving very popular, according to the deputation. In Brighton, the main National Kitchen was predominately used by the 'middle and lower middle classes' whereas in Leeds the city's two kitchens were located 'in a busy industrial area surrounded by many workshops in which girls are employed'. Sheffield had six kitchens, Nottingham eighteen, Middlesbrough three and Bootle five. The deputation recommended National Kitchens be adopted in Glasgow for three key reasons which mirrored the Ministry of Food's justification for the scheme: economy of fuel, the nutritious value and affordability of the food and economy of labour. Glasgow Corporation approved.[12]

In other areas of the country there were mixed fortunes for National Kitchens. In the south west of England, the kitchen in the small Devon market town of Cullompton seemed to thrive, selling 150 meals within a few minutes of opening on 10 May 1917 and continuing to trade well past the armistice. The *Western Times* visited the restaurant in March 1918, reporting that the fare was 'excellent'; its correspondent was delighted to have received a cooked dinner with meat, vegetables and potatoes followed by treacle pudding for just three pence.[13] The large market town of Taunton, in Somerset, also hosted a large and successful National Kitchen. Perhaps surprisingly, though, National Kitchens did not experience popularity in the larger neighbouring city of Exeter. Exeter city council formed a subcommittee, which visited Taunton's National Kitchen and recommended that Exeter should open one too. However, they faced stout local opposition. Critics pointed to a previous communal kitchen which had operated in a notorious slum area of the city named Exe Island, operating from a mission hall and serving poor food with utensils borrowed from the Exeter Penny Dinner Society. It had shut due to public disdain with one woman, when asked if she had been there, replying 'No I haven't come to that yet. It would be a disgrace if I were seen there'.[14] 'The taint of charity', as the Ministry of Food had termed it, was clearly persistent in this case, as was the lingering shame associated with the workhouse. Other southern towns doubted whether they had the population necessary to sustain demand and the scheme was turned down in Ilfracombe, Exmouth, Dartmouth and Newton Abbot. By contrast, seaside towns which experienced a large number on tourist visitors – such as Torquay – adopted the model. To return to Exeter, the council eventually refused to open a National Kitchen despite its subcommittee's enthusiastic findings. As well as the bad taste left over from Exe Island's slum kitchen, a more powerful disincentive was at work which ultimately swung the council against National Kitchens: an opposition to any municipal trading or state monopoly which would take away the livelihood of tradespeople in the city, whether greengrocers or restaurateurs. The argument went that National Kitchens were an affront to the shopkeeper and a traditional sense of 'fair play' in British commerce. It was a powerful point of view, and one which National Kitchen enthusiasts at the Ministry of Food would come up against repeatedly, as discussed later.

Yet despite regional differences, by April 1918 it seemed that there was no stopping National Kitchens' forward march. Even the secretary of the WNC had overcome his initially begrudging attitude to National Kitchens. Middleton wrote that kitchens were 'quite successful and have become exceedingly popular'. Middleton advised that 'the moment for starting them is when there is a scarcity in some particular class of food which the people regard as very important'. The extension of rationing provided such a moment, argued the secretary of the WNC, because it had forced people to cook more with vegetables. This meant that 'a National Kitchen should do better than the ordinary private person does' because vegetable broths and soups were their stock in trade.[15] The WNC, it seemed, were finally on board. Middleton wrote to Spencer in May 1918 promising Labour support for the further expansion of National Kitchens, telling him 'if you can only get the local authorities to move, our local Labour people in the main will be only too glad to assist'.[16]

Meanwhile, the values of National Kitchens were extolled at cinemas in propaganda organized by the Ministry of Food's Economy section. Providing 'object lessons' for the public in how to manage want, the campaign bore all the hallmarks of Kennedy Jones's 'Do-it-now' political ethic. Spencer announced that his division would avail of 'tactful speakers, quick witted and forceful, to educate the people' and show food economy films in schools.[17] The Ministry also recommended that National Kitchens incorporate cookery instruction, another departure from the earlier take-away model and a move towards educational expertise, as mentioned subsequently. It advised cooperation with Local Education Authority officials responsible for school dinners and insisted on female and labour representation at organizational level.[18]

School dinners had been provided since 1906 under the Education (Provision of Meals) Acts.[19] Pointing to the increase in food prices, left-wing voices demanded the abolition of means-tested school dinners and the roll-out of a universal national feeding programme in schools.[20] Rhondda, however, did not envisage the extension of National Kitchens into schools and pointed to the fall in demand for school dinners since the outbreak of war. This, he argued, was proof that poverty had actually diminished over the course of the war. At the same time, he advised local authorities to monitor closely local food supply and nutritional standards and, if necessary, to avail of National Kitchens if a noticeable drop in the 'health, physique and energy' of local schoolchildren occurred.[21] The health of local children was a yardstick by which some National Kitchens were measured. For example, the physical condition of Aberystwyth's children had undergone a marked improvement thanks to public feeding, it was claimed at the war's end, with the 'hot nutritious meal at midday' a 'boon' to the overall health of the town's young.[22]

With National Kitchens expanding their operation as 1918 wore on, longer-term considerations to do with nutrition and public health (rather than the immediate provision of calories) began to feature in writings about National Kitchens. A window into the contemporary operation and future prospects of National Kitchens was provided in memorandum form by Marion Phillips. Phillips, a member of the Women's Labour League and the Consumer Council, in the words of her fellow Fabian Beatrice Webb, adopted a 'critical attitude towards all persons and institutions'.[23] Her report therefore provides an honest account of how well National Kitchens were functioning by mid-1918.

Phillips was generally supportive of the principle of community dining, which she hoped would become a fixture of improved post-war working-class housing estates. She wrote that 'national school canteens' were in fact operating in London alongside what she called 'national restaurants'. Phillips reported on the Ministry's kitchen in Blackfriars in London, which took the form of a self-service restaurant with no waitress service. 'Poor cooking noticeable in some kitchens', she noted, but in general she deemed them to be operating well. The Ministry's Poplar kitchen was a notable success, too, in her opinion: 'well arranged, well-lit and beautifully clean', noted Phillips, but 'situated in one of the public baths so will not last post-war', she estimated.[24] And yet there were greater problems for National Kitchens than location and Phillips identified problems which were eventually to lead to the National Kitchen's demise. These challenges were borne of the extension of rationing, in particular meat rationing. With people receiving meat via their ration, Phillips reported several cases where recipients refused to give up coupons for the meat on offer in the National Kitchen. In response, the department was attempting to arrange a new system whereby certain types of offal would be provided coupon-free.[25] As detailed below, the National Kitchens division of the Ministry of Food came to devote considerable time to the question of cooking techniques, dietary habits and public nutrition. However, the steady introduction of a more comprehensive rationing system, as documented by Phillips, was later to sound the National Kitchen's death knell.

The Peripatetic Piewoman: A case study in female leadership in public feeding

As demonstrated by Phillips' interest in the matter, one of the most significant features of National Kitchens was female involvement. At every level – from the early female volunteers who inspired the state to sponsor social eating, to the paid kitchen staff and servers who ran National Kitchens, to the women who inspected them, to those who wrote about their social, political and nutritional significance – women were instrumental in the movement. One of the most enthusiastic, famous and unusual proponents of National Kitchens was a woman named Florence Horsburgh. Horsburgh, who would later become the

Conservative MP for Dundee, was the manager of Chelsea's National Kitchen and achieved her renown by distributing food from a donkey-pulled cart. Charles Spencer's vision of take-away tram kitchens may not have been widely realized, but the most notable example of the National Kitchen as 'travelling kitchen' was realized through the actions of this 'peripatetic piewoman', as the press came to term her.

Horsburgh was a determined and inventive National Kitchen manager before her well-publicized stunt in distributing food by donkey and cart. Chelsea was one of the more affluent London boroughs and when its kitchen opened in April 1918 she threw down the gauntlet by declaring 'I challenge any of the West End restaurants with their high prices to produce meals better cooked or more daintily served than those provided at the new Chelsea National Kitchen'.[26] This prompted *Tatler* magazine, chronicler of British high society life, to raise a wry eyebrow. *Tatler* responded to Horsburgh with faint praise, remarking on how 'customers shall even be able to order food in advance from the new Chelsea National Kitchen. All you have to do is fetch it hot and ready – which really does sound, doesn't it, a great solution to the awful servant question?'[27]

Although written in jest, *Tatler*'s coverage of Horsburgh's challenge may well have resonated with West London's upper middle class, who were feeling the pinch due to wartime conditions. Horsburgh's kitchen, which operated from the town hall of the west London borough, proved very popular. Too popular, in fact, as queues for food and seats started to form inside the venue. Her solution to the confines of space was typically eccentric: Horsburgh erected an enormous marquee on adjacent waste ground to increase capacity.[28] She was also good at communicating with other National Kitchens in the capital, responding to their needs by sending surplus staff and food to them by taxi. Horsburgh even opened a garden for growing vegetables served with the meals. Like most managers of National Kitchens, she was keen to make her venue as attractive as possible and recruited notable local artists to help her with signage and decoration; even the outdoor tent was decked out with blue tablecloths and vases of daisies. In designing her menu, Horsburgh received advice from professional chefs and, in doing so, was ahead of the later practice of London's National Kitchens, who received advice from the gastronomic experts of the Club Culinaire as well as Eustace Miles and company.[29] In line with the Ministry's guidelines, Horsburgh's kitchen was run as an efficient commercial concern, and not a charitable one.[30] Due to her forthright leadership and its affluent and bohemian surrounds, Horsburgh's Chelsea kitchen soon became an object of fascination for newspaper

Figures 3.1 and 3.2 Florence Horsburgh (1889–1969); Daily Mirror, 15 March 1918.

men. One newspaper reporter extolled its 'queer queues' (queer, in this case, referred to their cross-class composition) featuring

> artists, smart women, smart servants, professional men with silk hats, working women, boys from shops, and boys from public schools... it has already put out the evening fires in some of the big Embankment houses, the parlour maids bringing dinners home from the kitchen... if the present aristocracy is going to disappear and be replaced by an elite of talent the Dames of the Kitchens should have a special branch themselves.[31]

The Chelsea kitchen's salubrious location seemed to provoke titillation in the London press pack. Fascinated by the image of butlers from big houses on Green Park hurrying back to their wealthy masters with rice puddings and meat pies, numerous articles documented how all classes of people were to be found in the Chelsea kitchen, from ladies in frock coats to grubby little newsboys munching on treacle tarts. 'Fur coats vied with worn calicoes', as one article put it.[32] Since patrons of the Chelsea National Kitchens could either dine in or take food away, the *Evening Standard* duly came up with a spurious tale of a 'titled woman', allegedly well known in high society (but who wished to remain anonymous) who told one of their reporters (who also, unsurprisingly, also remained anonymous) how she had visited the Chelsea kitchen and

'Chose some vegetable hot pot, beans and onion, and a treacle roll… I then carried the lot home – a difficult feat as I had to travel by bus and then walk. As I was going down one of the small streets to the other side of Sloane Square I found myself the centre of attraction. "Ere's a smart lidy with a gold bag carryin 'er food home" called out one of the urchins in the road.[33]

Part of the attraction for the media was the fact that Horsburgh herself was from the world of the upper class. She was a middle-class Edinburgh woman whose former patron, Lady Ethyl Beatty, was the wife of Vice-Admiral David Beatty. Beatty led the first battlecruiser squadron at the Battle of Jutland in 1916 and would rise to First Sea Lord in 1919. For this reason, Horsburgh's activities soon gained particular attention, not least because in the summer of 1918 her enthusiastic embrace of public feeding came to embrace a new oddity. She began experimenting with taking dishes out to people in the poorer districts of Chelsea borough from a wagon pulled by a donkey. Piled high with sausage rolls, fishcakes, apple dumplings and jam tarts, Horsburgh's little cart would trundle slowly through the streets after the Chelsea National Kitchen had closed for the day, conveying surplus food and other treats specially prepared in the kitchen. Heralding her arrival by blowing on a battered old tin trumpet, Horsburgh and donkey would attract crowds drawn to the novelty and the cheap prices, and would usually sell out within half an hour.[34] Her activities soon won her a rechristening as the 'Perambulating Piewoman' and the 'Peripatetic Piewoman'.[35] Other newspapers reported in amazement how this 'Lady' would navigate the backstreets with a 'hawker's barrow': in travelling away from Chelsea town hall and into working-class areas, Horsburgh was crossing class boundaries as well.[36]

After some months Horsburgh was able to expand to sell hot food after a local business donated a stove for her cart. The cart soon became a large wagon with lanterns, a roof and several assistants inside. As the donkey pulled the wagon along Horsburgh, cutting an endearingly eccentric figure in long skirt and large hat, would stand on the outer rail and summon the hungry hordes with the shrill notes of her trumpet. The cold sausage rolls had been replaced by piping hot fish and chips.[37] Horsburgh was, by this point, travelling out to Chelsea's poorer neighbourhoods three evenings a week. By this stage press commentary had moved from amusement to something resembling adulation. One newspaper credited Horsburgh with affecting nothing less than a social revolution. She had not only proved that a woman could elevate the work of cockney whelk sellers and barrowmen into a social virtue, it claimed, but also demonstrated that upper middle-class women could take on useful occupations outside the house.[38]

Horsburgh's efforts were to gain her a royal audience. In early November 1918 she boldly declared 'I shall not be content until London's first travelling kitchen visits Buckingham Palace'. By the end of the month the invitation had duly arrived[39] and Horsburgh, wagon and donkey trundled through the gates of the palace, past saluting guards, to a waiting Queen Mary, who told her she was disappointed that she hadn't signalled her arrival at the palace by blowing on her famous tin trumpet.[40] Coinciding with Horsburgh's celebrity was a rise in prices with some hot dishes from her cart now being sold for six pence instead of the recommended two or three pence! Yet in every other regard her efforts stand as a shining example of the success of the National Kitchen model. It was managed locally and creatively rather than by centralized diktat. Food was available to take away, to eat in or to buy in the street. It achieved a cross-class appeal, regularly feeding 30,000 people a week with nutritious, cheap and appetizing food in attractive surroundings. In doing so, it achieved great economies in food and fuel. Moreover, Horsburgh seemed to be a natural when it came to public relations. The Chelsea scheme was privately run by Horsburgh but its net profit – which after the war stood at an impressive £2,709 – was duly given over to the local council's coffers. As a public servant, then, Horsburgh deserves great credit.

Food reformers: Nutritional instruction and egalitarian eating

Pre-war, British imperial might functioned around the ideal of free trade and the abundance it promised. Yet this nationalistic pride in free trade, and the cheap white loaf it delivered, simultaneously celebrated foreign production within a global market system while at the same time retaining a chauvinistic scepticism about 'alien' cultures of consumption.[41] Food reformers Cox, Bradley and Miles – authors of the *Public Kitchens Handbook* – were very much aware of the prevailing disdain for foodstuffs considered too exotic. In offering advice as to what sort of food National Kitchens should serve, they therefore considered that to ensure long-term popularity National Kitchens should 'bow to prejudice' by serving established British meat-based dishes. On reading the *Handbook*, one gets the sense that this practical advice was nonetheless galling for urbane vegetarian types like Eustace Miles. Accordingly, the guidebook could not help but take a swipe at the 'appalling ignorance' of the British people when it came to preparing attractive food. This situation, which the handbook's authors termed a 'national disgrace', had led to the neglect of many different cuisines, most notably those of the 'pleasant land of France – the shrine of all true chefs'. Yet foreign cuisines and the greater use of vegetables should be introduced only gradually, they instructed. Gravies should be prepared in the 'British way' – from the juices of their own meats – and not, 'as in many restaurants where foreigners rule', from a mixed meat gravy.[42] Begrudgingly, the Ministry's team of food reformers recognized that to foist nutritious yet unfamiliar fare on the British public at large would be to invite ridicule.

As mentioned, the *Public Kitchens Handbook* was spearheaded by Eustace Miles, very much the poster boy food reformer of the day. As a public figure, Miles was well aware of how strange the advocacy of health foods and vegetarianism sounded to the man on the Clapham omnibus: his fame had seen him lampooned in the music hall. Take, for example, 'The Mutton Chop', a popular ditty of the time:

> Let Eustace Miles find muscular force
> In carrot cutlets with Plasmon sauce
> Or other equally messy slop
> But give me my old fashioned mutton chop[43]

'Plasmon' was one of Miles's health food products. Another was 'Emprote': a nut-based energy bar marketed to cyclists and walkers. That great curmudgeon of the era, the writer G. K. Chesterton, rubbished what he saw as faddish consumerism masquerading as rugged authenticity. In a put-down aimed squarely at Miles, he deliberately mislabelled the name of his non-meat substitute as 'Nutter'.[44] Chesterton's may well be the first use of this derogatory term for a mentally unsound person in the English language. Chesterton, unsurprisingly, was not impressed by National Kitchens either, writing elsewhere that a 'communal kitchen' was not 'a real kitchen'.[45] Miles, though, was aware of such popular prejudice against him and the vegetarian image in general. He himself disliked the term 'vegetarian' due to such negative cultural connotations. 'It stands for cranks and bewhiskered gentlemen and other undesirable people' he once opined to a reporter, going on to claim 'my slogan is a balanced meatless diet'. Miles, seemingly at pains to emphasize his normality, also insisted 'I eat vegetables, eggs and cheese like yourself and others, in their right proportion'.[46]

Miles' awareness of a popular 'common-sense' disdain for vegetarian food was borne out in the *Public Kitchens Handbook*. If the desire among proponents of National Kitchens to transcend the Victorian philanthropy of the soup kitchen was palpable, so too was the worry that National Kitchens would be seen by the public as lofty avant-garde projects pushing trends like vegetarianism. The *Public Kitchens Handbook* duly noted the public 'suspicion' that soup kitchens only served bland 'bean-based dishes'. On the other hand, the wartime imperative not to waste food allowed Miles and his fellow food reformers some room for nutritional instruction. They warned about the negative nutritional effect of over-peeling and over-boiling vegetables: 'The peel, tops and outside leaves contain valuable salts which are lost when poured down the sink and boiling alters the composition of the salts'.[47] Instead simmering, stewing, frying or braising vegetables was recommended. Flavour, the handbook told its readers, was paramount, stimulating the digestive fluids and helping to extract the full nutritional value. 'Dull cooking', by contrast, would leave the digestive fluids 'inert'.[48]

The latest research on diet change during the First World War, which challenges some of the optimistic conclusions of the Working Class Cost of Living (Sumner) Committee of 1918, demonstrates how the British working-class diet underwent a reduction in the consumption of sugar, cheese, butter, butcher's meat, fruit and vegetables, and the increased consumption of bacon, sausages and margarine. This resulted in an overall shortage of vitamins A and B12 for skilled and unskilled workers and reductions in vitamins C, D and riboflavin for skilled workers.[49] Although vitamins were not understood properly at the time, such revelations would have disappointed the authors of the *Public Kitchens Handbook* who, in attempting to strike a balance between healthy eating and popular consumption habits, envisaged that the meat consumed in National Kitchens would compensate for potential shortages of foodstuffs which were not considered key. Therefore, although the handbook was co-written by Miles, a committed vegetarian, it devoted considerable time to explaining how to ensure meat was cooked properly and attractively. Even cheap cuts of meat should not be merely boiled 'for there is an unexplained repugnance to a grey hash', it instructed; 'instead, all meats should be lightly fried, then cooked slowly with a little stock and vegetables', with the unhealthy technique of deep frying recommended as the most economical means of cooking meat.[50]

All of this spoke to a broader desire to improve the national character through improving diet and reducing waste. The moral panic surrounding the poor physical standard of British recruits to the Anglo-Boer war of 1899–1902 had resulted in a mood of anxiety about how poor nutrition negatively impacted national fitness (and thereby fighting prowess).[51] The *Handbook* therefore combined patriotism, food culture and diet, its authors hoping that National Kitchens would

> avoid the tendency of all large kitchens to provide "factory food" and would instead be "centres of civilisation" fostering the "art and skill" of good food rather than its "manufacture".[52] Gas was favoured for cooking over electricity because "few persons familiar with its use were available" and the price too high;

Figure 3.3 Eustace Miles (1868–1948), Wikimedia Commons.

the latest technology such as roasting ovens, steamers and water jackets were to be used only where available.[53] It instructed that "odds and ends must be used" – peelings, stalks, outside leaves and tops of vegetables, to say nothing of bone and gristle.[54]

Ultimately, the final draft of the Ministry's official National Kitchens handbook was edited heavily by civil servants. Interestingly, favourable social consequences anticipated and explicitly identified by Eustace Miles as a corollary of the movement, such as the power of communal dining acting to quell popular demand for alcohol, did not make it into the final draft.[55] This is surprising because in the late nineteenth and early twentieth centuries addiction to alcohol was viewed as socially parasitic by not only temperance campaigners, but also the medical profession. Excessive consumption of alcohol was commonly seen as damaging not only to the individual but to the national body and alcohol, as a problem for both national and physical bodies, was seldom separated from other social questions.[56] Anxiety about alcohol was palpable in the 1904 Report of the Interdepartmental Committee on Physical Deterioration following the Boer war and was repeated in the Public Kitchens handbook compiled by Miles and his colleagues. Presumably, then, since National Kitchens were 'dry' venues and there were a raft of other wartime controls on alcohol, the Ministry of Food did not deem it appropriate to include temperance as a stated goal of public feeding. This seems a judicious decision, since the inclusion of any overtly pro-temperance aims within National Kitchens' remit might well have compounded the joyless 'bean-based' image problem identified by Miles et al.

Hippisley Cox, Bradley and Miles were not the only high-profile food reformers recruited by the Ministry of Food to assist in the National Kitchens movement. Three prominent women – Maud Pember Reeves, Constance Peel and Kate Manley – were recruited by the Ministry of Food to head a 'women's department', which became the National Kitchens advisory committee. Reeves was, like Marion Phillips, an antipodean suffragist and Fabian socialist, who in 1913 published *Round about a pound a week*, an influential survey of poverty in Lambeth which pointed to the structural causes of poverty rather than maternal negligence.[57] Her co-director Peel was familiar to the fashionable classes as editor of *The Queen*, a regular contributor to *The Lady* and, from 1918, editor of the women's page in *The Daily Mail*. Manley was an inspector of domestic subjects for the Board of Education.[58] Since Reeves' 1913 report had called for free school meals, Manley provided an important link between social reformers like Reeves and Peel and the educational authorities and colleges of domestic science. Reeves' role was interrupted by bereavement following the death of her son in June 1917 but Peel travelled nationwide on behalf of the Ministry, delivering almost 200 addresses promoting the economical use of food.[59]

Nutritional reform, then, was a central plank of the public-feeding message. Reacting to the mounting food shortages of late 1917, domestic scientists issued advice informed by contemporary ideas. For example, the British national conference of teachers of domestic science produced a pamphlet in May 1917 which not only contained the simple instruction that people must 'eat less food' but also advocated a technique known as Fletcherizing. Named after the American theorist Horace Fletcher, Fletcherizing was the technique of chewing food excessively in order to obtain the health benefits of better digestion. 'Well masticated, or in other words, well chewed food, yields more nourishment to the body than food which is eaten quickly and is not properly chewed', instructed Britain's teachers of domestic science.[60] Subsequently dismissed as a fad, British advocacy of Fletcherism nonetheless exhibits the wartime willingness to embrace alternative nutritional theories as a means of securing wartime efficiency and economy. Similar themes occurred in the works of Elizabeth Waldie, head-teacher at the Glasgow and West of Scotland College of Domestic Science, the largest of the three great Scottish cookery training schools, who published her best-selling *Economical Recipes suitable for War Cookery* in 1917. Cooking must respond to 'the greatest struggle of nations the world has ever known' by supplying energy for war work and achieving fuel economy, she wrote. She broke wartime nutrition into four food groups. 'Flesh Formers' – scarce sources of protein such as meat, eggs and milk – which could be replaced by cheaper meats, nuts, beans and dried fruit; 'Heat and Energy Producers' – fats which were in short supply – and which could also be obtained from suet, nuts, seeds and fish; 'Sugars and Starches' – for which Waldie recommended replacing jam with syrup and treacle; and 'Blood Purifiers and Bone Formers' – to be found in mineral salts and vegetable acids and now largely to be gotten from green vegetables. The message was the necessity of substitution and Waldie's book of *War Cookery* also provided a number of less-than-appetizing substitute recipes, including 'Poor Man's Goose' (made from pig liver); 'Brains on Toast' (made from sheep's brains); and 'Very Economical Plum Pudding'.[61]

Spencer's National Kitchens division was keen to harness the expertise of individuals like Waldie as well as using Britain's colleges of domestic science to its advantage. Cookery schools had been increasingly forced to adapt to the wartime ethic of egalitarian eating in instruction as well as recommendation. Waldie had redesigned her college's entire syllabus in the summer of 1917 in order to ensure that every course adhered to the imperative of cookery instruction 'of the greatest nutritive value at the least possible cost'. As part of the national Food Economy Campaign, the college dropped its Special Certificate in High Class Cookery in favour of free cookery courses to large audiences on topics such as 'meatless cooking'.[62] In general, Britain's schools of domestic science did their bit by publishing leaflets on wartime cookery, running cookery classes for widows, and even carrying out experiments into 'fatless dishes' and other nutritional innovations.[63] To the Ministry of Food, collaboration with the country's domestic economy schools was an exciting prospect.

The feeling, however, was not mutual. Whereas the Edinburgh School of Cookery resolved, in April 1917, to establish 'one or more communal kitchens', the Glasgow school worried that the autonomy of cookery training schools was threatened by the emergence of National Kitchens.[64] The Liverpool school sent a board member to inspect London's National Kitchens; after hearing her report the board agonized over the 'very great expenses' for 'equipment and upkeep' and hoped they would not end up being incorporated into the project and thus end up footing the bill.[65] These fears were, it turns out, well-founded. The movement towards a more statist political economy of food was underlined when, in May 1918, cookery colleges received instruction from Charles Spencer that all new National Kitchens 'in large populations centres' were to be located near to cookery training schools. The Ministry of Food envisaged that training schools were to educate future National Kitchen staff, providing them with professional standards. College principals were now instructed to liaise with their local education authority and food control committee.[66] In April 1918 the Ministry of Food took over the restaurant and training kitchens of London's National Training School of Cookery. The Ministry hoped that availing of the 'really first class cooking' of the training school would reinforce the point that National Kitchens were not merely cheap and cheerful.[67]

Meanwhile, the training schools had to come to terms with losing their autonomy as the interests of the war effort took precedence. Steadily, the leading teachers of domestic science were poached by the Ministry of Food, which sweetened the pill by improving the salaries of the best teachers if they agreed to leave their posts to become National Kitchen supervisors.[68] Thus, in May 1918, Scotland's war cookery guru, Elizabeth Waldie, was headhunted by the Ministry and appointed supervisor for National Kitchens in the south-west of Scotland.[69] Such head-hunting tactics revealed that the alliance between colleges of domestic science and National Kitchens was an uneasy one. The Ministry of Food on the one hand was keen to recruit the principals of domestic science colleges onto consultative committees but, on the other, was increasingly reluctant to release food to their institutions for educational purposes because to do so was seen as 'wasteful'.[70] Domestic science colleges, in turn, felt squeezed as their best people left to take up new posts created by the Ministry. It was not long, however, before National Kitchens raised the ire of another, and more influential, lobby group (as discussed subsequently).

'Civilizational Value'? Arnold Bennett versus GK Chesterton

The incorporation of educational establishments signified the expanding scope of the emergency public feeding of the First World War and raised the expectation that it might outlast the national emergency. The received wisdom that public feeding would become a permanent feature of British life was breezily repeated in press reports across Britain. In Wales alone, for example, various regional press reports of 1918/19 relayed the 'practical certainty that National Kitchens will long outlast the war', that they would form 'a permanent feature in English public life', and that the economic rationale, even after the war, was 'obvious'.[71] However, economic viability was one thing, long-term civilizational worth quite another, and a constant feature of British public-feeding experience was the disproportionate attention it attracted from public figures and celebrities concerned with the latter question.

There was something about the term 'communal' which was unpalatable not only of members of the establishment like Lord Rhondda but also of broadly traditionalist cultural figures. G. K. Chesterton's dismissiveness of the communal ethos was surpassed by his literary contemporary Arnold Bennett, who – writing about National Kitchens – praised the name change because 'Britons are too individualistic and too independent to like anything communal'.[72] Bennett's comments on National Kitchens, published in the *Daily News* in mid-1918, are significant because of the author's relationship with modernism, and literary modernism in particular. The futuristic, universalist bent of communal dining also chimed with the ethos of high modernism of the 1910s and 1920s and its impulse towards a radical break with the past.[73] Bennett's outlook, by contrast, was associated with the past, with much of his work drawing on his upbringing in the 'five towns' of the Staffordshire Potteries, old settlements subsumed into the modern polycentric city of Stoke-on-Trent in the early twentieth century. Bennett duly became a target of the literary and artistic modernists of the Bloomsbury set, who viewed him as symbolic of the old order. Well-fed and middle-aged when he composed his opinions on National Kitchens (one of his legacies was an omelette named after him by chefs at London's Savoy Grill), Bennett – who liked to think he knew a thing or two about gastronomy – went on to echo some of the sniffier verdicts of the *Public Kitchens Handbook*, claiming that the average British person 'does not understand either cooking or diet' and that French restaurants far surpassed their British equivalents.

Bennett, however, has also been represented in a more positive light as a champion of the expanding British working class. A popular author and journalist who was open about the fact that he wrote for money, he aimed his writing at a mass audience and aspired to be more in touch with 'the people' than his detractors of the intellectual avante-garde.[74] This aspect, too, is in evidence in Bennett's remarks on National Kitchens where, although critical of the term 'communal', he characterized resistance to the 're-baptized' scheme as 'reactionary', identifying middle-class snobbery as the enemy.

> I do not know how many national or municipal kitchens there are today. Probably not more than five hundred. There ought to be perhaps twenty thousand... municipal authorities ought to lead instead of waiting to be pushed. Innumerable towns are extremely sluggish... The impetus for them should and must come from the middle class. The lower class, for obvious reasons, is notoriously the class with the most adamantine prejudices about food. It has never had the chance to educate itself in diet and cooking. It is wants a huge, unmistakeable example, and that example it ought to have.[75]

That 'unmistakeable example', wrote Bennett, was the National Kitchen. They were eliminating waste, achieving economies of scale in buying and serving food cheaper, and offering ordinary people a greater variety of dishes than would otherwise be available. Anticipating the universalism and purchasing power of supermarkets, he saw National Kitchens as the way to overcome the small shopkeeper's refrain 'That is what I have to sell. You can take it or leave it'. What's more, Bennett (who, ironically enough, was to die of typhoid after defying the advice of a waiter not to drink water from the tap at a Parisian restaurant) identified expert nutritional advice as key to National Kitchens' success. Identifying the 'expert scientific management of their cooking processes' as favourable to the efforts of 'any single family – no matter how ingenious or up-to-date', he claimed

> A large proportion of the nation still has a secret contempt, and even hatred, of scientific methods and exact knowledge. Speak to it of calories and, like Lord Devonport, it will shy. Mention the theory of a scientific dietary and it will at once suspect that you intend either to starve it or to render the meal-table a purgatory. Say that the open fire and the saucepan are not the last word of culinary apparatus, and it will praise the cooking of its grandmother, who had nothing but the open fire and the saucepan. This reactionary spirit has got to be faced in the open and defeated by the force of proved facts.[76]

Bennett, it seemed, had changed his tune, and his praise for dieticians and food reformers would have been music to the ears of Eustace Miles. Some of these thoughts toed the official line, of course, and Bennett, who was at the time performing his war service as Director of Propaganda for France at the Ministry of Information, heaped the customary praise on Minister of Food Control Lord Rhondda. Like many people, his opposition to public feeding suddenly disappeared when it was wrapped within the patriotic priorities of the war effort. Yet Bennett's enthusiasm for the National Kitchen seemed to transcend wartime exigencies; insisting that National Kitchens 'ought to be encouraged and patronised and cried aloud for', he recommended that they continue after the war and not be written off as an extraordinary war measure.

Bennett's appraisal, though, also captured some of the problems that National Kitchens were starting to run up against with the end of the war in sight. Commenting on stories that National Kitchens had to be self-supporting, he urged that they do so, since any 'taint of institutionalism' would harm their popularity. Why, then, he wondered, were National Kitchens exempt from paying interest on the capital which they received via government? To continue post-war National Kitchens had to appear to be a 'business proposition' rather than a 'quasi paternal institution'. If the latter was the case, what Bennett termed 'distinctions of class' would take over:

> Nobody, not even a duchess, has the least hesitation about going into a post office; but ladies less majestic than duchesses will think twice about going into a National Kitchen to buy cooked food. This condition of things has to be altered. It is being altered to a certain extent. But in the puzzle-heads of large numbers of persons National Kitchens will continue to be confused with soup kitchens unless the guiding directors keep constantly in their mind that word "national" and constantly act up on it.[77]

However, as discussed later, the coming of peace would complicate the term 'national' and what it signified. Many would urge a return to the pre-war mantra of free trade as an essentially British value, something contrary to state-supported social eating whether dubbed 'national' or not. Moreover, the introduction of ration books issued to individuals and families had already started to damage National Kitchens. Bennett remarked on this, citing an instance in Salford where customers had criticized the quality of the meat served in the National Kitchen, claiming that their ration book coupons entitled them to better-quality meat than that on offer. Bennett blamed this on the managers of the Salford National Kitchen, giving examples from municipal kitchens in Hamburg and London where the ration value of a coupon could instead be spread over several days (and several meals). What he failed to appreciate was that the damage had already been done. With people adjusting to consumption via the rationing system, press coverage of incidents like this confirmed for some that National Kitchens, as Bennett would have put it, were 'quasi paternal' institutions meant only for the very poor.

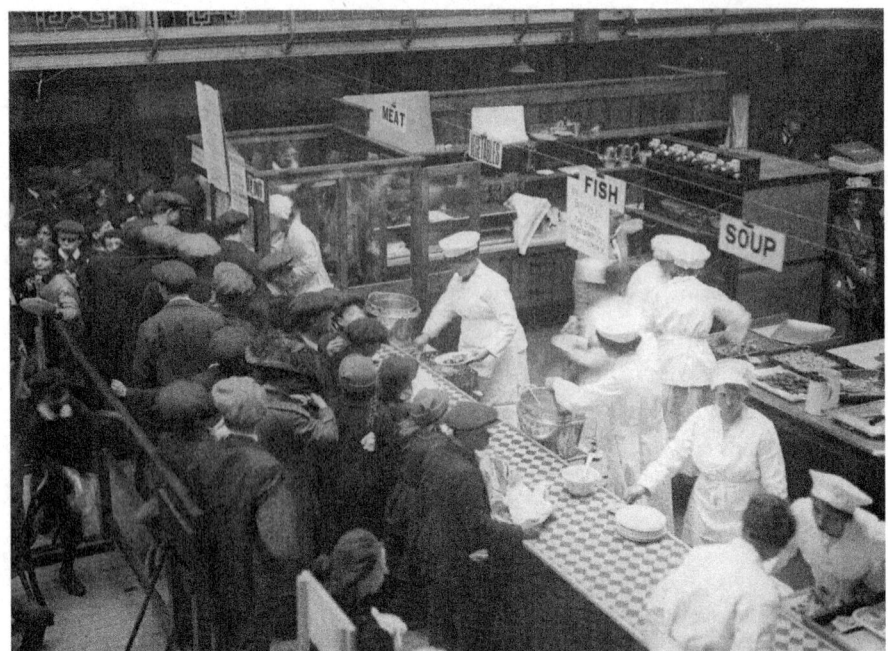

Figure 3.4 A bustling National Kitchen in Bow, London, 1918.

Resistance grows

In a Commons debate of June 1918 it was revealed that the Ministry of Food had been in discussion with a deputation of catering firms who had offered the use of their facilities as National Kitchens. Such collaboration was regarded as desirable given the expertise that the private firms would bring.[78] But while National Kitchens relied, then, to an extent, on private entrepreneurial initiative, they were increasingly seen as offensive to free trade. In August 1918 a deputation of Birmingham caterers met with the city's Lord Mayor to state their opposition to National Kitchens.[79] It was part of a coordinated campaign of resistance. The Birmingham scene was repeated in the same month in Glasgow, where the city corporation's special committee on National Kitchens met with a deputation from the Glasgow District Restaurateurs' and Hotel Keepers' Association. The restaurateurs had heard that the corporation was to buy a large restaurant in the city centre and run it as a 'national restaurant'. The terminology is significant: with the word 'restaurant' now increasingly creeping into discourse around public feeding, the restaurant trade reacted with alarm. The central location, claimed Glasgow's caterers, like their Birmingham counterparts, would be detrimental to the restaurant trade in the city. It was the location which mattered most – a 'national restaurant' would operate not in the city's slums, but on the bustling city centre Argyle Road.[80] Other owners of private enterprise, however, saw opportunity. Soon, private businesses were scrapping with one another in an effort to win contracts with the new public-feeding venue. Several Glasgow property owners approached the committee with rental offers for their premises. An iron works offered to rent their derelict canteen building to the Corporation at a preferential rate, and local ironmongers guaranteed a good quote on any kitchen equipment needed.[81] Naturally enough, though, a sizeable section of Glasgow's private food retail and restaurant trade cried foul at what they saw as the danger of state monopoly.

The resistance to national restaurants from the catering trade recurred throughout the country. This was not a matter of the trade trying to profiteer at a time of scarcity, maintained restaurant owners, rather the very principle of state-subsidized restaurants was wrong since it offended that quintessential British value – the notion of 'fair play'. A letter to the Ministry from London caterer John Pearce claimed that national restaurants, thanks to 'preferential treatment' from the state, had simply failed to 'play the game'. Pearce was the proprietor of the London-based 'JP' chain of cut-price restaurants, which suffered substantial wartime falls in gross profits.[82] Writing in late 1918, he claimed that Charles Spencer and the Ministry of Food could have fulfilled their duty by establishing national restaurants during dock strikes and hunger marches, but had preferred to concentrate on competing with, and undermining, private retailers like him.[83] This communique encapsulated another staple of popular pre-war free trade culture: the democratic ethic of the neutral state.[84] With the post-war return to normal trading conditions, proponents of 'fair play' like Pearce found the whiff of vested interests and the interference of the big state increasingly malodorous.

But could state-supported ventures co-exist with private ones? Spencer, for his part, failed to see the incompatibility. He did not see communal dining as a threat to private restaurants, insisting that they could co-exist and even buy cooperatively, through bulk purchasing reminiscent of centralized wartime conventions, in order to pass on savings to customers and reduce waste.[85] It was not an argument which held weight with Pearce and his ilk. Pearce, and other private retailers, claimed to have 'done their bit' for the war effort by providing hampers of food to the families of 'exasperated, hungry men', thus preventing a 'good deal of trouble'; Spencer, by contrast, had avoided addressing the 'real need'. And whereas he (Pearce) had 'four sons and a grandson fighting for King and country' Spencer 'apparently a young, strong man' with 'no knowledge of catering whatever' had enjoyed lavish state support and press backing for his advocacy of communal dining. Spencer had benefited personally from all this, claimed Pearce, since the publicity surrounding National Kitchens 'must have been worth thousands of pounds to him as an advertisement'. Spencer, according to this critic, was not only shirking his war duty, the Halifax-based businessman was also using his directorship of National Kitchens for personal gain.[86]

Spencer, of course, had attempted to merge public feeding with his own tramway empire and the accusation certainly wounded him. It appears to have compounded his growing doubts about the future of National Kitchens and his personal role in the project. If the introduction of full rationing in the summer of 1918, coinciding with the 'Spanish flu' outbreak, had diminished the appeal of communal dining, the opposition of the restaurant trade confirmed for him that National Kitchens had travelled a long way from his preferred model of the takeaway distribution of food. In October 1918 he penned a long memorandum on the future of state-subsidized communal dining. Looking to peacetime, Spencer contended that National Kitchens could not be left to local authorities to manage and subsidize. Wartime conditions had resulted in the negligence of local infrastructural priorities which would, he imagined, assume greater importance after the war. Post-war 'reconstruction' would mean that all available expenditure would be on infrastructure projects like roads and National Kitchens would therefore be deprioritized. And yet, in many cases, National Kitchens had also proved successful going concerns. Spencer pointed to the almost £3,000 profit that London's New Bridge restaurant had turned over in half a year as an example of the financial sustainability of the public-feeding model.[87] With one eye on post-war unemployment, Spencer cited factory workers used to canteen food who would be laid off in peace time and would need similarly cheap food. He therefore envisaged National Kitchens continuing on as centrally funded institutions which could work with the private retail trade in wholesale purchase and distribution, thus driving down the overall costs to the consumer. With the exception of financial assistance from the state, Spencer's vision – with its advocacy of large units to achieve economies of scale – bears some resemblance to the supermarket system today. Spencer's memorandum was still heavily coloured by wartime ideal of the 'national good' and assumed that the private retail trade would be amenable to working with the public sector in combating waste in all its forms: of labour, of material, of health, of energy. Spencer also envisaged National Kitchens enduring by taking over the large coffee houses of firms like Lyons in large towns and cities. His final recommendation, which echoed Marion Phillips' report, was that National Kitchens appear as part of post-war housing projects.[88]

However, two key factors intervened to dampen the appeal of eating collectively. First, as mentioned, came the mass outbreak of 'Spanish' influenza in the summer of 1918. Some local councils responded by ordering any places where people congregated collectively to close periodically to allow for cleaning and ventilation.[89] In venues which stayed open, it was reported that public demand for the schemes had diminished due to fears of transmission accompanying the pandemic, even in Hornsey in London, where Kennedy Jones – one of the greatest cheerleaders for the movement – was the MP.[90] Then came the armistice of November 1918, which was to provide another blow to the broad spirit of communalism. The announcement of peace was followed by the post-war winding down of the Ministry of Food and, with it, the forward march of the National Kitchen was steadily brought to a standstill.

At the turn of the year, a downbeat Spencer resigned as director. Before stepping down he recommended slimming down National Kitchens. Divisional directors were to be removed as well as the team of thirty engineers and architects responsible for the planning of new kitchens. A skeleton management would remain as well as a pared down central staff, but Spencer was pessimistic about the future. 'The National Restaurant', he wrote, 'was a war measure and could now be closed down with profit and credit to all concerned'. His idea of post-war cooperation with the private retail trade had now been abandoned. To keep going would 'merely set up national competition with the restaurant trade without any direct advantage to the state'.[91]

The politician Kennedy Jones, who took over Spencer as the Ministry's National Kitchens director, accused the Yorkshire businessman of reckless expenditure and announced a series of cuts to central funding. To save money, National Kitchen supervisors were no longer to be trained by the leading British domestic science colleges but were to receive their entire training back at headquarters in London.[92] Elizabeth Waldie, for instance, who had been so enthusiastic about taking up her post as supervisor of National Kitchens that she had turned down a substantial pay rise from her former employers in favour of the job, left her post shortly thereafter, taking up a new job as inspectress of the Scottish Education Department.[93]

The women of the National Kitchens advisory committee viewed the cost-cutting with alarm. With the lease on the flagship national restaurant at London's New Bridge Street set to expire in May 1919, the National Kitchens advisory committee declared that its closure would be 'disastrous' and the 'morale effect' of closure 'very bad'.[94] But the Ministry was by this stage busy selling on its national restaurants elsewhere, relinquishing control of sites like that on the Southampton docks while it wrangled over a price for New Bridge Street restaurant with the private food retailers Spiers and Ponds.[95] Councils were obliged to inform the Ministry of plans for the closure of locally run kitchens. The advisory committee frequently protested against the closure of local premises, citing social need, but could not force borough or district councils to keep their kitchens open without central support.[96] Large council-run kitchens such as those in Marylebone and Hammersmith were to receive eleventh-hour financial support from the Ministry but, continuing to make a loss, eventually shut up shop.[97]

And yet amid the closures there were still new kitchens opening, demonstrating that there was still demand for the service that National Kitchens provided in urban centres. In January 1919 the Ministry's kitchens advisory committee was discussing the possibility of taking over the capital's numerous civil service canteens.[98] Likewise, the *Manchester Guardian* claimed that National Kitchens were being established at a greater rate after the war than during it.[99] The postwar winding down of the Ministry of Food did not necessarily mean the end of public feeding, insisted Charles McCurdy, Liberal MP and the department's parliamentary secretary. It was possible for the state to provide cheap, hearty meals for the labouring masses in place of the 'sloppy tea and teacake' which was all that could be had for the same price before the experiment in egalitarian eating. Furthermore, by April 1919, National Kitchens were still turning over a net profit for the state averaging between £75 and £100 a week per unit.[100]

Within the Ministry, the idea of public feeding still enjoyed strong support. Resisting the winding down of their department, civil servants at the National Kitchens division produced a bullish internal newsletter boasting of the continued success of the 'NK movement'. The language used was indicative of the forward-looking spirit which had accompanied egalitarian eating in wartime Britain and which many involved were now loath to now abandon. Cheltenham, it reported, had opened a brand new kitchen in late January 1919, serving a range of 'mouth-watering foodstuffs from roast beef to apple puffs'. The cornish pasties and shepherd's pie on offer at Sunderland's new kitchen were, according to the newsletter, second to none. Newcastle had finally got its first kitchen in April 1919[101] and, while Liverpool was shutting its kitchens, new ones were opening up across the Mersey in Birkenhead. Similarly the first National Kitchen in Barrow-in-Furness opened long after the war, in March 1919; in this case, local authorities ignored government discouragement and pressed ahead, citing the acute local need in working-class areas.[102] There were those at the Ministry, too, who mocked the idea that National Kitchens were simply no longer needed. The NK newsletter rubbished a Scottish provost for claiming that British people were now well paid and well fed, and criticized one local authority for closing its kitchen because of the expense of hiring waitresses and table cloths. A thinly veiled contempt for the bourgeois character of the post-war world was clearly perceptible.[103]

National Kitchens may have been declining in Britain, but the newsletter breathlessly reported the growth of communal dining worldwide. Since War Office reports concentrated on activities in former enemy nations, news of communal dining ventures in cities like Vienna and Hamburg were marshalled by the newsletter's civil servant authors as evidence of the 'enormous public demand' for cheap dining and disdain for 'overcharging' across Europe. The 'movement' had even spread to the United States, according to the newsletter, where the school of medicine at Yale University had requested a copy of the British 'NK handbook'.[104] 'There are no rich people any more, we are all poor', it proclaimed.[105] Propaganda was needed to encourage large firms to provide canteens at their 'factories, works, docks, mines etc'. It recommended that all new local authority flats come with a 'common kitchen' to meet post-war public health priorities. The newsletter's authors envisaged 'competition with' the private trade insisting that trade opposition 'pales into insignificance' compared to public demand for cheap, nutritious food. Citing a Commons question where it was suggested that 90 per cent of post-war National Kitchens were running at a loss it countered that where 'suitable surroundings and efficient management' were in place National Kitchens were 'always profitable'.[106] There were 'immense possibilities' in the 'NK movement', the newsletter insisted, and it should be included in post-war 'reconstruction policy', assisting the educational authorities in giving children experience in gardening and cookery, and anticipating that the newly formed Department of Health take National Kitchens under its wing.

Yet central support was receding rapidly and more sites were closing than opening. It was claimed in parliament that several kitchens were running at a substantial loss.[107] In May 1919 George Roberts, one of Rhondda's successors as Food Controller, acknowledged the 'very large volume of opinion in favour of the retention and the development of National Kitchens' but announced that central support for National Kitchens in peacetime was not 'appropriate'. The risk would therefore be transferred, he announced, to local authorities who were welcome to keep them open if they wished but would no longer receive funding.[108] Opening the Poplar National Kitchen back in March 1918, Rhondda announced that there would soon be 1,000 National Kitchens and predicted that the number would double to 2,000 in three months.[109] However, at the signing of the armistice in November 1918 there were 363 officially registered National Kitchens in Britain; six months later there were 120 fewer.[110]

By early 1919 the National Kitchens division had taken over catering in royal parks: a further sign of the kitchens' journey from popular and cheap communal ventures to established institutions. Sure enough, these catering units were soon charging more than affordable restaurants like Lyons. Soon the National Kitchens division was doing handsomely from its running of refreshments in parks, reporting that £700 had been taken from four sites during the Easter holidays in 1919. The National Kitchens advisory committee urged that 'arrangements for poor children' be made through a special discount children's lunch[111] but it was clear that National Kitchens were, under Kennedy Jones' stewardship, evolving from cut-price communal ventures into highly profitable and expensive park cafes. Jones claimed that catering in royal parks had provided food at 'reasonable prices'.[112] The advisory committee's Maud Pember-Reeves countered that prices were 'excessive' and that they were unable to service large numbers of people.[113] Certainly, the sites at Kensington Gardens, Kew Gardens, Hyde Park, Regent's Park and Primrose Hill had turned over £4,000 in three months.[114] For all the committee's social concern, it was clear to all concerned that National Kitchens had morphed into something quite distinct from their original purpose. By late 1919, the vast majority of National Kitchens had closed their doors for good. The National Kitchens division was wound up, its advisory committee disbanded. While some kitchens persisted as non-affiliated ventures, the last instance of mass feeding carried out under the National Kitchens division's auspices was feeding hot cooked food to the thousands of police and lorry drivers called into London to take up the transport duties of striking railway workers.[115] In just two years, it seems, the National Kitchens movement had performed a 180 degree turn, heading firmly in the opposite direction to its communal origins.

Conclusion

Female-run, bottom-up efforts at egalitarian eating were the inspiration for the government's admirable experiment in attempting to feed everyone. But the roots of the scheme were soon forgotten as 'communal kitchens' were transformed into depoliticized, top-down 'National Kitchens' which, in turn, were eventually run down in favour of expensive mini-ventures based in royal parks. National Kitchens were part of an increasingly intensive state management of domestic affairs from late 1916 onwards.[116] With the government moving towards ever greater control of food pricing and distribution, communal feeding initiatives were swallowed up and regurgitated as National Kitchens, in the process becoming part of the state apparatus. By mid-1918 the Ministry of Food was talking confidently of public feeding, initiated as an emergency measure, instead becoming a 'permanent national institution'.[117] C.S. Peel, a co-worker with Maud Pember-Reeves, recalled the expectation that they would 'become a feature of the nation's life'.[118] Little more than a year later, however, their days were numbered. Spencer claimed that he had transformed a loose network of 'scrappy', 'back street' kitchens into a national movement.[119] His successor, Kennedy Jones, didn't see it that way and accused him of presiding over a division which kept incomplete financial records, was poorly organized and spent profligately in a vain attempt to get local authorities behind the scheme.[120]

According to Spencer, the demise of the National Kitchen was all about class. National Kitchens had suffered from deep-seated class and geographical divides. He noted that, for all the Ministry's efforts, many members of the working class still viewed National Kitchens as soup kitchens and that they were more popular with the middle class. They had also proven most popular in London and the south east where people were more inclined to dine out. This contrasted with the north of England, where the working-class man generally travelled home for dinner in the middle of the day. However, he maintained that this was changing, with northern workers now increasingly inclined to eat at canteens close to work.[121]

Spencer's observations on class culture, while valid, omitted how – overall – the economics of wartime heightened the appeal of the National Kitchen. Although wartime wages underwent an increase, so too did retail food prices[122]; National Kitchens, where prices were controlled, therefore provided an affordable slice of eating out for workers experiencing higher income. Moreover, with the wartime earnings of salaried employees hampered by inflation and tax rises, the National Kitchen was also an attractive option for the squeezed middle class. Eating out at a National Kitchen was also a patriotic act as it helped to conserve domestic supplies.

A more compelling reason for National Kitchens' decline was the stout opposition of the catering trade, which rejected any post-war moves towards cooperative purchasing and selling which would deliver efficiency and eliminate waste. In general, the private catering trade did not do well from the war, with nearly all companies experiencing substantial falls in profits compared to pre-war returns.[123] The Ministry held a meeting shortly after the armistice was signed on 11 November 1918 at which it proposed the establishment of public-private buying organizations for the collective purchase of foodstuff and the cooperative use of cooking equipment between National Kitchens/restaurants and private ventures. The caterers' trade association voted against the scheme at further meetings 'by very large majority'.[124] With the coming of peace, it was also expected that normal trading relations would resume and National Kitchens were viewed as interfering with 'fair play' in the market. Opinions like these marched in line with the state's broader movement towards de-control from 1918 onwards.[125]

Rationing, however, delivered the fatal blow to National Kitchens. The introduction of full rationing in 1918 guaranteed fair shares on an individual basis; this, in turn, dampened the demand for cheap *communal* dining. Spencer rightly viewed full rationing as a threat and insisted that further-reaching state controls on the price and distribution of food should not replace communal dining. Writing to Rhondda on the cusp of the extension of rationing in January 1918 he recommended 'taking over the House of Commons and House

Figure 3.5 A cheery Lord Rhondda (left) opens the shutters of a new National Kitchen in January 1918 (Getty). Within six months Rhondda was dead and his National Kitchens in terminal decline.

of Lords kitchens' and running them as National Kitchens. 'The effect on the country would be electrical, and it would be a real answer to the House demands for rationing'.[126] Just weeks later, though, full rationing was imposed and set about eclipsing communal dining. By December 1918 Britons were enjoying sugar-coated cakes and double meat rations. The gradual lifting of rationing restrictions, so soon after their implementation, had a similar effect in making communal dining seem less attractive. In January 1918, Spencer could write to Rhondda telling him that compulsion in food supply as a 'remedy' was 'worse than the disease' and that he could not conceive of 'any organisation which could feed the whole of the country without hopeless confusion'.[127] A month later, however, such a system was in place and beginning to function successfully.

Additionally, the impact of the 'Spanish' influenza pandemic of the same year has been completely overlooked in the existing historiography around public feeding in the First World War. Britain experienced its first wave of the disease in the spring of 1918 – a time, critically, when the country was adjusting to the new rationing system – and the death toll worsened over the next months. Ventilation was identified as a priority in combating the 'flu and the gathering of people in large communal venues, like cinemas, theatres or halls, was prohibited by the Medical Officers of Health of local authorities and boroughs.[128] Although consuming a healthy and hearty diet was recommended by some experts of the day,[129] and although community kitchens were a fixture of the public health response in some large American cities,[130] in Britain many National Kitchens – like schools and other workplaces and institutions – were forced to close, and many never reopened.

Despite these trends, there is plenty of evidence to suggest that National Kitchens could have persisted in the post-war period. To quote the great contemporary economic historian R. H. Tawney, 'it did not follow that because some controls had had their day, others had no useful part to play in the post-war world'.[131] Against a backdrop of increased unemployment, demand for cheap and nutritious dining was certainly widespread. Yet with the post-war downsizing of the Ministry of Food, leading to its 1921 disbandment and transfer of functions to the Board of Trade, the National Kitchens division failed to find a new home. Contrary to what Arnold Bennett had urged, the National Kitchen was written off as an extraordinary war measure, the 'national restaurant' – as National Kitchens had effectively become – would not be revived until the next world war. The strange death of the National Kitchen was, then, a question of political will rather than public indifference.

4

British food and feeding in the interwar period

Introduction

Some National Kitchens did survive the war and continued service as communal restaurants during the interwar period. One in Blackfriars in London, renamed as the 'VC Restaurant', kept its doors open for demobilized servicemen.[1] Yet, shorn of state support, there was no disguising the relative decline of public feeding in Britain during the interwar period, despite the widespread unemployment of the Depression years of the 1930s delivering fresh demand for such schemes. This chapter explores how, by contrast, elsewhere in interwar Europe social eating thrived as a popular activity; it also chimed with the ideological priorities of authoritarian polities and received state endorsement in both fascist Germany and communist Russia. Although some saw this as further evidence of its insidiousness, social reformers and nutritionists were meanwhile increasing pressure on the British state to address diet and nutrition as a national priority as war crept inexorably over the horizon.

Public-feeding limps on as British society changes

Although the war had served to magnify the social and scientific link between poor nutrition and health, government support for public feeding rapidly receded with the resumption of peacetime patterns of public expenditure. As the role of the state lessened, the interwar period witnessed the increasing involvement of the private sector in research into diet as healthy food became marketable once more. Meanwhile, the scientific understanding of nutrition spawned dietary surveys and dietary campaigns became more prominent. Thus one of the most notable government feeding initiatives from this period – the subsidized Milk in

Schools Scheme set up in 1934 – was based on several key influences: not only the better scientific understanding of the importance of vitamins to child health, not only the clamour of social reformers, but also the economic needs of the dairy industry (the scheme itself was a revival of a commercial campaign by the Milk Publicity Council).[2]

Persistent class disparity in nutritional standards continued, as outlined below, along with the class consciousness that regulated social distinction in Britain and which was clearly displayed around individual consumption habits when 'eating out' (put plainly, whether one headed for the chip shop or the restaurant). But despite dogged class division, post-war British society and culture were undergoing change as well. A 'modern' and 'self-conscious' middle class occupied new professions based around scientific advances and the office worker suffered less from the unemployment that stalked the working class in the period. The British middle classes also experienced relatively greater purchasing power coupled with the expansion of 'leisure time', leading to the expansion of consumer choice when it came to food. A cultural Americanization was accompanied by more efficient technologies around the distribution, preservation and production of food. The new consumerism stressed pleasure over necessity and the experience of 'eating out', even at accessible venues like Lyons' tea shops, became an aspiration for many.[3]

While the new middle-class consumer was spending more, the government was tightening the purse strings. School feeding was proving too expensive, complained the Board of Education, which warned, in 1921, that it was becoming 'indiscriminate'.[4] The state was, then, reverting to a targeted approach to feeding, with many keen to relegate the wartime ethic of 'fair shares for all' to posterity and to focus once again only on those 'deserving' of support. The rise in unemployment following the 1929 stock market crash intensified the debate over the state's proper role. Pressure to reduce public spending contributed to the fall of the Labour government in 1931 and the formation of successive National Governments. Public feeding was now targeted not at the general populace, but towards schoolchildren. But against a backdrop of worsening unemployment, aversion to 'indiscriminate' state spending sometimes conflated feeding with learning itself, with neither considered an efficient use of public funds. In a 1932 Commons debate around the expansion of secondary education a Conservative MP complained that free secondary schooling threatened to 'turn the whole country into a vast educational soup kitchen from which few would get proper rations, and still fewer people would be able to digest what they got.'[5]

As this quote suggests, for all the advances in the public perception of public feeding delivered by National Kitchens, the social stigma of 'pauperism' once again emerged after the war. Demonstrating both the influential political opposition to 'indiscriminate' feeding and the growing prominence of nutritional science, as outlined below, there were increasing calls for entitlement to school meals to be determined by medical evidence. In 1934 the British Board of Education responded by introducing the policy of medical selection for supplemental feeding in schools based on evidence of malnutrition. This drew criticism from the political left, which ridiculed the idea, as summarized by Britain's leading nutritionist John Boyd Orr, that food deficiency could only exist if people were seen to be dying of starvation.[6]

Targeting feeding by medical need dovetailed with income restrictions, ensuring shades of Edwardian means-tested feeding re-emerged. When it came to school meals, many Local Education Authorities effectively separated children by income, operating 'canteens' for paying students and cheaper 'feeding centres' for those in receipt of free school meals. Feeding centres were usually to be found in central locations and, in a blurring of public provision and private charity, often occupied the same site as mission halls run by the Salvation Army and other Christian voluntary groups. Evidence suggests that many children who used these publicly prominent feeding centres learned to be ashamed of the fact and the food on offer was frequently nutritionally substandard too.[7] Illustrating the lack of a uniform and consistent approach to interwar school feeding, which varied considerably by local authority, in a Commons debate of 1937 it was revealed that the number of children in receipt of free school meals in England and Wales was 88,761, but an additional 32,000 needy children were paying for food in school canteens or feeding centres.[8] There were signals of the more coordinated approach shortly to come, nonetheless. In 1937 the Board of Trade Food Department was renamed the Food (Defence Plans) Department. With a major war potentially looming once more, its functions were reconceived to resemble something closer to what had existed in the Great War, with its brief expanded to plan for the 'procurement, control and distribution of food' by the central state.[9]

Nutrition, the body and national health

The interwar period witnessed the re-emergence of anxieties over national fitness, a concern broadly analogous to those which had appeared prior to the First World War and which served to amplify the voices of those, like the LSE's renowned economist and social reformer William Beveridge, who called for a greater role for the state in sustaining the population. Beveridge would write as early as 1928 that 'the great food policy lesson of the First World War' was that 'an alternative to competitive private enterprise' had to be found in wartime, replacing 'economics by human laws'.[10] Beveridge's later memorandum 'Wider Aspects of Food Control' (1936) pressed home this point, arguing that it was important for the government to 'think out in advance *and as a whole*, that the civilian side of the next war is as important as to design measures of military attack and defence'.[11]

Beveridge's use of military terminology supported the wearying conclusion of the social reformer Eleanor Rathbone, made in 1936, that it was not 'humanitarian, nor social, nor even business or economic considerations' which had made the widespread problem of malnutrition of public concern, but 'considerations which are fundamentally military'.[12] Rathbone's reflection helps to explain the focus of this book, for public feeding 'for all' reached its apogee in the emergency conditions of the world wars. Beveridge's call for the state to take food policy seriously, though, also reflected the fact that across Europe state-inspired approaches to combat economic depression focused on bodily health and efficiency through better nutrition. Against a cultural-political backdrop in which eugenics was advanced as a means of social deliverance by both voices on the left and the right, the 'fit' body assumed ever greater importance. In the 1920s and 1930s the notion of adolescence, identified by early century psychologists as a developmental stage between childhood and adulthood, gained greater popularity, illustrating the cultural emphasis placed upon the notion of youth in the interwar period. As the notion of 'leisure time' became a fixture of European society, British public health reformers urged greater bodily discipline. Echoing the Edwardian period, when personal attention to diet and lifestyle was embodied in Eustace Miles, vegetarian restaurants and health food shops underwent something of a mini boom in 1920s Britain. Such campaigns appealed to the individual quest for the 'body beautiful' but were also increasingly underpinned by eugenicist fears about national degeneration and, as such, inspired public health campaigns such as the British National Government's 'National Fitness Campaign' of the late 1930s.[13] National responses also included the clamour for better youth nutrition and a number of governments adopted the nutritious 'Oslo Breakfast', to which we shall return, as a model school meal.[14] In Britain there were similar demands for better childhood nutrition and in 1934, as detailed above, the Milk in Schools scheme was introduced by the National

Government following lobbying from food reformers and voluntary pressure groups focused on the issue.[15]

Despite the disappearance of emergency public feeding, the state's role in providing sustenance was quietly expanding. After all, as Beveridge had insisted with a grim inevitability, the nation had to be better prepared for 'the next war'. However, war or no war, the economic and social problems of the Depression era had been thrown into sharp relief by compelling nutritional evidence. In interwar Britain, understanding of human nutrition had improved greatly since the days of Edwardian food reformers like Eustace Miles, but policy still tended to lag behind the science. The characterization of the interwar political attitude to malnourishment by John Boyd Orr (1880–1971) – pioneer in the field of nutrition and later first Director-General of the United Nations Food and Agriculture Organisation – bear repeating; many politicians in the interwar years, Boyd Orr lamented, genuinely held the opinion that food deficiency could not exist if people were not visibly dying of starvation.[16] A lifelong campaigner for better food for the masses, Scotsman Boyd Orr compared his crusade to 'the anger an Englishman feels when he sees a horse or dog maltreated' and set out to expose this fallacy. He composed a 1935 report 'Food, Health and Income' which documented malnutrition in Britain. In it, Boyd Orr claimed that the diet of up to half of the British population was nutritionally inadequate according to the standards of the time. While average calorie intake had improved compared to some of the Edwardian surveys, Boyd Orr identified deficiencies in vitamins and minerals and concluded overall that extensive malnutrition existed among the British working class.[17]

Communal feeding as communism and the female call for 'permanent relief'

But was communal eating the best way to combat malnutrition? During the interwar period a familiar bogey would return to discussions around public feeding due to its association with the overbearing and authoritarian state. In particular, the linking of communal feeding with communism would become more entrenched in sections of the British press. Like in the First World War, social eating in the Soviet Union was seized upon by its detractors. In 1931, for example, the *Daily Mail* published a sniffy report detailing that some twelve million Russians were fed at central kitchens and dining halls. Not so the British populace, the *Mail* proudly noted.[18] Here was the association between social eating and austere tastes that the food reformers of the National Kitchens movement had been so keen to break. Amid the tense labour relations of interwar Britain, the link between public feeding and communism was explicitly asserted in the House of Commons, too. Conservative politicians, in a 1934 debate, complained that the bulk of funds raised by the National Unemployed Workers' Movement were being used to *feed* participants on its 'hunger marches' to London. While the hunger marches were a protest against the means-testing of state support rather than simply hunger itself, conservative voices tried to show that communists wanted to not only steal the cake but eat it too.[19] The reality was that the relative absence of state support in northern hotspots of unemployment led to the formation of communal kitchens by local working-class people.

An aversion to a loosely conceived 'totalitarianism', a term which entered into usage in the interwar period, underpinned such political opposition. In this context, philanthropic feeding continued to plug the gaps in state provision. In the 1920s Evangeline Booth specifically oriented the Salvation Army's 'soup and salvation' model towards emergency feeding (following war and natural disasters).[20] For other female activists, by contrast, the well-worn linkages between poor nutrition and poverty demanded that the problem be viewed as a long-term measure rather than an emergency one. In common with socialists and communists, they viewed feeding as the state's long-term responsibility. Eleanor Rathbone's lament about nutrition only being taken seriously when war loomed is an example of the persistence of female lobbying on the question of food and feeding, much of which pressed for permanent reappraisal. For Rathbone, who came from a wealthy nonconformist background and became an influential independent member of parliament, the question of diet, poverty and nutrition would be principally addressed through her long-term campaign for family allowances.[21] Muriel Paget, too, who continued her humanitarian emergency food provision in central Europe in the 1920s, anticipated later debates around humanitarian food aid by urging that public feeding look beyond short-term relief to 'permanent' questions of welfare and health.[22] Likewise the Fabian Barbara Drake, who in 1913 had investigated the working conditions of the 'tea-shop girl' and for whose 1937 study *Nutrition: A Policy of National Health* Eleanor Rathbone had penned an introduction, claimed that collective feeding provided *long-term* economies which justified the full provision of school meals to all children under fifteen. Such a measure, argued Drake, would go beyond providing milk to mothers and children because freeing adults from the economic burden of nourishing children would enable them to better nourish themselves.[23]

Interestingly, it was in part thanks to the unlikely intervention of an extraordinary Russian woman – Flora Solomon – that the association of public feeding and communism would be challenged. Solomon, as mentioned earlier, was no communist, arriving in Britain during the First World War as the daughter of a multi-millionaire Jewish banker exiled from his native Russia after the Bolshevik takeover. As an enthusiastic Zionist, her first experience of public feeding came in 1920s Jerusalem where she established a milk depot for the local poor. In the following decade she was recruited to improve conditions at the retailer Marks and Spencer by the store's founder, Simon Marks, whom she knew through Jewish networks in London. Her most significant innovation at the high-street business was the introduction of staff canteens in every Marks and Spencer store, staffed by experienced cooks, and distinguished by bright colour, comfort and cleanliness. By the end of 1932, as she recorded in her memoir, 'a girl could have a substantial hot meal for sixpence – discreetly waived if she couldn't afford it – and tea in a cup with a saucer and a biscuit for a penny'.[24]

As the next chapter details, at the outbreak of the Second World War Solomon would go on to urge Minister of Food Frederick Marquis (Lord Woolton) to restart public feeding on a national scale. Woolton, a retail guru of working-class roots, had forged his career at another Jewish family retailer – Lewis's – and during the interwar period had himself run a social experiment sponsored by the firm which provided food and bedding to the poor of Liverpool.[25] He was naturally receptive to Solomon. Notably, against a backdrop of widescale civilian bombing and the successful incorporation of retail expertise, the clash of private retail and public feeding would come into play less pronouncedly in Second World War Britain. Whereas the private retail trade had helped to kill the National Kitchen of the First World War, then, private enterprise would, at least initially, be instrumental in its resurrection during the Second.

International comparisons

Although a feature of both world wars, British governments did not endorse public feeding in the interwar period in quite the full-blooded manner in which it was witnessed elsewhere in Europe. As discussed, the association of communal dining with authoritarianism would be repeatedly resurrected by its detractors. It is therefore worth noting the extent to which it was embraced by Europe's dictatorships in the interwar period and into the Second World War, but also the fact that similar public-feeding schemes also thrived in democracies. As detailed in greater depth in the second half of the book, the social eating phenomenon of the twentieth century was something which was at times endorsed by the political right and at times endorsed by the political left.

In Europe's fascist dictatorships of the interwar and wartime period, the traditionalist emphasis on the homely mother cook coalesced with the role of food as an expression of the modern national community. In Fascist Italy, for example, the mother-nourisher was held aloft, but so too was diet as a public duty. Adherence to an austere diet alongside others in the community, symbolic of the rejection of selfish indulgence, became an expression of alimentary sovereignty.[26] In Nazi Germany, similarly, the thrifty yet nutritious *Eintopf* (one pot) meal was the subject of a major state-sanctioned campaign to get people eating together in order to foist national communal spirit. As part of the *Eintopfsonntag* campaign, the money saved in swapping a more lavish Sunday meal with a vegetable-based broth was donated to war veterans. The *Eintopf* genre duly emerged in cookbooks of the Nazi era. In photograph and film, great communal *Eintopfs* became useful propaganda; restaurants were required to offer a cut-price *Eintopf* on a Sunday, and the dish became a staple in factory canteens.[27] Fascists in France, meanwhile, who would attain a degree of power with the establishment of the Vichy regime in 1940, argued in the 1930s that French people should turn to *pot au feu* simple fare. Such eating was symbolic of a healthy national spirit of communitarianism and anti-epicurianism, they imagined, and was a corrective to the culinary overindulgence that had corrupted the French national character in the liberal period.[28]

While British public dining shared similar patriotic communal overtones to the above examples, it never possessed the same level of ethnocentric communalist insistence. Neither did it assume the all-encompassing dimensions of the great Soviet example of the 1920s and 1930s.

In the Soviet Union, state-run canteens were embraced both as an efficient use of resources and as representing the freedom of women from domestic slavery. Following the revolution, many of the Tsarist-era restaurants and taverns were nationalized.[29] These new social eating spaces – *stolovayas* – shared some similarities with the emphasis on civilizational improvement to be found in their British counterparts: fresh flowers, chess, reading rooms, music, artwork, public lectures and ornate plaster mouldings. The organization of nutrition and the ordered consumption of food in the Soviet Union of the 1920s and 1930s mirrored aspects of British public feeding in the world wars: an emphasis on eating vegetables and generally healthy nourishment, economies of energy and resources and dining-out which was reasonably priced and thus accessible to all. On the other hand it has also been argued that *stolovayas* shared some of the dystopian features of communal dining imagined by British naysayers: rats, propaganda posters, ideologically pure yet incompetent chefs, vile soups, dank environs and the 'eternal reek' of stewing cabbage.[30] These unappealing features naturally intensified during the serious Soviet food shortages of the interwar and war periods. Another important difference with the British experience of public dining was the sheer utilitarian scale of canteen eating across Soviet society: communal restaurants existed in residential apartment blocks (a vision of some of its British proponents never realized in a meaningful way) and in enormous 'kitchen factories' (factory canteens were part of the British experience, of course, but on nothing like the Soviet scale).[31]

The occurrence of organized social eating during the great left-right showdown of the interwar period, the Spanish Civil War (1936–39), is a significant example of non-state commensality which is comparable to the pioneer efforts of London's working-class women during the First World War. *Comedores populares* (popular dining rooms), a common feature of Latin American societies, were established in Republican areas following the resistance to the right-wing army coup of July 1936. In cities like Barcelona a social revolution took place, taking the form of worker self-management and collectivization and captured by George Orwell in *Homage to Catalonia* (1938). Symbolically, in Barcelona the Ritz Hotel's vast and elegant dining halls were transformed into a huge canteen for blue collar workers renamed 'Gastronomic Unit No. 1'.[32] In examining the use of hotels during the early stages of the conflict historian Anthony Beevor implies that Gastronomic Unit No. 1 – spearheaded by the anarcho-syndicalist CNT and socialist UGT unions – represented a truer bottom-up socialist vision than that of the Soviet communists, contrasting this canteen 'for all' with the luxury dining retained by the Communist Party in elite Madrid hotel The Gaylord, which was reserved for the exclusive use of its senior functionaries and Moscow advisers.[33] The Gaylord was 'too good for a city under siege' wrote Ernest Hemingway in *For Whom the Bell Tolls* and it seems that in the eyes of its Communist occupants it was too good for the common people as well. This implies the authentically socialist character of bottom-up social eating in defiance of the Stalinist charade, and does much to rescue its romantic image from the cabbage-smelling bleakness of Soviet statism. Yet it is notable, on the other hand, that canteen dining also featured in parts of Nationalist Spain occupied by the Falangist forces of Francisco Franco and that independent humanitarian food relief during the conflict – that is feeding administered by global faith and public health agencies – took this form as well.[34]

The United States of the Depression era provides some useful comparisons with the British experience as an example of how social eating functioned in a liberal democratic capitalist system in time of crisis. Although British civil servants enthusiastic about National Kitchens noted that the trend had spread to America, in fact the wariness of the big state witnessed in British discourse was, unsurprisingly, even more pronounced on the other side of the Atlantic. While the self-sufficiency principles of the thirty-first US President Herbert Hoover are often juxtaposed with the interventionism of his successor Franklin Roosevelt, the latter was initially ambivalent about the federal government feeding people, insisting during his election campaign against Hoover that the immate responsibility for feeding was local and voluntary, then that of individual states, and only in last resort that of the federal government.[35] Much American social eating during the Depression, therefore, was provided by private initiative. Alongside charitable canteens and soup kitchens, privately run 'penny restaurants' reappeared, offering cheap and usually meatless meals at very low prices. New York even had its own Eustace Miles: Bernarr McFadden. McFadden, like Miles, was an early proponent of fitness culture and a vegetarian who advocated radical dietary solutions. This weightlifting businessman ran a four-storey penny restaurant on New York's West 44th Street offering plain healthy fare such as vegetable soups, prunes and wholewheat bread.[36]

But if state-supported social eating did not take off in America as markedly as it did in Europe, the central state's ordering of public consumption was occurring in subtle yet significant ways as the 1930s progressed. Like in First World War Britain, female instructors of the US Bureau of Home Economics carried out nutritional lessons for housewives on low budgets. These women's title – they were 'agents' of the Home Economics Bureau – carried more swagger than that of their British wartime counterparts, but the principle was the same.[37] More significantly still, and like in Europe, modernity was now coalescing with scarcity, through the propaganda of the interwar food reform message. The fictional character the federal government devised to promote the nutritional reform credo was 'Aunt Sammy', a homely female version of Uncle Sam, who took to the airwaves in the 1930s to advise Americans on food waste, calories and diet, recommending frugal yet nutritious recipes.[38]

Conclusion

As the next chapter shows, during the Second World War Britain's Ministry of Food was to use similar modern media techniques to promote the second coming of the National Kitchen: the British Restaurant. Aunt Sammy's avuncular equivalent was to be the real-life Lord Woolton, whose tenure as wartime Minister of Food has been viewed in a generally positive light by historians. The character of Britain's second Ministry of Food, however, was not just shaped by the man at its helm but by First World War precedents and the hungry interwar years. The interwar period had illustrated not only the popular demand for forms of public feeding and its statist excesses, but also the pressing need for joined-up thinking and organization when it came to questions of nutrition and diet. These concerns helped shape Britain's food story during the Second World War and would emerge after it as a great policy theme: collectively, the National Health.

5

The birth of emergency public feeding in the Second World War

Introduction

Twenty years after the death of the National Kitchen, the prospect of public feeding re-emerged in 1939 with the coming of war against Nazi Germany. At this point it is worth quoting once again Flora Solomon – the redoubtable Russian émigré who revolutionized Marks and Spencer's staff canteens in the 1930s – and who claimed that in 1939 the idea of a communal restaurant was so 'alien to the mentality of the British people it could be likened to replacing the brick walls of the Albert Hall with glass and turning the place into a nudist colony.'[1] Solomon's colourful recollection raises the question of how, given the mere twenty-year remove from National Kitchens, this sort of collective amnesia or revulsion towards public feeding could have set in. On the one hand, Solomon's claim is credible given the much-desired return to normality following the 'war to end all wars', in which many so-called wartime exigencies were quietly and conveniently forgotten. On the other hand, Solomon is to be taken with caution.

Although her role in public feeding was important, Solomon was of the ilk of the 'Peripatetic Piewoman' Florence Horsburgh: an upper class 'Lady Bountiful' or, to employ the epithet attached to her specifically, 'Lady of the Ladel'. She was a 'no-nonsense' woman who got things done in an eccentric yet inspirationally efficient manner and was not afraid to confront male authority. According to her rather self-serving memoir, she had been appointed to her role at Marks and Spencer's after telling Simon Marks flatly 'it's firms like yours that give the Jews a bad name'. Likewise, she claimed credit for re-igniting the communal restaurant in the Second World War by, in her own words, 'penetrating' the 'bastion of government' that was the Ministry of Food. Solomon's thrusting memoir tells of how she simply marched into the Ministry's offices on London's Page Street resplendent in her mink coat, demanded an audience with Minister of Food

Figure 5.1 Flora Solomon (1895–1984), courtesy Marks and Spencer PLC.

Lord Woolton, and told him and his officials that if they didn't feed the bombed-out people of London's East End 'they'll rush this place and tear it to bits'.[2]

While Solomon undoubtedly lit a spark, the reality, of course, was also a more soberly bureaucratic one. If the age of the 'Lady Bountifuls' had evidently not yet quite passed, their role in feeding the wartime public had been subsumed by the much larger British state apparatus operating during the Second World War. The National Kitchens movement of the First World War *did*, in fact, provide inspiration for public feeding in the Second World War, even if the forward-looking policymakers of the day did not like to admit as much. The foremost public-feeding scheme operative between 1940 and the early 1950s was the 'British Restaurant': a national network of state-subsidized public dining rooms which were part of the Ministry of Food's broader feeding programme. As discussed subsequently, they were christened by Prime Minister Winston

Churchill (who claimed that the Ministry of Food's original title – 'communal feeding centres' – was 'redolent of communism and the workhouse') and there were over 2,000 operating across the country at their peak, some of which continued to function beyond their wartime context and into the next decade.[3]

If the patriotic rebranding of communal eating provides an example of history repeating itself, there were other instances, too, of how the public feeding of the First World War inspired that of the Second, not least in the use of mobile canteens, publicity, the attendant political debate, and the nutritional battle. The historiography pertaining to these public dining spaces has undergone a marked transition from the upbeat early official histories, which pointed to their popularity and success, to later revisions which have cast them as of only marginal importance.[4] Like the National Kitchen, the British Restaurant has suffered a relative poverty of historiography, the subject of book chapters rather than thorough interrogation.[5] This second part of the book therefore critically reconsiders the British Restaurant, providing a fresh perspective on this significant chapter in British economic and social history while examining its operation alongside alternative public-feeding measures of the day.

The British Restaurant is born

The second Ministry of Food came into existence on 8 September 1939 with Conservative politician W.S. Morrison, formerly Minister of Agriculture and Fisheries, as the new Minister of Food. Morrison is said to have viewed his move from Agriculture to Food as a demotion and his bitterness, according to one historian, 'greatly coloured the first period of the food ministry' during the conflict.[6] Despite Morrison's unhappiness at his new post, his Ministry's staff and functions soon ballooned, a trend that continued after leading retailer Frederick Marquis – Lord Woolton – took over from him as Minister of Food in April 1940.[7]

Although he would come to possess a benevolent appeal to the British public, Woolton was initially unenthusiastic about taking up the post, telling Prime Minister Neville Chamberlain he knew 'nothing about food except as a consumer' and insisting (as Charles Spencer had to Lord Rhondda) that he would only take on the role if he could operate as a businessman, untrammelled by red tape. Chamberlain's successor, Winston Churchill, would later disabuse Woolton of the idea that he was regarded by the public as a businessman, telling him 'they think of you as a philanthropist'.[8] Churchill's implication was that the public afforded a fond deference to 'Lord Woolton', who was simultaneously 'Uncle Fred', because of his title rather than his entrepreneurial prowess: in the Churchillian imagination the days of the Lord and Lady Bountiful were not quite over after all.

In reality, Woolton was from a firmly working-class Manchester background and could appear to some as rather austere; he was a Unitarian with a puritan streak and a weak constitution who disliked rich and extravagant food; Churchill, by contrast an epicure, liked to goad him, claiming that he overly enjoyed restricting the enjoyment of food and was unduly harsh on petty black marketeers.[9] As mentioned, Woolton had prior experience of urban anti-poverty programmes and the idea of public feeding would become a firm fixture of his Ministry of Food. A ready blueprint for public feeding existed, of course: the National Kitchens of the First World War, which signified Britain's first foray into state-funded social eating.[10] However, the idea of reviving the schemes of the previous war was initially sniffed at by some of Woolton's officials at the Ministry of Food and the uptake was slow at first.[11] The official history of wartime feeding notes that the idea of reviving National Kitchens afresh did not really take off until the formation of the national coalition government on 10 May 1940, the implication being that the ideological influence of the political left was decisive in getting the idea off the ground once again.[12]

One of the most influential voices from the left, of course, was LSE's William Beveridge and it is fitting to return to his 1936 memorandum 'Wider Aspects of Food Control'. In urging greater state intervention in feeding, Beveridge had presciently envisaged problems not encountered in the First World War such as the logistics of mass feeding following intensive aerial bombardment. The evacuation of people from London, Beveridge wrote, ought to be conceived not only on the basis of housing, but of public feeding, and this should operate 'on a free communal basis at first'. Such a programme, Beveridge urged, must come under the central control of the National Food Controller.[13] And yet, in an example of the typical back-and-forth dialogue between government departments over expenditure, the newly formed Ministry of Food initially regarded communal dining as none of its business and was keen to leave the responsibility to the Ministry of Health.

The Ministry of Food's initial reluctance to take on a public-feeding role is reflective of two key points: firstly, left-right political tensions within the department and the government as to how extensive its 'proper' role ought to be, and secondly the generational shift in the conception of food consumption as a long-term health issue, itself allied to the question of the extent to which the state ought to concern itself with public health.[14] It would take the changed circumstances of war, and some cajoling by the Ministries of Health and Labour, to force the Ministry of Food to take on a wider public-feeding role more closely resembling that recommended by Beveridge in 1936. In marked contrast to the First World War, as Beveridge had predicted, the mass targeting of civilians in German bombing raids would change everything. Flora Solomon, according to her own account, felt compelled to burst into Woolton's office following the first air raids on London during the Battle of Britain, in September 1940. She was angry at the absence of state-led public feeding in the East End. She had been running communal restaurants there since early 1940, 'commandeering church halls and other empty premises and borrowing Marks and Spencer personnel to set up each little establishment until the locals could be persuaded to run it'.[15] Like in the First World War, then, public feeding in the Second would first emerge as voluntary female initiative, only this time the role of the private retail trade in aiding working-class communities would be more pronounced. In London at least, much of this is attributable to Solomon, who described the scenes of bombed-out East Enders as 'stolen from Dante's inferno: everything a person needed for his day – a change of clothing, a hot beverage, a sense of order, had been blown sky high, along with the friendly neighbourhood grocery store'.[16]

The obliteration of the grocery store is important. Unlike the First World War, food rationing was introduced early in the conflict (January 1940) and, as many studies have emphasized, was based around exchange over the counter at the grocery store.[17] The destruction of the neighbourhood grocer seriously compromised this system of food supply, as the example of the British midlands city of Coventry would prove. After the Luftwaffe's blitz of Coventry in November 1940, 120 food retailers were destroyed and a further 180 forced to close, but public food relief was slow to arrive. Mobile canteens arrived late and the first 'municipal restaurant' was not opened until a fortnight later. As the official history of British wartime food policy implies, the state was initially sluggish in recognizing that war on a new scale necessitated a proportionate response, one where food aid would be provided centrally 'as a matter of right' and 'freed from the odour of the poor law'.[18] Once again, it would take the private initiative of the likes of Flora Solomon to fill the gap in provision. Under her auspices, Marks and Spencer set up mobile canteens, grocery stores and communal restaurants in bomb-ravaged Coventry.[19]

As more British cities underwent the Blitz, however, it was increasingly clear that private voluntary and commercial initiative were no substitute for public communal feeding, as urged by Beveridge, and the Ministry of Food took on the role. Under the direction of Woolton the Ministry was, by this point, already carrying out an 'experiment' on a London housing estate, offering hearty and nutritious food such as roast beef and stews at cheap prices. In practice this was a revival of the National Kitchen model, with diners buying tickets, then queuing up and exchanging them for food from a series of hot plates. The pilot was well received and the Ministry looked forward to the roll-out of what they termed Community Feeding Centres.[20] Thereafter London County Council took the lead, establishing sit-down communal dining through the 'Londoners' Meal Service' which by Christmas 1940 was supplying over 80,000 meals a week to people in the capital. The pricing was up to local authorities, but the Ministry recommended the following formula: 'the cost of food + 25 per cent + halfpenny for fuel', usually working out at an inexpensive 9d or 10d for a two-course meal.[21] There were parallels with the Croydon kitchen pioneered by the Workers National Committee in 1917; however, this time the involvement of the central state was more pronounced.

Elsewhere in the country, too, communal feeding was reappearing. The 1940 bombing raids on Coventry and London had heightened the sense of urgency and by end of the year similar schemes were operative in Britain's major cities. Gwilym Lloyd-George, son of First World War Prime Minister David Lloyd George, and Woolton's parliamentary secretary, stated in a Commons debate of 1940 that the 'communal kitchens' of Newcastle-upon-Tyne, which had been running since the Depression era, ought to be 'copied' in other big cities.[22] Manchester and Birmingham were selected by the Ministry as sites for what were still being called 'National Kitchens'. The Ministry originally envisaged using industrial caterers for canteen dining and an independent Home Guard unit for mobile canteens, but both ideas were dropped as it assumed control of public feeding as a comprehensive national project under its own aegis.[23] Illustrating its new importance, the Communal Feeding Division of the Ministry of Food was relocated away from the bombs, to sleepy Colwyn Bay in Wales.[24]

In November 1940 the campaign became nationwide and the number of British Restaurants gained pace. The Ministry guaranteed financial assistance with over four million pounds set aside and a dedicated infrastructure and information service.[25] In a letter pressing civic heads to apply to run these new facilities, Woolton wrote

> If every man, woman and child could be sure of obtaining at least one hot nourishing meal a day, at a price all could afford, we should be sure of the nation's health and strength during the war, however long it may last, and the fitness of the next generation.[26]

Figure 5.2 Public feeding on Clydeside following a bombing raid, 1941.

Although policymakers of the Second World War were sometimes dismissive of anything associated with the First, National Kitchens provided the obvious blueprint and the wartime logic of public interest remained essentially the same: to ensure members of the general public 'have at least one hot nutritious meal a day at a reasonable price' with all the accompanying benefits in economies of food and fuel.[27] The imperative to use price-capped dining as a tool in the wider effort to control inflation remained the same too.[28] As we shall see, some of the old conservative anxieties about all things 'communal' persisted, but improved nutritional understanding would hasten the impulse towards the country's largest ever roll-out of public feeding.

Nutritional reform

As mentioned previously, research by the Scottish physician and biologist John Boyd Orr in the 1930s had highlighted the persistently high levels of malnutrition in Britain. Boyd Orr's criticisms were not well received by the government of the day and, according to him, a national food policy based on nutritional needs did not arrive until Woolton's tenure as Minister for Food from 1940.[29] Woolton, according to one biography, was especially receptive to nutritional reform because he remained haunted by the death of a neighbour from starvation as a boy in late Victorian Manchester. A man of plain tastes who scorned eating to excess and was constantly teased by Churchill for his neglect of the 'lightness' of life, Woolton was committed to improving national nutritional standards, especially amongst expectant mothers and children.[30] Boyd Orr's work was recognized by Woolton in 1940 when he was included in a special committee to advise the Ministry on food policy. Writing in that year, Boyd Orr noted that cheap milk and meals in schools had much improved rates of deficiency diseases and infant mortality, but claimed that by the British Medical Association's 'minimum cost' and League of Nations' 'optimum diet' yardsticks a third of the population was still undernourished.[31] The result of the committee's work, in his own words, was the first comprehensive food plan in modern history guaranteeing that 'every child in the slums got his orange before a millionaire could get one'.[32] Woolton affirmed this egalitarian nutritional mission in 1941, stating that he wished to see every schoolchild as well fed as pupils of Eton or Harrow.[33]

Scientific understanding had changed considerably for the better since the last global conflict. Since the First World War it had become established science that the absence of vitamins and minerals led to deficiency diseases like scurvy and rickets, that these deficiencies had mental effects and that malnutrition also led to increased susceptibility to infectious diseases like tuberculosis.[34] As one of the Ministry of Food's Scientific Advisers, Jack Drummond, put it 'we are now in a much more favourable position for dealing adequately with the problems of feeding the people during wartime than twenty-five years ago'.[35] A meeting of food scientists convened by the Ministry during the middle of the war agreed, noting that the ignorance of the dietary role of vitamins had almost proved 'disastrous' in the last war.[36] Yet the Ministry did not always follow the recommendations of the men of science. One of the earliest pieces of advice from the scientific advisory committee on food policy was the plan to feed the nation a 'basal' diet, whereby individuals received 'essential elements and minimum quantities' per food group, thus ensuring that everyone received basic nutritional requirements.[37] These plans would be dismissed by Ministry officials as impractical, but the basal diet continued to influence scientific thought on public feeding, as evidenced by the influence of men like Boyd Orr and Drummond.

A contemporary of Boyd Orr, Drummond was a brilliant biochemist; made Professor of Biochemistry at University College London aged just thirty-one, he was responsible for breakthrough research on vitamins. In 1939 Drummond's *The Englishman's Food: A History of Five Centuries of English Diet* was published; the closing chapters of this book convey his sense of mission that improved scientific knowledge must be used to improve the nation's diet and wellbeing. In February 1940 he was promoted from the Ministry's chief adviser on food contamination to its scientific adviser, becoming the leading nutritional adviser on rationing.[38] But what of his opinions on emergency public feeding? In an upbeat memorandum on public dining written in August 1940 he cited the increased professionalization and knowledge around social service gained in the interwar years but emphasized the 'nutritional knowledge' (much of which he was responsible for) as the critical factor. He might have added the increased ability of the Ministry of Food to avail of the broadcast media in getting its point across, as discussed later. Nutritionally, Drummond saw the wartime revival of mass public feeding as 'an opportunity'. He was an advocate of the 'Oslo breakfast' or 'health dinner' (where, in one sitting, most or all of the day's needs for animal protein, vitamins and minerals were met). Pioneered by Norwegian food reformer Carl Schiøtz, the 'Oslo Breakfast' was rolled out across Norway in the 1920s, replacing hot school meals with a combination of wholemeal bread, cheese, milk, green leaves and fruit. As mentioned previously, milk had been introduced to British school dinners in the 1930s and Drummond was a strong advocate of the 'simple and fundamental' nutritional benefit of public-feeding programmes which provided a balanced diet to those on 'poverty diets'. The original Oslo breakfast, wrote Drummond, supplied 'nearly, if not quite, all the vitamins A,B,C, calcium and iron required by a growing child' so that 'it is of no importance, therefore, if home conditions are so bad that the child receives little more for the rest of the day than white bread and jam'. He urged the same model to be used in mass public feeding.[39] Echoing food reformers of the last war like Eustace Miles, Drummond was aware of public suspicion of the 'food crank', but argued that the Oslo model had proven nutritional benefits, unlike the then-trendy 'Hay diet' (in which food was separated into alkaline, acidic and neutral groups) which Drummond dismissed as a fad. He urged that the hot, meat-based mid-day meal be replaced with one based around cheese, salad and wholemeal bread. This, he wrote, 'can be done cheaply and without disturbing to any significant extent ordinary food habits'.[40]

As in the First World War, some saw public feeding as a way to counter what they saw as the undesirable effects of alcohol and to achieve social improvement. The British Women's Total Abstinence Society, for example, campaigned nationwide for the late opening of British Restaurants because they thought they could provide young people with an alternative to the public house.[41] With improved understanding of nutritional science, however, the desire for civilizational improvement was increasingly couched in medical, rather than moral, terms, and the British Restaurant was never seriously advanced as providing a disincentive to go the pub. Indeed the pub was regarded by policymakers as too important in terms of morale and culture to be displaced by state-led food-based alternatives.[42] Although British Restaurants allowed for the mixing of the sexes as well as the classes, Nadia Durbach's verdict that they presented 'an ideal wartime pickup spot' for unmarried men and women seems over-romanticized; the pub still remained the primary 'pickup spot'.[43]

Like in the First World War, the changes desired by food reformers came dripping slow. If glimpses of the Brave New World of nutritional improvement through public feeding were starting to reappear, nagging trends from the First World War would persist. Regional variations in nutritional standards persisted too. Meals 'out' were not evenly distributed throughout the population and regional differences in cultures of consumption were still marked. It was observed that regional differentiation in consumption habits was frustratingly persistent. In Scotland, for instance, the consumption of fresh vegetables in British Restaurants remained 'obstinately low'. While dishes made from less desirable organs such as hearts, liver and kidney were popular with patrons, vegetarian 'substitute' options such as lentil cutlets proved less so.[44] The poor take-up of foodstuffs aimed at vulnerable groups – such as orange juice and cod liver oil – also disappointed nutritional experts.[45]

Unsurprisingly, Drummond's recommendation that hot mid-day meals be replaced by healthier cold ones was not taken up in British Restaurants, where the fare remained healthy but stolidly 'canteen'. But this was not necessarily a negative, the nutritionists decided. Assessing the situation midway through the war, the nutritional impact of public feeding was deemed largely satisfactory by the Ministry's food scientists, who pointed to the high levels of Vitamin C contained in typical British Restaurant fare such as cabbages and potatoes. Perhaps the eternal reek of cabbage was not such a bad thing after all.

Naturally, war aims also influenced the fare offered. Cartoon tuber 'Potato Pete' – a masochistic spud in a hat who called on the public to slice him up and eat him in many different ways – was a staple of wartime propaganda, and Woolton would write to all his divisional food officers instructing that potatoes be served at all times of the day, even at breakfast, in order to relieve the pressure on bread as a staple food.[46] In sample menus from British Restaurants, potatoes feature in nearly every main meal, always accompanied by either 'greens', which usually referred to cabbage or beans. After a series of experiments on how to guarantee high Vitamin C content in meals, the scientific advisory committee recommended that potatoes be served roasted rather than boiled, that cabbage, rather than salad, constitute the main 'greens' in the typical meal and that metaphosphoric acid be added to counter the loss of Vitamin C through boiling cabbage.[47] The Ministry's food scientists also urged the inclusion of parsley, beans and pulses in cooking. In sampling meals from British Restaurants across the country, the scientists were chiefly concerned – perhaps over-concerned – with Vitamin C content. The inclusion of cabbage in meals therefore emerged as a key recommendation.[48] Since the appeal of the British Restaurant rested largely on the square 'meat and two veg' type of meal, the ubiquity of cabbage does not appear to have met much popular resistance.

The official history of food supply records that 'the diet theoretically available to the British civilian was not only maintained but actually improved during the war'. The fall in consumption of animal proteins was remedied by the arrival of Lend/Lease supplies from 1941. While supplies of vitamins and minerals increased too, the official History sounded a note of uncertainty when it came to 'vegetable supply statistics' which explains the Ministry's emphasis on providing vitamins A and C through public feeding.[49] Nutritionally, therefore, the British Restaurant was considered by contemporaries to be an integral part of the battle to improve the health of Britain. Although public feeding might appear 'marginal' relative to the monolith that was rationing, it is worth considering that 79 million meals a week were eaten outside of the home in May 1941, with the figure rising to 170 million by December by 1944, roughly equivalent to four meals 'out' a week for every man, woman and child.[50] Although the number would fall short of the Minister's preferred vision of 10,000 British Restaurants, to the diet-conscious Woolton and his nutritional reformers, public feeding was a prominent contour on the food map of wartime Britain.

British Restaurants: How they looked and how they worked

Like the National Kitchens of the First World War, British Restaurants were managed by local authorities, who also employed the staff, but received their start-up capital through a grant from the Ministry. The local authority would apply to the Divisional Food Officer, who considered the proposal on behalf of the Ministry. In terms of covering costs by selling meals, they had to at least break even but 'reasonable operating deficiencies' were guaranteed against by central government. The location of British Restaurants generally depended on the willingness of local authorities to apply to the Ministry for capital funding to open one. As with National Kitchens, central government urged local government to think big and locate these new centres in attractive local premises (usually halls or schools, or hotels on public thoroughfares). The principle of 'fair shares' pervaded the scheme – it was intended that people obtain one meal at a time, and reports of people dining 'in' before purchasing food to 'carry out' were frowned upon.[51]

A noticeable difference to their First World War predecessors was the government's provision of large corrugated steel Nissen huts in the case that no suitable venues were available. At first glance the Nissen hut restaurant may appear austere, but these prefabricated British Restaurants were often the site of murals by local artists and art students, the Ministry insisting – as it had in the First World War – on good decoration, fittings, lighting, pictures and posters. From 1942 onwards professional artists were recruited through Arts Council to paint murals on London's British Restaurants. The Ministry also recommended that music be played during meal service from a wireless.[52] In some cases schoolchildren had carried out the designs. The subject matter of murals tended to be depictions of events in the history and traditions of the neighbourhood. Where original artwork was unavailable, local authorities hung artwork such as lithographs, collotypes and stencils donated by artists. The lithographs were original artworks; the collotypes were often reproductions of famous paintings which would have been recognizable to the general public, and the stencils were based on pastoral motifs designed by the special art advisor to British Restaurants, artist Clive Gardiner.[53] Even the colour scheme of tables was given consideration by a small panel of so-called 'colour experts' who advised that table cloths be dispensed with in favour of tables in four colours – red, green, blue and yellow – replacing the need for cut flowers and tablecloths as recommended by the Ministry in the First World War.[54] An atmosphere of 'brightness and cleanliness' was the object, with woodwork painted in 'cheerful colours' and floors polished.⁵⁵ Gardiner, Principal of Goldsmith's College of Art and himself a muralist, was employed to offer advice to local authorities on interior design. He commissioned lithographs and posters from contemporary artists and continued the murals initiative begun by Lady Elizabeth Clark, wife of director of the National Gallery Sir Kenneth Clark. Lady Clark had campaigned for the commissioning of murals to decorate British Restaurants and borrowed artwork from national collections, including Buckingham Palace, to hang on the walls.⁵⁶ The attention given to the design of British Restaurants points, once

Figure 5.3 A British Restaurant in Ilford is decorated with a painting from the royal collection, Buckingham Palace (The Sketch, 10 March 1943).

again, to the desire that public feeding fulfil a civilizational and morale role rather than a purely calorific one.[57] Illustrating the spirit of wartime reciprocity, public artwork in public dining spaces would inspire the private trade. Just after the Second World War, inspired by a desire to emulate the British Restaurant, the Lyons chain of cafes commissioned various war artists under the guidance of lithographer Barnett Freedman to produce artworks for its corner houses.[58]

The Ministry put the average staff of a British Restaurant at a manager, two chefs, six kitchen maids and two porters, together with drivers for the transport of food.[59] Wages were agreed with the Joint Industrial Council for the area.[60] Those who volunteered as managers for British Restaurants continued to be paid by their existing employer during the three-week training course and those without an employer were paid and fed by the Ministry during the training period.[61] Cooks were trained on courses by professional advisers and the Ministry employed its own Cook Advisers from 1942. Interestingly, training courses were limited to women over thirty – clearly with the priority of reserving younger female workers for industrial labour – and those who had to travel significant distances to work were granted a lodging allowance.[62] These courses for 'older women' were, according to *The Times*, 'one of the most interesting social developments of the war'.[63]

Food was procured wholesale and at discount since public-feeding ventures were deemed 'priority establishments' by the government. As in the First World War, most diners ate in, but patrons were free to 'take out' the food if they wished. Meals normally consisted of a meat and vegetable option, a sweet and a hot drink or soup, and cost between 8d and 10d.[64] Whereas the government introduced a 5 shilling price limit on private restaurant food in 1942, the Ministry did not insist on price limits in British Restaurants, instead strongly urging adherence to the following price structure:

Soup with bread 2d
Soup 1d
Meat and vegetable 6d
Sweet 2d
Tea or coffee 1d[65]

Anecdotal evidence suggests that regularly dining at a British Restaurant was regarded as too expensive for some working-class families, with one Liverpool air raid warden recording in his diary the criticism of a mother of three, who claimed that to dine at a British Restaurant every day of the week would cost her around 12 shillings. This amount was simply out of reach for her and Lord Woolton was 'living in the clouds', she said. Other evidence from Mass Observation (the social research project which sought to inform policy by recruiting volunteer observers to anonymously document people's everyday conversation, behaviour and attitudes) points to similarly scathing opinions about the success and popularity of the schemes from certain respondents.[66] Similarly, a 1942 survey of housewives revealed that only 40 per cent of the 2,430 interviewed approved of British Restaurants. While just 4 per cent actually disapproved of them, the overwhelming opinion conveyed in that particular survey was one of indifference.[67] Nonetheless, the overall opinion on British Restaurants provided by Mass Observation – which is impressionable, contradictory and should not be over-amplified – also contains much praise. As discussed later, a Mass Observation survey of 1942 recorded that 96 per cent of people who had eaten in a British Restaurant regarded it as a positive experience.[68] Indeed the majority of Mass Observation diarists who ate in these venues on a regular basis recorded positive experiences. Regularity of use appears to have been key. While certain of Mass Observation's female volunteer observers, or 'diarists', were not gushing in their praise, none of these women appear to have eaten in one with much regularity; this may explain why they did not recall the food on offer or the surroundings with any great passion or enthusiasm, despite (or maybe due to) the fact that one of the diarists actually worked in a British Restaurant as a volunteer.[69] Revealing the central importance of food in wartime, Mass Observation diarists would often describe their dining experiences on a certain day in great detail. Consequently, the experience of communal dining could be, for the same woman, in December 1941 'not so bad' with generous helpings of soup, meat, vegetables and a sweet for just nine pence; in March 1942 her public-feeding experience got even better, with a lunch of beef, potatoes, bread pudding, custard and coffee at a Women's Voluntary Service canteen costing almost twice as much but proving tastier and more satisfying; or the next month, by contrast, dreadful, with the liberal use of sage and onion in the mock goose causing her 'hours of pain and discomfort' afterwards.[70] As these excerpts suggest, Mass Observation evidence – in all its subjective detail – is of only limited use in assessing the broader success of wartime public feeding.

As in the First World War, the schemes were initially known as 'Community Kitchens'. In November 1940 the Ministry of Food issued a circular to all local authorities urging them to 'set up and operate Community Kitchens'. The model owed much to its First World War predecessor. The Ministry would cover all the capital expenditure of these new ventures and cover any initial shortfalls in revenue; in return local authorities would ensure that these ventures could be 'self-supporting' by reducing or removing any rent and rates. This time round, though, some things were different. The Ministry was clearer when it came to its return, insisting that any profits be at *its* disposal. Accounts had to be submitted monthly along with statistics detailing the number of meals sold. As indicated in the case of the Mass Observation diarist, the Ministry also encouraged the participation of volunteers and voluntary organizations in providing free labour (albeit with full insurance against war service injury), something which National Kitchens supremo of the First World War Charles Spencer had strongly urged against.[71]

Woolton urged staff to remember 'the Ministry's prestige was very closely associated with the efficiency of British Restaurants [and] he was anxious that the quality of the service and other meals served should be maintained at a higher level'.[72] Despite empowering local authorities to requisition buildings for purpose and despite the financial assistance, the Ministry of Food noted that local authorities were initially 'somewhat slow in taking action' and the British Restaurants did not gain momentum as a new national movement until the early months of 1941.[73] As in the First World War, local authorities had to receive the Ministry's blessing before qualifying for funding and using the title British Restaurants. By August 1941, 766 ventures nationwide were operative, outstripping the 400 or so non-affiliated feeding centres such as community kitchens set up by voluntary groups; this number rose to 1,140 by the end of the year.[74] At 1943 peak, there were 2,160 British Restaurants: a number significantly higher than earlier histories record.[75] Like in the Great War, there was a strong technical, as well as financial, incentive for local authorities to convert their existing provision into a nationalized social eating space. Cafeteria that continued on a voluntary basis, run by independent voluntary groups such as the Women's Institute, did not qualify for central funding. British Restaurants, by contrast, availed of the best technical advice and the very latest labour-saving devices, such as potato-peeling machines, electric ranges and ovens, dishwashers, gas boilers, deep fat fryers, electric mixing machines and hot cupboards.[76]

Although more centralized and organized on a bulk stock basis with four Chief Divisional Food Officers, the organization of public feeding on a local level remained largely in the hands of Divisional Food Officers (as it had in the First World War).[77] Initially, the Ministry worked with retailers and wholesalers through so-called 'mutual assistance pacts' via which, when the threat of invasion appeared imminent in 1940, the private trade was called upon to lay in stocks.[78] These arrangements were exposed as inadequate after the most intense air raids of that year, and thereafter food distribution was further centralized.[79]

The destruction of food retail premises in bombing raids, which is discussed later, further strengthened the case for municipal dining. That notion – the *municipality* of social eating – had been stressed in the First World War, when it was urged that new housing estates incorporate communal restaurants. There are shades of Soviet residential canteens here and the incorporation of public restaurants into housing developments was realized in the case of several new housing estates in the early stages of the Second World War. However, there was at least one case where wartime shortages of steel and timber delayed the construction of a British Restaurant on a new estate.[80]

The Second World War equivalent of the *Public Kitchens Handbook* was *Canteen Catering* (1941) which offered practical hints and sample recipes. It reiterated much advice from its predecessor, including the instruction that vitamins and minerals in vegetables were lost when soaked overnight, that all possible parts of the vegetable, including outer leaves, be used and that water used in cooking vegetables be recycled for use in gravies and soups.[81] As in the First World War, the scheme benefited from the technical advice of nutritionists, food scientists and dieticians. There was a reappearance, too, of the gap between the loftier ideas of food reformers and the public preference for plainer fare. In 1942, for example, newspapers reported public resistance to attempts to introduce meals in the 'Oslo style' championed by the Ministry's scientific adviser, Jack Drummond, as mentioned previously.[82] An internal memo noted that when it came to breakfast 'the more solid alternative' to Oslo breakfast or 'Pieces' – as it was called in Scotland – was 'infinitely to be preferred' and the Oslo breakfast 'not appreciated by most schoolchildren'.[83] Moreover, as the Ministry of Food began to take on the running of nearly all the various public-feeding schemes from school canteens to evacuee feeding, it also acquiesced to the Ministry of Labour's appeal – of August 1941 – that British Restaurants open beyond midday. Opening beyond midday meant, at many British Restaurants, the inclusion of a pudding course to follow what was essentially a 'meat and two veg' meal. Demand for suppers far outstripped demand for breakfast from war workers and proved a further nail in the coffin of the Oslo breakfast.[84]

The instruction that public dining function on the basis of one meal per person at any one time was underpinned by scientific advice as well as the notion of 'fair shares'. The Ministry had intended that a main meal in a British Restaurants be hearty enough to constitute one third of a person's recommended daily calorie intake; however, a 1943 report found that a typical meal accounted for less than this – around a quarter of the day's energy needs.[85] As in the First World War, though, differences in culinary opinion were generally negotiated successfully by the Ministry, which reported that 'better off people' as well as 'the industrial section of the population' were patronizing public dining.[86] As well as the general public, a good proportion of custom appears to have been from war workers of all types sitting down for their evening meal before starting the night shift.[87] In 1940 *The Daily Mail* interviewed patrons at a site in Kensington, featuring one man who worked night shifts and whose wife worked days, leaving him with the responsibility of feeding himself and their infant son; for this enthusiastic communal diner, public feeding enabled him to save considerable money, time and effort.[88]

Although the appreciation of food is inherently subjective, an article in *The Times* published post-war, and therefore unshackled by censorship, even claimed that the food on offer in British Restaurants was superior to that served in the restaurants of the Sorbonne in Paris.[89] This account chimes with the opinions of a *New York Times* restaurant critic who visited London in March 1942 and remarked on the surge in popularity of dining out at midday, noting that public restaurants were so popular that there were long queues to enter. Private restaurants, by contrast, he found overpriced and unsatisfactory, one serving shepherd's pie which 'looked like, smelt like, and probably was canned stuff sold in the U.S. for feeding cats and dogs'.[90] Government restrictions on eating out in private restaurants, which really came into force in 1942, further enhanced the cross-class appeal of public dining.[91] In an interview that further illustrated the gulf between Woolton and Churchill when it came to the appreciation of food, Woolton told the *Daily Express* in July 1940 that he wanted to end 'ostentatious eating' at private restaurants.[92] At first, restaurants were urged to restrict meals to one main course, then ordered to do so; Woolton's assault on dessert was to follow, with further restrictions on icing sugar, cream and ice cream.[93]

While the National Kitchens of the First World War were not rolled out across schools, British Restaurants sometimes took the form of school canteens (expanded to feed the general public) and evacuee-feeding centres. From the outset of war, British Restaurants were conceived of on a much greater scale than National Kitchens and at their peak there were 2,160 overall: comfortably over double the number of National Kitchens. Once again, the majority (around a third) were located in and around London and nearly every local authority with a population over 50,000 had at least one British Restaurant.[94] These venues proved so popular that the Ministry insisted that canteens have an 'in' door and an 'out' door so people would not become stuck in the doorway.[95] Local political will again proved decisive, a point which the official history of food control emphasizes. For example, Liverpool, which had all but shunned National

Kitchens, adopted British Restaurants enthusiastically. Similarly, coordination between local food officers and central command did not always run smoothly, especially when – as in Bootle and Portsmouth – local offices and their entire records were destroyed by enemy action.[96] Affluent Chelsea boasted one restaurant per 8,000 people whereas working-class Stepney had one per 70,000 people. That a city the size of Manchester served daily only one third the number of meals served in Canterbury reflected the fact that, once again, a regional/class culture of eating out habits varied, as did local enthusiasm and amenities.[97]

Historians have scratched their heads over statistics like this. It is clear that eating out was more popular in the south, where it was more culturally established, than the north in both wars. When it comes to the specific example of Chelsea – on the surface something of an aberration given the relative wealth of its residents – one historian attributes the popularity of public feeding there to civil defence planning deliberately oversupplying facilities in west London because evacuees from the south coast would have flooded there in the event of an invasion.[98] To the current author's mind, however, the reason might also be simultaneously more prosaic and more colourful: the fond local memories of Chelsea's 'peripatetic piewoman' Florence Horsburgh ensured the local authorities were better disposed towards the idea of British Restaurants. In short, local action and enthusiasm were decisive in determining how well public-feeding schemes fared and, despite the degree of amnesia or disdain about First World War precedents, local collective memory ran deeper than many realized.

Chelsea also stands as a good example of the successful cross-class appeal that the Ministry of Food had always insisted be a feature of emergency public feeding. Achieving cross-class popularity was a consistent policy of the Ministry of Food in both wars. Nadia Durbach's *Many Mouths*, an overview of state feeding in modern Britain, fails to recognize this key point. For all its imperfections, state-supported wartime public dining marked a clear break with the Victorian institutional feeding programmes that preceded it (such as prison, workhouse and prisoner-of-war camp feeding) which targeted specific populations. While other government initiatives of the Second World War, like the Welfare Food Service, maintained this 'targeting' approach by concentrating on the working poor, National Kitchens and British Restaurants functioned as a complement to rationing and, as such, explicitly aimed for a much broader appeal, even if they didn't always achieve it.

Durbach seems caught between acknowledging, on the one hand, the anomaly presented by these 'eating out' sites relative to the targeted institutionalism of the Poor Law era and, on the other, the need to justify their very inclusion in her study.

But instead of recognizing that the state's role had in fact progressed some from the Malthusianism underlying the New Poor Law, she instead awkwardly argues that British Restaurants not only 'paralleled previous state-feeding programs targeted at specific populations' but were also a novelty which pre-echoed a Blairite vision of bottom-up 'citizen consumerism' in which collectivism was left behind in the supermarket car park. Notwithstanding the involvement of private retailers in wartime social eating, this anachronistic verdict completely ignores the First World War precedent of National Kitchens, which her book ignores. 'That they came to serve a much broader cross section of the home front population was not the result of coherent government policy', writes Durbach.[99] To reiterate, this is incorrect; in both wars, in fact, achieving a cross-class appeal very much *was* the result of government policy.

The conversion into a British Restaurant of one of Cambridge University's most exclusive and traditionalist undergraduate societies, the Pitt Club, provides more evidence of the social levelling achieved by the scheme.[100] Ultimately, however, cross-class appeal was achieved through the quality of the food offered relative to the rationing system. As mentioned previously, rationing was introduced much earlier, and more successfully, in the Second World War than in the First.[101] This allowed some of the tensions that had arisen in 1918 around the quality and quantity of food served in National Kitchens vis-à-vis ration allowances to be ironed out early on. Part of the misconception around British Restaurants exclusively targeting workers seems to be based on the fact that venues received allowances for rationed food on the same basis as commercial catering establishments, and more if they could prove that their clientele was chiefly composed of heavy manual labourers. This ensured that some British Restaurants attracted heavy manual labourers who would, in the First World War, have generally visited industrial canteens rather than National Kitchens. However, when the Ministry introduced restrictions on the sale of rationed food in cafes, restaurants and clubs in 1941 it ensured that the British Restaurant (which was exempted) underwent a surge in general popularity. For instance, in Bicester in Oxfordshire a large number of mothers and young children evacuated from London were convinced that they should stay in the town rather than return to the city only after a British Restaurant offering cheap and nutritious food off-ration opened up.[102] It wasn't just the 'lower orders', though, who were supposed to patronize these sites. Early in the war Ministry of Food officials, conscious of the social stigma attached to poor relief, noted that some emergency rest centres were being avoided by the general public because of a 'supposed poor law taint' and therefore were emphatic in their insistence that there be 'no question of a

Figure 5.4 Queue at a London Citizens' Kitchen, 1940 (Getty).

Means Test' associated with emergency feeding schemes, nor price differentials according to the class or occupational status of the patron.[103]

Left/Right political divisions

Winston Churchill was to make a decisive and telling intervention in March 1941, recommending the name change to British Restaurants 'because the word "restaurant" is associated positively in people's minds with a good meal'.[104] Churchill's remarks were telling of left-right political divisions within the wartime coalition government over communal feeding. The author Edward Blishen, who was later to achieve fame through children's literature and memoir, thought British Restaurants 'anonymous' places because of their air of uniformity.[105] Perhaps unsurprisingly, Blishen was a disciple of fellow author G. K. Chesterton (who was, as noted earlier, no fan of the National Kitchens of the First World War), but his criticism of anonymity chimed with Churchill's fears that the very idea of communal feeding conjured up the misery of the Victorian workhouse or the conformity of the Soviet Union. Conservative MP Sir William Bell called state-sponsored canteens 'brutal in their cooking, brutal in their presentation of food. One needs to be British to "take it" in a British Restaurant.'[106] Frances Partridge, a famous writer of the liberal Bloomsbury set, agreed with Blishen and Bell. She described Swindon's British Restaurant as:

> A huge elephant house where thousands of human beings were eating, as we did, an enormous all-beige meal, starting with beige soup thickened to the consistency of paste, followed by beige mince full of lumps, and garnished with beige beans and a few beige potatoes, thin beige apple stew and a sort of skilly [porridge]. All very crushing, and calling up a vision of our future Planned World, all beige also[107]

The cultural uncomfortableness of what might be loosely termed conservative and liberal sections of British society with communal eating was underpinned by a fear of the growth of the big beige state; after all, they reasoned, wasn't the point of the war to combat the tyrannical excesses of the state over private enterprise and private initiative? The US-based British Food Mission, a Washington relief effort, observed that the extension of public dining in Britain represented 'the acceptance by the state of a foster-parentage of considerable social significance'.[108] Communal feeding was contributing to the disintegration of the home 'before our eyes', moaned one *Daily Mail* columnist.[109] The *Coventry Evening Telegraph* thought that communal dining would bring about a psychological shift in women, threatening their domestic and familial roles; after the war, the 'new wife' would be 'opposed to domestic drudgery' and would instead use 'a central restaurant attached to the estate or block of flats in which she lives', a development which might even lead to her 'requiring such conveniences as a bar'. Other commentators worried that 'for a woman to sink her individuality into a common pool [would be] to deprive herself of an essential requisite to her natural development.'[110]

The perceived growth of the state's 'foster parent', or even 'nanny', role was viewed by some conservatives as offensive to the British way of life, echoing the traditionalist voices that had opposed National Kitchens in the First World War as threatening the family and the female domestic role. These complaints were amplified in 1942 when the Ministry introduced restrictions on the price and type of meals served in private restaurants but not British Restaurants, arguing that British Restaurants' cheap prices meant that they relied on a higher volume of customers to break even and so were exempt from such controls.[111] In time-honoured tradition, the private trade cried foul, criticizing such monopolistic action as offensive to the British notion of 'fair play'. A 1942 op-ed in *The Times* newspaper went one further, opining that the ideals of collective feeding were precisely foreign ones, at odds with British individualism and class distinctions.[112] Although Ministry of Information reports from 1940 to 1941 in fact demonstrate a marked British public distaste for 'individualism' (whether apparent in reports of heroic individual Royal Air Force pilots or occurring elsewhere in society).[113] *The Times* was attempting to hit on the same vein of populist patriotism that had led to the rebranding of communal dining as 'National Kitchens' or 'British Restaurants': communal dining was foreign muck and inherently offensive to the free-born Englishman.

In another light, by its very name the *British* Restaurant chimed with a vein of populist and reactionary nationalism excited by the war. Back in the First World War, anti-German riots had targeted German pork shops across the country following the sinking of the *Lusitania* in 1915 and the rabble-rousing *John Bull* newspaper told readers 'if by chance you should discover one day in a restaurant that you are being served by a German waiter, you will throw the soup on his foul face'.[114] Likewise, in the Second World War, anti-Italian riots occurred in London with Italian restaurants in Soho targeted. A number of Italian restaurant owners were consequently forced to conspicuously declare their support for the British war effort and their own Britishness by placing signs in their windows and taking out newspaper advertisements to the same effect.[115] Moreover, the greater surveillance and restrictions on private restaurants led to a disproportionate number of their non-British staff – Austrian, German, or Italian waiters and chefs – being interned for the duration of the war as enemy aliens. British Restaurants, by contrast, were unequivocally *British*, and it is not unreasonable to conclude that notions of patriotic virtue impelled some people to patronize them.

By contrast, and turning to the left wing of the British political spectrum, Labour party figures such as Minister for Labour Ernest Bevin were much more comfortable with the notion of communal feeding. In fact, Bevin advocated the roll-out of public feeding along explicitly class lines, envisaging the division of public feeding by occupation: industrial canteens for manual workers (who required more calories) and community restaurants for clerical workers.[116] These designs were shared by some civil servants within the Ministry of Food, who wanted public feeding prioritized for workers. They pointed to the fact that a British Restaurant might appear in a town or village with a small population but not in a busy city district where war work was concentrated.[117] This lobby scored a victory in March 1941 when it was agreed with the Ministry of Labour to urge the opening of what the Ministry of Food termed 'community kitchens' in areas where factories were located, and evidence suggests that certain sections of the public associated public dining as something exclusively for manual workers, as noted previously.[118] As the war progressed, these political divisions began to surface, with a 1944 Ministry of Food memorandum complaining that Labour MPs and councillors were taking instruction from the Labour Party, and not it, on the proper function of British Restaurants.[119]

Lord Woolton, a successful high-street business executive performing a very public duty as Minister for Food, sat more or less in the middle of this ideological divide. Like his First World War predecessors Rhondda and Spencer, he was against the idea of the British Restaurants as sites solely for the working class, or for any particular type of worker, arguing instead that they should be 'open to all members of the public'.[120] Above all, Woolton did not want them to take on 'an "institution" atmosphere'; he wanted them instead to be 'bright and jolly'.[121] The term 'community feeding' ought to be 'killed', Woolton would write in 1941, because of its inherent 'coldness'. Flora Solomon's claim that Woolton demanded to know of her 'are you a communist?' because she had named her centre a 'Communal Restaurant' is probably spurious since it appears only in one edition of her autobiography[122]; but her yarn at least captures the fact that anxieties around associations with Soviet Communism first witnessed in the First World War still very much lingered in official circles. Woolton was not averse to the rationalizations and efficiencies demanded by wartime organization, but he was opposed to any attempts by his ministerial staff to 'draw a line of distinction between the people who use British Restaurants', insisting that they be available to the *general public*.[123] Due to the very fact that this sentiment recurs again and again in policy documents of the time, it is worth repeating the point that cross-class appeal remained paramount. Although members of the working class represented the majority of customers, the Ministry insisted – as their predecessors had done with National Kitchens –

that these were not to be spaces solely for 'the very poor', that they be attractive and open 'to all', and that 'no taint of charity' be attached to them.[124] The writer J. B. Priestley, a regular broadcaster during the war, supported the government's initiative, writing that British Restaurants had a 'real social value of their own' and presented the opportunity of making 'a civilised social virtue out of war necessity'.[125]

Yet what might be termed the left-right divide on public feeding (apparently left *for*, right *against*) was not nearly as clear-cut as might be assumed. Margaret Thatcher's father, Alf Roberts, a grocer and local politician – to whom Thatcher, as the premier of the modern age most associated with the creed of privatized individualism, would pay constant lip service – ran a British Restaurant in Grantham, Lincolnshire, and was a vocal proponent of public feeding.[126] Edward Blishen, who objected to communal feeding, was no straightforward conservative but rather a conscientious objector who objected to the war on pacifist grounds as recalled in his memoir *A Cackhanded War*. Then there was the right-wing voice of *The Daily Mail*'s Montague Smith, who argued in favour of the British Restaurant because, quite simply, he considered 'we are all better for human contacts at meal times'.[127]

There were also those – on the political left – who criticized communal feeding because they saw it as representing a certain contradiction of the domestic ration. Similarly, there were those in government who thought it inappropriate that vast quantities of meat be allocated to these public canteens off-ration, worrying that it would undermine the domestic system. In fact, British Restaurants were always ancillary to the domestic ration; the official history of food supply in the war goes as far to claim that even if 10,000 had opened they would not have compromised domestic rations.[128] However, it was the system of bulk purchasing – a combination of big government and big business working together to ensure wholesale economies – that irked some voices attached to the Fabian Society, the left-wing collective with whom the very notion of communal cooperation was much associated.

In January 1942 the Ministry promised to inspect on the spot whenever retailers complained that a British Restaurants would compromise business: a promise, smaller retailers complained, which was rarely kept.[129] The Ministry disagreed and cited instances where the objection of private retailers had delayed progress.[130] The rather petit-bourgeois concern for 'fair play', which had emerged in the First World War, now found an echo in some writers from the Fabian left whose concern was often not with *how* people were fed but with the muffling of the democratic 'bottom up' voice by those controlling food policy (capitalists and the big state). While generally supportive of British Restaurants, there was more than a hint of wistfulness in Fabian Barbara Drake's observation that they had transformed domestic service from 'skilled handicraft' to 'mechanised and mass produced industry'.[131] In a similar vein, a 1940 pamphlet by Fabian Charles Smith entitled *Food in Wartime* claimed that during the First World War this system of bulk purchase worked to exclude cooperative enterprise and the same was the case in the Second World War. The cooperative movement in Britain, he wrote, did not undergo as impressive a growth between 1914 and 1919 as in France, Germany or Belgium because food supply in the war was 'unfair': supplies were allocated to retailers on basis of the number of customers that retailer previously had, economies of scale which nudged aside the small man or the cooperative business. Smith charted how the 'discrimination' wrought by monopoly control and high prices led to the founding of the Cooperative Party in 1917. Instead of communal feeding, he looked to Food Control Committees (composed of consumers and small retailers) as the crux of wartime democracy in feeding. In short, monopoly capitalists and big government were hand in glove, throttling a broader 'struggle for democracy' with unfair wartime controls, and public feeding was part of their compact.[132]

Writing in the same pamphlet series, John Boyd Orr reiterated these concerns when he rued the fact that the war had resulted in 'big trading interests' (the likes of Marsh and Baxter, Tate and Lyle, and Ranks) 'getting a more complete grip on the food of the country'; he called for a Food Council composed of experts to counterweigh commercial self-interest, something at least partially realized when he was invited into the fold by Woolton later that year.[133] To his list of 'big trading interests', Boyd Orr might have added Marks and Spencer, which had a hand in many food relief ventures, as documented before. Flora Solomon, a regular visitor to the Ministry, was to write that Lord Woolton 'grew tired of my mink-lined coat' but his indulgence of her was, perhaps, another example of favouritism. Woolton was wounded by this very accusation in May 1941 when the Labour MP for Dunbartonshire, Adam McKinlay, alleged that restaurants in Lewis's, the department store that Woolton had left to take up his wartime role, had been selling cooked meats while its rivals couldn't procure any. 'I cannot explain to the public outside that it is only a coincidence that the noble lord who presides over the ministry was at one time connected with Lewis's', he stated.[134] Indeed, some voices from the left seemed to resent the cross-class nature of public feeding, with allegations that wealthy people were 'using feeding centres to obtain cheap meals and dodge meat rationing'.[135]

There was a fork in the road, then, between left-wing voices critical of the wartime government and those defensive of it. J. B. Priestley was critical of the over-intrusive state yet enthusiastically championed the state's role in spreading British Restaurants. Other left-leaning voices, by contrast, tempered their enthusiasm, aligning themselves more closely with the small retailer than the big state. In many ways, these dissenting voices of the left and the private retailer made strange bedfellows since the latter's concern was primarily profit. For example, commentators like Charles Smith looked to Food Control Committees (FCCs) as the essential bastions of fair play and democracy, yet private retailers often complained that these bodies blocked private ventures from opening, and that FCCs favoured British Restaurants.[136] And Boyd Orr, somewhat schizophrenically, could simultaneously call for the extension of centralized controls like rationing and price fixing while lamenting the squeezing of the small retailer by central government.[137]

By contrast, Boyd Orr's colleague Jack Drummond did not share these qualms and his wartime experience of industry working with government for the general good led to a faith in the ability of large-scale commercial enterprise to meet the public interest.[138] Similarly, another voice from the Fabian left, Bill Clark – secretary of the Children's Nutrition Council and a prominent figure in the struggle against hunger in the 1930s – wrote that concerns about the small retailer were relegated in importance by the necessity of mass feeding for all. To Clark, who lost his eyesight in the First World War but was a key member of the Labour Research Department and the Spanish Medical Aid Committee, emergency public feeding represented a new spirit of social cooperation, one which was 'democratic in price and clientele', offering a fair and equal service to all regardless of class and status.[139]

Although private businesses were allowed to operate in air raid shelters (where the bulk of shelter catering was undertaken by private traders large and small) the decline in bombing after the Blitz meant that profit margins were so small as to seldom justify the employment of a sizable paid staff. Flora Solomon recalled how Marks and Spencer met demand by running canteens in London's air raid shelters, with 'plates of rich stew available as cheap as the price of the proverbial packet of Woodbines'.[140] Solomon's recollection would seem to contradict the notion that firms favoured by the Ministry were profiteering and corroborates the observation – made by William Beveridge back in 1936 – that in the first 48 hours following a heavy air raid, food simply had to be given away free since displaced people did not carry cash on them. Nonetheless, the Ministry did note sceptically that prices in shelter canteens run by private caterers were sometimes double those in public venues, as private suppliers desperately sought to retain profit margins in such circumstances.[141] This practice ran contrary to the Ministry's instruction that private caterers prominently display a list of maximum prices as determined by the local authority. Therefore, in answering criticism that the big state was colluding with big business, the Ministry could simply point to the economies of scale involved in meeting public-feeding needs. Still, the Ministry estimated that private restaurants, teashops and cafes accounted for a substantial proportion of all the meals served in the country, with the highest estimate placing them at 40 per cent of total national meal provision.[142] Given these figures, private retailers could claim to be carrying out – from a commercial disadvantage – quite the public service.

Conclusion

As in the First World War, the political debate around communal dining did not conform neatly to the left/right dichotomy. Many of the contradictions and grievances between public and private enterprise outlined above, which coloured ideological responses, were addressed by the British government's introduction of points rationing in December 1941, which allocated a points value to foodstuffs which changed according to availability and demand. This had the effect of placing public-feeding schemes on a more equal footing with private caterers.[143] Despite protestations to the contrary, the private retailer was not destroyed by public-feeding initiatives but rather continued to play a vital and symbiotic role in wartime public feeding.

The British Restaurant of the Second World War surpassed its First World War equivalent through more systemized central and local management, more comprehensive nutritional guidelines and a better planned and coordinated approach from the Ministry of Food. Problems witnessed twenty years previously recurred: regional disparities in popularity, the perception that these were exclusively spaces for war workers and the lingering taint of the Poor Law. And yet the more positive aspects of the state's commitment to communal dining also came about more thoroughly: the insistence on cleanliness and good decoration, the notion of fair shares for all and the measured insertion of nutritional imperatives into public life. The next chapter outlines how emergency public feeding developed as the conflict continued, encompassing more than the British Restaurant and firmly establishing the interventionist role of the state.

6

The development of emergency public feeding in the Second World War

Introduction

There is a clear lineage from Beveridge's 1936 memorandum, grim yet accurate in its prediction of aerial destruction, to the Ministry of Food's emergency feeding schemes of the Second World War. Beveridge had predicted the extensive aerial bombardment that would materialize so spectacularly during the Blitz. In implementing emergency feeding, the Ministry was to find itself frustrated by local authorities' sluggishness in establishing feeding centres until the moment of attack. Local authorities, for their part, found the distinctions between different public-feeding centres hard to comprehend. These distinctions between feeding schemes, the official history hints, were unnecessary, resting on 'purely historical reasons' and the Ministry's preference for 'static' over 'mobile' feeding, which it attributed to 'ambitious plans for community feeding to which the Ministry was wedded'.[1] But if the Ministry was generally in favour of nutritious sit-down dining, in practice it supported a number of emergency feeding schemes operating on a more mobile snack-in-hand model.

As this chapter outlines, the context of aerial bombardment and the extension of the state's role led to a plethora of schemes. In assessing public feeding during the war historians have been guilty of focusing disproportionately on communal restaurants, when in fact emergency public feeding comprised much more than sit-down dining. This chapter details how the government negotiated the gap between its public health priorities and often oppositional popular tastes through slick propaganda. The scale of the national crisis ensured that there was an effective blurring of boundaries when it came to public and private sector responsibility for feeding people followed by a ballooning of the Ministry of Food's responsibilities. Finally, this chapter considers the overall usefulness of public feeding during the Second World War.

Figure 6.1 Eating out in Whitehall, London, 1943 (Wikimedia Commons).

Nutritional reformers versus the sausage roll

The Second World War would witness an expansion in the number and variety of public-feeding schemes. Although trams, carts and vans had been used to feed people in the First World War, a key difference in the Second was the increased use of motorized transit and, of course, the frightening reality of aerial destruction. Overseen by the Ministry of Food's Wartime Meals Division, field kitchens and mobile canteens were located beside air raid shelters. These provided emergency food, delivered by great convoys of lorries, to blitzed city dwellers in heavily bombed cities such as Coventry, Portsmouth, Plymouth, Liverpool and Birmingham. In early twenty-first-century Britain, the basic food bank parcel provides, in the words of the main food poverty charity the Trussell Trust, three days' 'emergency food'. Interestingly, although this book considers wartime public-feeding schemes obvious examples of 'emergency feeding', the same term was rarely used during the Second World War, despite the clear state of national emergency. Public feeding was an established means of ensuring fair shares; it only became 'Emergency Feeding' in official parlance when it accompanied the very worst blitz destruction. Therefore, after the heavy German bombing of Plymouth and Belfast in April 1941, 'emergency feeding centres' provided 'emergency food' to tens of thousands of people bombed out of their houses.[2]

On the Blitz night of 23 April 1941 alone, these air raid canteens served a total of 186,000 people nationwide.[3] The greater incidence of civilian bombing in the Second World War demanded a quicker emergency feeding response from the state than in the First World War and the use of motorized convoys carrying supplies meant that specific emergencies were addressed more quickly and fully. For example, the Ministry responded to the Luftwaffe's blitz of Greenock, Scotland, on 6–7 May 1941 – which resulted in high civilian casualties with 271 people killed – by feeding 25,000 people at mobile feeding centres outside the town.[4] In large towns and cities, the food served in British Restaurants was delivered by lorry in heat-retaining containers, the food having been prepared in cooking depots located in safer areas. In smaller towns, less at risk from aerial bombardment, food might be prepared on site.[5] Around the country, the government also undertook an enormous subterranean feeding operation. Hundreds of thousands of civilians were fed in tunnels as bombs reigned down, whether in the sprawling Tranmere Tunnels underneath Birkenhead, the shelters beneath Cardiff's castle walls or in the bowels of the British Museum.[6] The ghost of Charles Spencer's National Kitchen trams even appeared when, in November 1940, the Ministry launched its first 'Food Train' on the London Underground. The food train ran through the underground network, halting to feed people huddled on station platforms. It would run during periods of heavy bombing, between 7 and 9 pm each evening and 5:30 and 7 am each morning.[7]

The Ministry's Shelter Feeding Division also created a central pool of cooking equipment – urns, cans, pots, pans, heating devices – which local authorities could avail of. Royal physician Thomas Jeeves Horder (the unfortunately named Lord Horder – hoarding, of course, being a cardinal sin in the moral economy of wartime) was chosen by Woolton to head the division.[8] In contrast to British Restaurants, which provided hot cooked meals, 'emergency food' provided by the government was similar to today's non-perishable food bank package: tins of soup, beans, rice pudding, corned beef and biscuits.⁹ The supply of tinned American food through lend-lease arrangements also aided the government's emergency feeding efforts as, by the third year of the war, Britain was receiving over 5,000 tonnes of canned condensed milk a week from the United States.¹⁰

In analysing emergency feeding arrangements, the Ministry's nutritionists urged that 'thick, nutritious soup' be the staple in air raid shelter feeding. Characteristically, Flora Solomon claimed credit for this, recalling how she came up with the idea of canning Marks and Spencer's trademark stew and renaming it 'blitz broth'. The ingredients – beetroots, carrots, potatoes, soya beans – were typical of the Russian *borscht* of her childhood, and she sent several tins to Woolton for his approval.¹¹ It is more likely, however, that the Ministry's nutritionists came up with the idea of their own accord. Evidence suggests that they were almost constantly agonizing over how to get people to eat more vegetables. They also fretted over the fact that hot drinks were more popular than fruit squashes and mineral waters, and expressed concern that the consumption of 'starchy foods (buns, slab cake etc.)' was the norm in shelters.¹² In July 1941 Jack Drummond, champion of the unpopular Oslo breakfast, complained to the Ministry of Health that the standards of the British Medical Association's 'minimum cost' diet – a baseline advocated by Boyd Orr and others – were not being met when it came to evacuated children, pointing to supply disruption, rising prices and the costs involved. The BMA's scale looked to the amount of money spent on food per week and recommended a minimum of eight shillings and sixpence a week for children under ten, ten shillings and sixpence for those aged ten to fourteen and twelve shillings and sixpence for those over fourteen. Instead an 'adjusted' index had been composed based on more minimal nutritional requirements which was 'just about adequate to provide sufficient nourishment'. Drummond's revisions reduced the figure of twelve shillings and sixpence for individuals aged fourteen and above down to nine shillings and sixpence.¹³

These anxieties prompted the Ministry's scientific advisors to place renewed emphasis on meeting nutritional standards through emergency feeding. 'In an endeavour to guide tactfully the tastes of people', they instructed that 'posters are to be placed in the air raid shelters instructing the people as to the type of food to take'.¹⁴ Within the Ministry, this reflected the influence of the Food Economy Division which, with its 'Kitchen Front' propaganda effort, was the most enthusiastic proponent of posters, pamphlets and paraphernalia as a means to educate the masses.¹⁵ In London a leaflet composed by the Ministry's scientific advisers on the comparative nutritive values of shelter foodstuffs was also circulated to all local authorities.¹⁶ It was up to local authorities to licence caterers and set prices but the Ministry oversaw all efforts, provided money for the fitting of piped water, electric heating, cupboards, sinks and counters, and guaranteed councils against reasonable operating deficits.[17] Caterers received recipe advice for 'wholesome, nutritious and attractive food' in a Ministry booklet prefaced by Lord Horder which recommended healthy snack foods such as vegetable pies, oatmeal scones, potato patties, mixed vegetable cake; it also included new dainties such as 'Scotch Sprout' (a cooked Brussel sprout split at the stalk end, stuffed with sweet pickle and enveloped in mashed potato) and 'Woolton sandwich' (raw carrot, raw cabbage, raw celery with chutney or pickle).[18]

Yet the urging that shelter feeding be based around thick soups and vegetables was met with public preference for meat pies and sausage rolls when eating underground.[19] Practical constraints meant that sit-down dining was often not possible in shelters and the Ministry discouraged the supply of drinking utensils and cutlery to people due to instances of theft.[20] As the war progressed, the demand for cooked meals in air raid shelters underwent further decline and the number of British Restaurants increased, indicating public preference for restaurant meals when above ground and snacks when below ground. Similarly, the fluctuations in the number of people using air raid shelters complicated the planning process because it was never certain how many people would gather in an air raid shelter at a given time and during the summer months demand for hot food naturally declined.[21] Indeed, a snack and a hot, sweet tea were recommended by every first-aid manual of the time as an elementary treatment for shock.[22]

The standard fare served in air raid shelters was therefore jam tarts, biscuits, meat pies, pasties, sausage rolls, slab cake, cocoa and tea. Occasionally a baked potato was to be found.[23] Only one licensed caterer per shelter was allowed and trading had to cease between 10 pm and 5 am to allow for sleep, but the popularity of fish and chips ensured that 'visiting fish and chip merchants' gained an exemption to this rule.[24] Against the wishes of food reformers like Jack Drummond at the Ministry, then, air raid shelter dining (mainly a London phenomenon) would largely remain an 'unhealthy' snack-in-the-hand experience. Defying the nutritionists, the Ministry of Food's most eloquent, humorous and mischievous civil servant – Brian O'Brien – even composed an elegiac celebration of the wartime value of the humble British snack:

> When John Montagu, fourth Earl of Sandwich, invented the sandwich to sustain himself while continuing uninterrupted his card playing, he can hardly have foreseen the far-reaching consequences of what must even then have seemed a

gastric revolution... Since then the sandwich has suffered the natural fate of an elegant improvisation gradually descending and percolating through the social scale... its relegation from the silver plated sandwich box... to the labourer's 'butty box' has been, for a British institution, comparatively rapid. This is in no way to decry his Lordship's inspiration, but rather the reverse, since there can hardly have been an innovation in the realm of 'eats' of such universal appeal and usefulness... the sandwich has thrown out branches as well as roots, if one may include in its family tree such equally convenient delights as the meat pie and the sausage roll... the essential quality of portability explains its importance to the modern worker [who] cannot always avail themselves of 'sit down' canteen facilities... What rich food for the social philosopher is presented by the traditional choice displayed, from the caviar of the connoisseur to the corned beef of the hungry Home Guardsman, the cool cucumber of the vicar's leisurely lawn tea party to the spiciest delicatessen of London's darkest underworld of snack-bars![25]

Time and again, experience showed that the 'essential quality of portability' and the reassurance of comfort food trumped nutritional qualms when it came to public demand for food in air raid shelters and O'Brien's poetic lines accompanied the opening of canteens without cooking facilities, which the Ministry launched in 1942, granting allowances of rationed food and catering licences to places of employment where the nature of the work was not compatible with 'sit down' dining. In these venues pre-prepared snacks – sausage rolls, sandwiches, Cornish pasties, cakes and buns but seldom a Scotch Sprout or Woolton sandwich – were sold to workers who then took them away to consume 'on the go'. In agricultural areas, too, a 'pie scheme' – providing portable and quickly consumed pies and pasties – operated for rural labourers, with the pies prepared at local bakeries or British Restaurants and brought to the fields in vans.[26] The necessities of wartime had once again, it seemed, prevailed over the nutritional reformers' designs. As in the First World War, nutritional improvement was often counterweighed by the imperative of maintaining morale. The sausage roll had proved defiant.

There were too, though, the Ministry's 'Emergency Feeding Centres', which were stocked through vast local 'Wartime Meals Dumps'. Following air raids gas and electricity supplies were often disrupted, putting both public and private restaurants out of operation. Emergency Feeding Centres, by contrast, were powered through solid fuel (coal, wood, charcoal) and provided 'hot food of a simple kind' and hot drinks.[27] Woolton instructed all towns and cities with populations above 50,000 people and vulnerable smaller settlements to provide at least one of these centres, which were intended as venues where people could

Figure 6.2 London tube shelter canteen, 1942.

congregate for a meal cooked using portable ranges and boilers. The Ministry insisted that in Emergency Feeding Centres – which, understandably, served comfort foods such as biscuits and cocoa – people could also sit down to eat a 'specially prepared nutritious pea soup and vegetable stew' to ensure bombed-out people were eating as many essential nutrients as possible. All Emergency Feeding Centres were equipped with a week's emergency food supplies which included the following: margarine, baked beans, condensed milk, cocoa powder, rice pudding, tea, biscuits, beef hash, sugar and Ministry of Food soup.[28]

Unlike British Restaurants, Emergency Feeding Centres were envisaged as a temporary feature of the public-feeding landscape, meeting feeding needs following bombing raids. For example, whereas British Restaurants were not usually permanent located in schools (due to the interference with education), Emergency Feeding Centres could take over school premises and avail of school kitchens to provide dinners to people over a matter of days.[29] As with British Restaurants, there were regional disparities and anomalies. A 1941 report claimed that apart from in Glasgow, there was no Emergency Feeding Centre on the densely populated north bank of the river Clyde.[30] On the other hand, emergency centres were much easier to establish than British Restaurants, ensuring their spread. The Ministry calculated that there were over 4,000 of these feeding centres in operation at peak, catering for over 10 per cent of the net population of Britain's large towns and cities (two million out of a population of twenty million): a very significant aspect of the wartime feeding effort.[31]

Noting that bureaucratic overlaps in administration could occur, the Ministry asked county councils (as well as district and borough councils) to collaborate with them in opening more of these centres – a request met with refusal by some, with others pleading confusion: were Emergency Feeding Centres now to replace so-called Rest Centres (discussed subsequently) and, if so, what exactly was the difference?[32] Could a British Restaurant, a Rest Centre and an Emergency Feeding Centre operate under one roof and if they did so, what would distinguish one from another?[33] Although some arms of local government were unwilling to shoulder more expenditure, the confusion seems to have been genuine. The term Emergency Feeding *Centre* was taken by many to imply a sit-down meal service, when in fact the Ministry's instructions on how to construct the stoves for these venues – telling people to requisition spare outdoor items such as bricks, oil drums, bins, buckets and door scrapers – really conveyed *emergency and temporary* feeding – the rather more apocalyptic extremes of public feeding.[34] It is clear that in operating so many different public-feeding platforms, the Ministry was in danger of overkill, as is discussed below.

A plethora of schemes

As the war continued, the Ministry of Food gradually took on responsibility for all public eating – everything termed 'community feeding'. This did not include occupational feeding: the Ministry of Labour operated factory and dock canteens and the Ministry of Home Security fed air raid wardens, for example.

In March 1941 it took over the running of Evacuee Feeding Centres (previously organized by the Ministry of Health) and got the assurance of the Ministry of Education that school meals would be opened up to the general public if emergency conditions demanded so. The Ministry of Food's milk supply scheme had ensured that the vast majority of Britain's five million schoolchildren were drinking milk at school every day and by 1942 it was providing a mid-day meal to a million schoolchildren a day.[35] Similarly to the First World War, civil servants envisaged public feeding as providing civilizational, as well as strictly nutritional, benefits. Writing about the school meals service, one Ministry official called it 'valuable not only on nutritional grounds, but as an important form of social education'.[36] As well as providing economies of time, fuel and food, communal feeding 'helps to create confidence, health and a sense of wellbeing'.[37] Once again, the ideological drive towards 'civilized' sit-down dining was at play.

A key difference from the preceding war was the increased involvement of voluntary organizations in feeding schemes. While the National Kitchens Division of the First World War had been critical of well-meaning amateurs, in the Second the scale of destruction and civilian displacement meant that the Ministry readily worked alongside groups such as the Salvation Army and various other faith-based voluntary groups in feeding people in need. In 1941 the Ministry reassured church leaders that church premises were not to be requisitioned for use as public-feeding venues without prior permission being granted. This followed a complaint to Woolton from the Baptist Union of Great Britain and Ireland, who cited a case in Monmouthshire where a local official had entered a chapel and begun the work of measuring up the premises with a view to the removal of the pews and its conversion into a British Restaurant.[38]

British Restaurants still made up quite a significant proportion of public feeding: by June 1941, the Ministry estimated that every day 208,000 people ate in one. Regional variations persisted, however, in part determined by population density. Thus in April 1941 North Wales (roughly 4,000 square miles) did not have a single British Restaurants whereas London local authority of West Ham (roughly eleven square miles) had thirteen.[39] Local political inaction again proved significant, with Liverpool, for example, agreeing to pioneer communal dining in early 1940 but not opening a restaurant until the late autumn.[40] It was also reported that the take-away or 'cash and carry' form of feeding was more popular in the north-east whereas seated dining was favoured in London.[41] 'Cash and carry' feeding was also the preferred method of feeding agricultural labourers, where mobile canteens visited farms and fields.[42] Regional variations in menu were also noticeable. In Lancashire venues, hotpot was a staple, in Cornwall,

Cornish pasties, the Ministry even developed a set of menus specifically geared towards 'Scottish tastes' featuring Scotch broth and haggis.[43] Like in the First World War, where Charles Spencer had allowed for 'special kitchens' for Jewish communities, some venues were provisioned with kosher food. Such local considerations did much to further secure popularity.

A post-war enquiry found that by mid-1944, British Restaurants were providing around 7.5 per cent of the meals consumed by the British public.[44] The statistics, however, are inconsistent and complicated by differing definitions of 'a meal'. Overall, historian Peter Atkins adjudges British Restaurants to have contributed only 'marginally' to wartime feeding, a verdict with which another historian of wartime food, Natacha Chevalier, concurs.[45] However, it is important to note that Atkins' judgement is based upon the strict definition of a 'British Restaurant'. By 1941 the Ministry was running what were variously termed in official correspondence Community Kitchens and Community Feeding Centres as well Dock Canteens and 'Cash and Carry' Centres for agricultural labourers, not to mention Emergency Food Kitchens, Evacuee Feeding Centres, Air Raid Canteens and Emergency Meals Centres and in some cases Rest Centres (for those displaced by bombing).[46] Then there were the public-feeding initiatives which did not always feature in the Ministry's statistics but were supplied by it, such as canteens run by the London Passenger Transport Board and the London Meals Service. Works-based canteens were aimed at war workers such as miners and dockers rather than the general public and are therefore not considered here, but it is important to note Pit Head Canteens (run by the Miners' Welfare Commission but supplied by the state and feeding over half a million miners per day nationwide). Many of the above schemes eventually came under the British Restaurants umbrella, yet it is again important to emphasize the fact that the extent of public feeding extended much further than the British Restaurant. By the end of 1941 – and alongside the plethora of public-feeding schemes listed above – the Ministry calculated that there were a further 172 canteens serving food daily run solely by local authorities, ninety-four canteens run by voluntary organizations and sixty-nine canteens administered by local educational authorities and serving the public from large schools.

The overriding point is that in the Second World War, in contrast to First, when it came to public feeding the lines were blurred and the bureaucratic overlap considerable; commensurate, of course, with this ballooning of emergency public feeding into a messy amalgam was the increased demand wrought by aerial bombardment. Altogether, in 1941, the Wartime Meals Division estimated that some 325,000 members of the general public availed of some sort of public feeding on a daily basis from 1,148 public-feeding centres (of all kinds).[47]

Naturally enough, this plethora of public-feeding schemes proved confusing. In a Commons debate of 1941 clarity was requested, on behalf of local authorities, as to what was the essential difference between a British Restaurant, an emergency feeding centre and a rest centre. It had proved 'impossible', it was claimed, to distinguish one from another and to know which Department to deal with.[48] As late as June 1941, the Ministry of Food was still insisting that the Ministry of Health ran the rest and emergency feeding centres and it ran communal feeding facilities.[49] In practice, however, the Ministry's all-too-neat division between different types of feeding centre was exposed after the 1940 Blitzes of London and Coventry when rest centres became overwhelmed by tens of thousands of hungry homeless people, and the Ministry of Food was to assume the overarching responsibility for public feeding.[50]

That the Ministry of Food had effectively taken on responsibility for feeding the nation's young is emphasized by a number of recollections about British Restaurants by people who were children during the war. One man recalled how, as a teenager in Plymouth during the conflict, he would eat his main meal (beans on toast) at a British Restaurant because his school did not provide dinners. For another, a schoolgirl in London, the fortnightly trip to a British Restaurant was a treat, leaving her with memories of 'the smell of mince and the condensation', whereas a boy in Scotland was regularly brought to the local British Restaurant by his grandmother, who favoured bread and dripping over 'posh' restaurants and the foreign 'horses doovers' (hors d'oeuvres) 'that that lot eat'.[51] A girl in West Yorkshire visited one in her town with her mother but they did not return because 'mother felt it was really meant for "the workers"'. This class-based verdict on British Restaurants runs against the consistent aim of the Ministry of Food to ensure that public eating was 'for all'. It was an opinion shared by at least one Mass Observation diarist, who considered them places of the working class, patronized by people below her social class.[52] On the other hand, an American observer noted that communal dining showed the British behaving 'like a united family', and 'willing to sit beside each other regardless of station in life, the greasy overall beside the well cut suit, the unmannerly beside the fastidious'.[53]

Although public feeding in the Second World War availed of the increased ability to provide mobile supplies, as in the First World War grand plans for mobile National Kitchens did not really take off as the conservation of petrol supplies was always a concern. The Ford Motor Company placed thirty-five vans equipped with containers for hot food at the Ministry's disposal, with these vehicles garaged and maintained by Ford dealerships[54] and in 1943 the Ministry planned a series of regional mobile food shops which would require patrons to bring their own dishes (much like the National Kitchen trams of the First World War). However, a survey found that many Divisional food officers had already taken such steps, earmarking furniture vans to act as mobile canteens when needed.[55] There were occasions, such as the influenza epidemic of Christmas 1943, where food was transported direct to sick people's homes.[56] However, there was also resistance from local authorities to the mobile supply of food. The scientific advisory committee was also concerned at the loss of vitamin C in transit in insulated containers. The Ministry responded by providing steam sterilizers. But local authorities still largely resisted the Ministry's desire that all food supply be conveyed by car and van from depots rather than prepared on-site.[57]

Convoys of food were operated by the grandiloquently termed 'Queen's Messenger Service', a branch of the Women's Voluntary Service entitled to wear their own special badge. They were supposed to bridge the gap between an air raid and static feeding arrangements in the first 48 hours or so following a bombing raid. The idea of diligent, royally appointed uniformed young women – getting behind the wheel and screeching off at a moment's notice to feed the masses – seems to have struck a real chord with some at the Ministry, and the Queen's Messenger Service are often referred to in breathlessly admiring tones in official correspondence. The regal romance of the image has affected some historians too, with one gushing over the idea of the Queen personally paying for eight of the convoy vehicles and crying tears of pride at the resilience of British women, with crowds cheering the 'fleet' on its way wherever it went as it 'ploughed' its way to those in distress.[58] In practice, civil defence vehicles were often used for this purpose and many Queen's Messenger Convoys were never deployed; those that were suffered high rates of breakdown and despite the Ministry's enthusiasm for them they remained a largely unused reserve.[59]

Eating out with Tommy Trinder (and Barbara Cartland)

Like in the First World War, state-supported restaurants received royal endorsement, with George VI touring three London sites in October 1940.[60] Arguably, however, endorsement from actors via wireless and film was more valuable to the state in communicating its message to the general public than periodic royal visits. One notable feature of public-feeding schemes in the Second World War was the ceaseless promotion of communal consumption via Home Front propaganda. Food was part of an overriding state narrative of wartime collectivism played out on screen in which public feeding assumed central importance. Driven by a government keen to achieve economies in food and fuel, Britons were 'eating out' in public as never before. Mass Observation testimony includes evidence that the fuel-saving imperative emphasized by the government was getting through to the public, with one diarist noting people dining together in order to economize on fuel and quoting a colleague of hers on 'the saving of time in washing up, mop + sink cleaning + and so on after a meal'.[61] In line with the food and fuel message, many British films of the era contained scenes in which meals were consumed in the public arena. Among other examples, the hit British movie *Millions Like Us* (1943) features many critical scenes set in a canteen, where the film's heroine works.[62]

In early 1941 the Ministry of Information recruited the popular music hall actor Tommy Trinder to promote British Restaurants. Cockney Trinder, whose catchphrase was 'you lucky people', starred in the short film *Eating Out with Tommy Trinder* in which Trinder's fiancé and in-laws had the fortune of being treated to a British Restaurant meal with the eponymous star. Trinder was an established star of light entertainment, a familiar face and voice to wartime audiences, the recent star of the 1940 Ealing Studios comedy hit *Sailors Three* in which three drunken Royal Navy sailors accidentally capture a German battleship while on shore leave in Brazil. Trinder's public eating propaganda piece was less exotic, beginning with the entertainer relishing the prospect of a Saturday night dinner date, only for his fiancé to insist that he comes to dinner 'with mother and the family' instead. At her mother's house Trinder suffers not only the company of his fiancé's mischievous younger brother and overbearing mother but a dinner that contains tiny portions of tough lamb ('that was all they had at the butchers') and no vegetables ('couldn't get to the shop on time'). 'I'm sorry if the dinner wasn't too good' apologizes his fiancé afterwards, 'you know it's difficult in wartime'. 'Of course it isn't' insists a chipper Tommy, and the following Saturday takes the whole family out to a British Restaurant. Bizarrely, since the film is clearly set in London, Tommy and company turn up at the Byrom Restaurant in Liverpool. There, by contrast, the plates are full. 'Look what you get for four and tuppence' enthuses Trinder 'blimey, they're giving the stuff away!'

Eating Out with Tommy Trinder also reiterated the economical and scientific logic of communal dining as first set out in the *Public Kitchens Handbook* of the

First World War, as Trinder explained the time-saving gadgetry to his future mother-in-law:

> Now look, you eat at home… your one oven cooks for four… this restaurant uses four ovens and cooks for 800 people. If all these people ate at home like you do it would take 100 ovens and 100 times the gas or electricity to feed them. And they'd all be peeling the spuds in the old fashioned way! But here they've got a machine that does it all. In go the potatoes, on goes the switch, and off come their overcoats! I used to think that I was a bit of a masher, but this machine's got me beat every time… and *this* machine does all the carving, so instead of you doing all the work while everyone else eats, here you sit down and eat… do you know what, Mrs Jones? You should get around more. How is it you've never heard of these British Restaurants?

There were distinct echoes of Arnold Bennett's advocacy of National Kitchens here, when he criticized a 'reactionary' cultural spirit resisting scientific improvements in the preparation and service of food. The film was aimed squarely at the woman of the house, as the above narrative suggests, urging her to embrace the new and dispense with old habits. Like its equivalent First World War propaganda, the film was also at pains to point out that public feeding was not the preserve of the very poor. 'Department managers, shop-girls, clerks, all kinds of people come here', narrated Trinder as a distinctly middle-class couple come into shot, 'even actors like me'…

> I know what you're thinking Mrs Jones. The place is alright, the service is alright, the cutlery's alright, but what about the food? What did you have last Saturday? Roast lamb. The Saturday before that? Roast lamb. The Saturday before that? Roast lamb. Five Saturdays running you've had roast lamb. It's time that roast lamb was mutton. Now look what I've been sacrificing for roast lamb. I could have come here, this is one place where they never let bygones be rissoles. They're continually changing the menu. Look at this – we've as much as we can have to eat, with rice pudding and cups of tea to follow for four and tuppence. And another thing – it helps the country. It saves food, fuel and time.

The film ends with Trinder correcting his father-in-law for suggesting that the family needed to move house to be closer to a British Restaurant. 'Don't be a twerp!' exclaims Trinder, explaining that anyone could get a public canteen in their own district by petitioning the council to apply for central funding. 'It's up to you – all you've got to do is ask your local council'.[63] Of course, getting a British Restaurant in your locale was not as easy as Trinder suggested, with the local authority, if willing to open one, having to find premises and staff.

Nonetheless, the seven-minute film – broadcast in cinemas nationwide in May 1941 – provided a significant propaganda boost to the government's communal dining programme.

British Restaurants also received celebrity endorsement from an unlikely quarter: romantic novelist Barbara Cartland. The long-lived, colourful and prolific Cartland would go on to earn a reputation as something of a snob, churning out high-society romances and inhabiting an affluent world far removed from communal restaurants. Yet the war brought tragedy for the author when her two brothers were killed at Dunkirk in 1940, impelling Cartland to contribute to the war effort as a welfare officer with the Women's Voluntary Service (WVS).[64] The WVS had a specialist section dedicated to British Restaurants, run by fellow female society figure Lady Iris Capell, who publicly urged women to volunteer their cookery services gratis as part of the war effort. In September 1941 Cartland took up the crusade, writing a long letter to the editor of *The Daily Telegraph* registering her support for communal feeding centres and urging that instead of being restricted to badly bombed cities they should be extended to as many towns as possible. Cartland, who had already made her name as a gossip columnist and writer of romances, went on to explain that she had recently broadcast to Australia endorsing British Restaurants, arguing that

> The food is well cooked and nicely served, and the dining rooms are sprayed with disinfectant after use. Busy housewives can send children there alone, knowing that they will be looked after and their choice of food superintended... While deprecating any injustice caused to private enterprise by the inevitable injustices of war, the common good must be the final criterion of judgement. The good done by these feeding centres can be seen by the difference in health in those children who attend them regularly, rosy cheeks, increased vitality, straightened limbs and smiling faces being a most obvious argument in their favour.[65]

Notwithstanding the reference to regular disinfection (which may have raised initial doubts in the mind of her readers about dirty and crowded restaurants full of people with doubtful hygiene) it is remarkable that Cartland – a staunch conservative, anti-socialist and eulogizer of the aristocratic order whose food was usually served to her by a butler – could advocate British Restaurants with such an appeal to the public good. Endorsement from the likes of Cartland was critical in winning over middle-class housewives to the idea of public feeding.[66] Whereas some working-class housewives had expressed concerns over the expense of dining out at a British Restaurant, the concern was that middle-class women would adopt an aloof attitude. This fear is supported by Mass

Observation evidence, which reveals that social class played a central role in how public feeding was viewed. In analysing the Mass Observation evidence, Natacha Chevalier points out that women who did not have children to feed on limited rations and did not need communal feeding to help with their children's diet tended to be sceptical. In contrast, respondents for whom having access to a British Restaurant could have helped with their main wartime difficulty – feeding the family – tended to be more upbeat about the idea. There was also noticeable class-based difference in opinion between female Mass Observation observers who could afford to dine out in expensive private restaurants and those for whom cafés, tea rooms and canteens were the norm.[67] According to Zweiniger-Bargielowska, only 1.3 per cent of housewives dined in a British Restaurant, compared to the 2 per cent of the general population claimed by Peter Atkins.[68] Although these statistics are only estimates, and appear to be overly conservative estimates at that, they illuminate the importance of winning over the housewife to the idea of dining out at such venues. It is therefore significant that Tommy Trinder's mother-in-law in *Eating Out* is a decidedly house-proud middle-class woman and it was to this type of woman – whose home standards were high, and to whom the idea of communal eating might have appeared unclean and undesirable – that Cartland was appealing. For its part, the Ministry recognized that winning over this demographic would be critical to the success of the British Restaurant; therefore, endorsement from the right personalities was invaluable.

Celebrity endorsement, then, was critical in bridging the class distinctions that dogged the Ministry of Food's central message: egalitarianism in consumption. Many of its initiatives were launched from smart hotels and restaurants so that the public would perceive that not only were the rich undergoing austerity like them, but that everyone – regardless of class – was eating the same. Woolton pie is a case in point. The pie was an unappetizing mixture of carrots, swedes, potatoes and cauliflower. According to the manageress of a British Restaurant in Ipswich, which is supported by other accounts, it 'was not a favourite'.[69] Named after the Minister of Food, it was launched at London's upmarket *Savoy* in 1941. 'In hotels and restaurants, no less than in communal canteens, many people have tasted Lord Woolton pie and pronounced it good' chirped *The Times*.[70] Churchill wasn't one of them, upsetting Woolton by sending his back at the *Savoy* press launch of the dish, grumpily requesting beef instead. The differences between the two men were again laid bare and one can appreciate Woolton's exasperation at Prime Minister's pig-headedness. Woolton himself could be maddeningly stiff, though, such as the occasion when served Woolton pie at the opening of a British Restaurant in Hackney in 1941, only to send it back because – contrary to the bland official recipe – it contained sausages.[71] Such behaviour was unbecoming of his PR persona 'Uncle Fred'. With ministers acting in this way, the Ministry of Food's use of celebrities to promote public feeding is understandable.

Utility – 'marginal' to the war effort, or more significant?

The disruption to civilian life during the Second World War far outstripped the experience of the First. Justifying communal dining schemes early on, the Ministry noted the large number of women employed in war work for whom cooking at home was no longer possible; of men unable to return home for a mid-day meal due to extended working conditions and hours, of evacuees displaced and in want of a meal, munitions workers billeted to unfamiliar towns and, of course, the ascending prices and descending bombs. Similar to the First World War, the British press noted the successful running of communal feeding schemes in enemy Germany; for example, a *Telegraph* report of February 1943 cited a 'huge communal feeding centre with its own slaughterhouse'.[72] Rather than deriding enemy efforts, there was an element of competition in such reports.

And yet a common theme re-emerged. Public feeding was conceived of merely as a wartime expedient by some, with a Ministry memo of 1943 concluding wistfully 'it will be for post-war governments to decide whether to leave to private caterers all arrangements for eating away from home or to continue the wartime experiment.'[73] From 1943 onwards Allied victory in the war was looking ever more assured and with thoughts inevitably turning to post-war organization, the question of the utility of communal feeding arose. The following year, a House of Commons debate concerned the Ministry of Food requisitioning of a billiards hall in Carlisle for use as a British Restaurant, an action which had resulted in the eviction of its seventy-five-year-old proprietor, who was left to live, it was claimed, on less than a £1 a week. Woolton had left the Ministry of Food in November 1943 to become Minister of Reconstruction and his successor, J. J. Llewellin, defended the action as regrettable but 'in the interest of the majority of the people'. But the public interest argument was becoming harder to sustain, particularly in Carlisle, which was already home to a number of government-run pubs and hotels. 'Better to have no British Restaurant than to have this injustice' snapped back his fellow Conservative MP, Edward Keeling.[74] Like in the First World War, there were cases where public feeding was beginning to militate against the expected return of 'fair play' in peacetime.

In considering the overall utility of public feeding, the Ministry had previously looked to a Welsh case study. The small and rather sleepy town of Tenby, in South Wales, had a wartime population of just 6,000. Yet it became the unlikely subject of debate within the Ministry of Food as to the usefulness of British Restaurants and other feeding schemes. From the outset of public feeding's reinvention, there was a consistent lobby within the Ministry for feeding schemes concentrated around areas of vital war work rather than on every high street. Carlisle, for example, was home to war industries, but somewhere like Tenby – with no war industries to speak of – was cited as an example of the sort of place where a public cafeteria was not needed.[75] But Tenby's British Restaurant had its defenders, too, within the Ministry. While conceding that the population of the Welsh town was small, they pointed to the fact that like many other rural settlements it played host to evacuees (in this case 400) and that the public canteen had justified its

Figure 6.3 Frederick James Marquis, 1st Earl of Woolton (1883–1964), Wikimedia Commons.

existence, turning over a small profit and serving between 150 and 200 meals a day.[76] Similar examples came from Scotland, where the Ministry noted that the authorities of a town of 120,000 denied the need for communal feeding despite possessing heavy industry and high rates of poverty; a small town of a few thousand, by contrast, boasted that it had community-feeding facilities and emergency feeding would be deployed at half an hour's notice.[77]

As mentioned earlier, at the outset of his tenure as Minister of Food Woolton wanted public feeding to be exactly that: public and open to all. However, by 1943, the Ministry was recording cases in central London where 'genuine workers' had been crowded out by 'visitors'.[78] In Croydon it was reported that town councillors and corporation officials were being favoured, receiving better meals than the 'small and half cold' dishes served to the general public.[79] In some parts of the country the lack of provision of school meals meant that British Restaurants were flooded by noisy schoolchildren, for whom – the Ministry considered – menus and arrangements were unsuitable.[80] In others, educational authorities opened school canteens to the adult population, irking the Ministry of Food by serving food at prices which undercut British Restaurants.[81] And while some local authorities operated Emergency Meals Centres, in others already existing British Restaurants performed this function. Elsewhere, the Ministry's cooking depots for emergency feeding were being used to supply schools.[82] Clearly, the public imperative to feed everyone did not adhere to the Ministry's neat divisions between different types of feeding scheme.

The protestations of the retail trade were mounting, too. They gained the support of senior civil servants like Sir Henry French, who pressed for enquiries to be established in any case where a British Restaurant had been established to the detriment of private caterers and, by 1942/43, Woolton agreed.[83] The Minister met with representatives from the catering industry in early 1942 and pledged 'if their associations came across cases where local authorities proposed to establish British Restaurants and where the catering trade could demonstrate that it could handle the problem alone, he would be prepared to send an inspector to the area to make an enquiry on the spot'.[84] Woolton – a retailer, after all – was wedded to the idea of the high street and even considered the opening of 'emergency shopping centres' where bombing had destroyed all shops within an area.[85]

Woolton also instructed that all profits from British Restaurants were now to be split between local authorities and the Ministry. According to Woolton's team, staffing was becoming the greatest problem: 'the type of staff available is such that there is a good deal of unavoidable absenteeism', a situation which often led to the late and inaccurate reporting of accounts.[86] New instructions tightened up the finances available to local authorities running British Restaurants, restricting the salaries of catering managers and staff and reigning in capital expenditure as well as requiring greater detail in monthly accounts submitted to the Ministry.[87] Criminal behaviour does not seem to have been unduly associated with public-feeding schemes during the war, although there were cases of employees stealing and, as documented earlier, the theft of utensils and cutlery by members of the public. Flora Solomon recalls petty criminality and violence at some public-feeding spaces in London's East End but, in keeping with her sometimes madcap management style, she dealt with these through recruiting her own East End toughs to act as a sort of unofficial police force, led by a respected local character known as Mickey the Midget.[88]

By 1943, British Restaurants were registering a net profit nationwide, suggesting both popularity and long-term viability.[89] For the financial year 1942–3 net profit nationwide was £97,500 and for 1943–4 this figure stood at an impressive £170,000.[90] Several were making profits so substantial that they repaid the Ministry their entire original loan for capital costs plus interest.[91] If we are to consider British Restaurants in isolation, their peak of 2,160 was determined by the Ministry itself rather than by public demand alone. They were reaching a point of ubiquity which is illustrated by comparison to the number of McDonald's restaurants operative in the United Kingdom at the time of writing, which is around half that figure. And yet in September 1943 – with the overall supply situation in the war looking much rosier and British Restaurants recording record profits – Woolton applied the brakes, instructing Divisional Food Officers to cease campaigning for their opening.[92] Two months later, Woolton was to depart his post at the Ministry of Food, taking with him some of the avuncular charm that seems to have been popularly associated with him and which had provided a tonic to the occasional excesses of statist intervention.

Conclusion

The official history of wartime food describes community Kitchens as 'novelties' and claims that the contribution of British Restaurants to wartime feeding was not 7.5 per cent but an unremarkable 3 per cent, going on to suggest that those who thought communal dining might replace home feeding in peacetime were [leftist] zealots.[93] Some of this scepticism has naturally crept into the historiography, which repeats some of the Ministry's mistakes in too neatly dividing up public feeding into its separate schemes (such as solely considering feeding sites strictly termed British Restaurants) rather than the broad sweep of public-feeding initiatives. As the official history puts it, a 'revolutionary development in communal feeding' did not take place. While the opposition from some commercial caterers was predictable, the Ministry also complained of only 'luke-warm acquiescence' from local authorities.[94] As usual, and like in the First World War, everyone was concerned about who was footing the bill. History repeated itself, then, when it came to the strongest lobby against British Restaurants – businessmen of the catering and restaurant trade – who often vented their opposition through their local chambers of commerce. The cry was the same: 'it's not fair'. British Restaurants benefited from interest-free loans, their equipment was centrally purchased and expertly equipped, and the state was there to support them. Woolton, himself from a high-street retail background, eventually acquiesced. Furthermore, as in the First World War, the lofty goals of the nutritionists and food reformers like Jack Drummond would remain only partially realized via public feeding, with rationing restrictions providing the real boost to health. In May 1943 it was announced that British Restaurants must pay their way or close down and proposals for new ones were more carefully scrutinized. The 1946 Civic Restaurants Act allowed local authorities to compulsorily purchase feeding centres from central government. Although communal eating continued under local authorities well into the 1950s, the legislation led to the rapid closure of 460 British Restaurants 'proper' and the following year the Ministry relinquished control of all cooking depots as well.[95]

As with the winding down of National Kitchens after the First World War, proponents of public feeding within the Ministry of Food reacted with outrage. Jack Drummond wrote a spirited defence of social eating in the *British Food Journal* in 1944, claiming that it had proved 'almost universally popular', was 'economic', 'low wastage' and 'nutritious'. After the war, claimed Drummond, communal dining 'with competent handling and appropriate guidance' would become 'one of the most vital foundations' of British economy and society, ensuring the 'health and efficiency of the workers'. Interestingly, Drummond's defence broke with the official line in that he defended the utility of public feeding in explicitly class terms, referring admiringly to the example set by the Soviet Union. Nonetheless Drummond (who would be brutally, and bizarrely, beaten to death alongside his wife and ten-year-old daughter on a family holiday to France in 1952) envisioned the emergency feeding of wartime continuing beyond the factory canteen to the benefit of the general public, fulfilling 'as essential a role in peace time as under war conditions'.[96]

While Drummond overstated the case, there is much evidence to suggest not only the necessity but the popularity and medium to long-term profitability of public-feeding schemes during the Second World War. After the Second World War, the ethos of public feeding lingered longer than after the First. As mentioned previously, by 1919 National Kitchens had morphed into rather more select venues in London's royal parks where prices exceeded cheap tea houses like Lyons. In 1946, by contrast, the Ministry of Food estimated that a standard meal cost one shilling and threepence in a British Restaurants was exceeded by an average cost of one shilling and ten-pence in a Lyons outlet.[97] Like in the First World War, loans and subsidies from central government enabled the British Restaurant to succeed; unlike the National Kitchen, the cost of public dining was kept down by up to 40 per cent of the labour in them being voluntary and by the expanded role of the private sector in supporting the model.[98] Another important legacy of the National Kitchen was the morale-boosting imperative to make eating in a British Restaurant a civilized experience. Ministry officials paid great attention to ensuring that decor was light rather than dingy and that the font of the signage was consistent and appealing. There was live music in some venues and many had artwork adorning the walls, some of it specially commissioned.[99] Like in the First World War, the mobile, 'take away', or 'cash and carry' model of public dining amounted to less than 10 per cent of service in British Restaurants; it is clear that the majority of people liked to 'dine in' in comfortable surroundings, and that this was also the ideological preference of the Ministry of Food.[100]

What is clear is that the early introduction of rationing in the Second World War – in contrast to the First World War – diminished the relative importance of communal dining when it comes to the base consideration of ensuring people were fed. It is interesting to note that relatively few housewives availed of British Restaurants because the rationing system made preparing meals at home cheaper and more convenient.[101] At the same time the disruption of war and the extension of working hours meant eating out was very popular. Even with low profit margins, communal dining could pay its way thanks to the high turnover of customers: 100 people a day could be served at a price as low as a shilling and the restaurant would still break even.[102] The Ministry estimated that 14 million meals were served outside the home every day in wartime Britain and, contrary to the received wisdom that British Restaurants were 'marginal', it is clear that public feeding – taken as a whole – was an important complement to rationing. It was a means of 'deliberately and officially easing the pressure on the domestic ration', as the Ministry put it, while at the same time extending the principle of equality and boosting morale.[103]

Although overriding opinion is hard to gauge, as mentioned, a Mass Observation survey of 1942 recorded that 96 per cent of people who had eaten in a British Restaurant had had a positive experience.[104] In contrast to the lukewarm appraisals of much of the historiography, one historian of wartime morale in Britain considers British Restaurants 'one of Woolton's most inspired innovations' and judges them an 'immense success'; from a morale perspective 'British Restaurants, by giving some relief from the constraints imposed by the basic rations, were a powerful force for public contentment'.[105] The historian Angus Calder considered them popular places where good food was served. Although this verdict is questioned by Natacha Chevalier's study of Mass Observation diarists, she points out that Calder is not 'wrong' but that contemporary appraisals of British Restaurants tended to be coloured by taste, preference and social class – in other words, they tend to be highly subjective, with judgements on the food varying from good to terrible.[106] There are some signs, too, that the historiography surrounding British Restaurants is shifting, with more recent work considering the phenomenon 'particularly significant' in the wider history of state feeding.[107]

Alongside rationing, the state's endorsement and promotion of the British Restaurant and other forms of emergency social eating symbolize what another historian calls a 'communalist gastronomic paradigm'[108] and it is within this paradigm that British Restaurants deserve to be judged. As this analysis has demonstrated, British Restaurants were but one arm of a greatly expanded wartime public-feeding network, something which historians have largely been guilty of overlooking. They were the most eye-catching form of public feeding but were also, from their original design, an ancillary service to other forms of communal eating (such as factory and dock canteens and emergency feeding in shelters) and never a primary food provider. Nonetheless, in frequently citing Churchill's early dislike for the term communal feeding, historians have perhaps overlooked the prime minister's later defence of British Restaurants 'which had served a most useful purpose and should not be allowed to disappear'.[109] And yet, like National Kitchens before them, disappear they gradually did.

Conclusion

Emergency feeding in historical perspective

Back in 1917, the *Public Kitchens Handbook* confidently declared home cooking a thing of the past. This futuristic prediction of a civilizational ascent towards communal dining found an echo in the 1960s. J. G. Davies, a leading food scientist, told London's Royal Society of Arts that home cooking would disappear by the year 2000. Instead, he claimed, 'instant' food, pre-prepared and served in large communal feeding spaces, would be the norm, reflective of profound sociological changes. Davies anticipated an ageing population living largely in high-rise flats; combined with higher numbers of working women and students, the net result would be sterile food, wrapped in plastic and needing only to be warmed. This was, in large part, a reaction to the American 'TV Dinner' emergent in the 1950s and 1960s but, interestingly, Davies felt that the greater concentration of people living in cities would lead naturally to 'the development of communal feeding' rather than the 'atomization' of mealtimes. Davies's observations raised the ire of restaurant critic Egon Ronay, who protested 'home cooking will never come to an end – unless the way to a man's heart is through a pill … if this does come about I am glad I shall be dead by the year 2000.'[1]

Ronay (who died in 2010, aged ninety-five) need not have worried. Home cooking has persisted and, by the end of twentieth century and the post-war rise of individualism and consumerism, it was instead the notion of communal eating that had become somewhat passé. As this book has shown, public feeding has always suffered from something of an image problem. George Orwell's novel *Nineteen Eighty-Four* (published in 1949) reimagined the popular BBC Eastern Service staff diner at 200 Oxford Street as a dystopian cavern in which apron-clad functionaries of the totalitarian regime ladled out regulation pinkish-grey stew: an image from which the reputation of canteen dining has arguably never recovered. The columnist Michael Wharton, who wrote under the pseudonym

Peter Simple in the conservative *Daily Telegraph*, enjoyed deriding communal feeding and in 1956 penned a ditty pillorying the willing submissive within Orwellian society, a man

> Who had no surname, just a number
> Forgoing all the bourgeois lumber...
> Possessing what he stood up in,
> Feeding at communal canteens,
> And buying drinks at slot machines...
> His feet in due course did not fail
> To kick the suicidal pail
> Saving the bankrupt NHS
> His cost in second childishness.[2]

Remarkably, Simple even attacked Winston Churchill for having insisted on the name British Restaurant, writing 'to give fine-sounding names to nasty things is to give jewellery to a drowning man. It cannot save him and he takes it with him as he sinks'.[3] In the post-war period, public feeding would undergo further reputational damage when it became linked to outbreaks of food poisoning. In 1951, sections of the British press attributed a rise in the number of such cases to the reheating of meat dishes in large containers at the remaining communal feeding sites that had survived the axe.[4] In 1979, on the eve of Margaret Thatcher's prime ministership, communal feeding of any type was identified by the right-wing press as a public health hazard, an activity through which participants ran the risk of contracting food poisoning.[5] Nevertheless, as a response to the poverty experienced in London communities in the early 1980s, the Labour Party-controlled Greater London Council (GLC) 'seriously considered' the reintroduction of civic restaurants before its disbandment in 1986.[6] And subsequently, as outlined in the introduction, the opening two decades of the twenty-first century would witness the slow but steady return of the social feeding phenomenon in Britain, this time through private charitable means.

In the years since the end of the Second World War there have been periodic moments of crisis: the industrial unrest of the 1970s, the riots and labour disputes of the 1980s, the foot-and-mouth outbreak of the 2000s: the riots and Brexit division of the 2010s. But none of these witnessed the same *emergency* status and national *emergency* measures as the Coronavirus crisis of 2020–21. While stopping short of calling a formal national emergency, as many other countries had done, in March 2020 the British state introduced emergency powers so wide-ranging that a former British supreme court justice described them as 'coercive powers over citizens on a scale never previously attempted... the most significant interference with personal freedom in the history of our country'.[7] Accordingly in 2020, and for the first time since the Second World War, the UK government introduced, alongside other feeding measures, an eating scheme that applied to 'everyone in the country'.

History – to employ once more one of Karl Marx's most abused pieces of purple prose – repeats itself first as tragedy and then as farce.[8] The first repeat of history came with the scale of the national feeding effort in 2020 following the national 'lockdown' announced by Prime Minister Boris Johnson on 23 March 2020. Consequently, a great surge of public-feeding efforts saw local and state actors coordinating the delivery of food packages to the doorsteps of people 'shielding' or 'isolating', supermarkets employing a system of informal rationing to prevent panic buying, the government funded a food voucher scheme aimed at low-income parents and, later, came Chancellor Rishi Sunak's headline-grabbing 'Eat Out to Help Out' through which the state footed 50 per cent of over 100 million restaurant bills at a cost to the Treasury of £52 million.[9] Despite Sunak's assertion that such a public-feeding scheme was unprecedented, this was history repeating itself. As the human tragedy of the 'first wave' of the Coronavirus started to slowly recede and the attendant cultural and economic tragedy of restaurant closures took centre stage, state-subsidized dining again became part of British public life.

Leaving aside the Churchillian 'wartime leadership' which Prime Minister Boris Johnson aspired to,[10] the similarities with feeding the people in wartime were striking. The public-feeding schemes of the two world wars were rolled out, similarly, on a national scale. They excited great political and cultural debate: welcomed by some as symbolic of a heartening shift towards collective action, they were derided by others as expensive state overreach.[11] On 15 June 2020, in an open letter to MPs, Manchester United footballer Marcus Rashford called on the government to extend the free school meals vouchers scheme over the summer holidays. The growth in 'school holiday hunger' had been well documented in the preceding years.[12] At the time of Rashford's appeal, 1.3 million children from the lowest income backgrounds were in receipt of free food at school, a measure first introduced nationwide in 1906 and detailed earlier in this book. In urging the government to extend their voucher scheme, Rashford pointed to the extraordinary circumstances of the national emergency. The following day the government relented, extending the food voucher scheme over the school summer holidays.

This was an extraordinary moment. Firstly, in terms of celebrity intervention on public feeding Rashford's was perhaps the greatest example since Charles Dickens implicitly attacked the food policies of the New Poor Law (1834) in his *Oliver Twist* (1838) and *A Christmas Carol* (1843). In terms of long-term nutritional impact, Rashford's campaign – restricted, as it was, to school summer holidays in 2020 – may not have been as substantial as the 2009 rule change on healthier canteen meals achieved by celebrity chef Jamie Oliver. Nonetheless, Rashford's goal was achieved in the context of a national emergency and, as this book demonstrates, *emergency* public feeding has long been marked by celebrity involvement. Secondly – and most importantly – in meeting Rashford's demand the UK Government was acknowledging the scale of the national emergency by moving away from *targeted* feeding (in school) and towards a position of *food for all*, because the vouchers could be used *outside* of school and *outside* of term-time. The point made above, which outlined this dichotomy, bears repeating. As is detailed extensively in this book, 'targeted' feeding (essentially institutional) has been the preferred method of feeding pursued by the British state since the Victorian period. In providing food only to certain subsections of the population rather than 'the people' at large, central government not only saved money but stayed comfortably within the ideological boundaries of political economy forged in the nineteenth century which cautioned against wasteful public spending on the feckless poor. These principles were enshrined in 1834's New Poor Law, which standardized poor relief and introduced the workhouse system in an attempt to deter the lazy and restrict provision to those in real need. Only during the wars (and in their aftermath) had public feeding *for all* been applied. In line with the government's other public-feeding measures of the Coronavirus pandemic, then, extending free school meals over the holidays was an emergency measure which whiffed of a wartime 'we're all in this together' ethic.

But then came the farce. On 27 October 2020, to public outcry as the 'second wave' of the pandemic roared, Boris Johnson rebuffed Rashford's call for the government to again extend food vouchers over the holiday period. In refusing a relatively inexpensive and resoundingly popular call, the government may have scored 'an own goal' in terms of public opinion, as *The Guardian* put it,[13] but by reigning in one plank of the greatest effort in emergency public feeding since wartime, the government was retreating to an ideological comfort zone it has occupied for much of the modern period, with the great exception of the world wars.

The political debate around feeding during the Coronavirus crisis resembled closely a century-old left-right division around the state's proper role around feeding. However, and despite the similarities, it would be ahistorical and greatly amiss not to reiterate the fact that the emergency public-feeding schemes of twentieth-century Britain operated in vastly different contexts and with varying degrees of success. While wartime public feeding is of relevance to early twenty-first-century 'food poverty', the significant difference in market conditions, types of emergency, political climate, technology and demographics must be strongly emphasized.

The history of public feeding in both wars does, nonetheless, provide some common conclusions which may be of use to future architects of food policy in Britain. Firstly, public feeding functioned best when top-down state support and finance were combined with bottom-up expertise, voluntary action and, occasionally, private commercial input. Secondly, as this book has demonstrated, the noble desire for nutritional improvement had to be tempered by the consideration of popular consumption habits and regional cultures of consumption. Next, in order to overcome the persistent image problem of beige uniformity, decoration, design and celebrity endorsement proved desirable, particularly when coupled with an inventive media campaign. Lastly, and as the Ministry of Food urged in both conflicts, public feeding met its definition by not remaining confined to the very poor and instead aspiring to cross-class, and indeed cross-cultural, appeal.

As this book has argued, the public-feeding schemes of wartime Britain were more successful and popular than previously acknowledged. The measurement of such success and popularity is, of course, relative, with the heightened value of wartime morale transcending reductive measures of profit and loss, nonetheless many proved viable going concerns. National Kitchens fared better in London, where there was a greater concentration of clerical workers and less of the entrenched prejudice to restaurant dining witnessed in northern England. In this regard, their popularity amongst the middle class mirrored that of preceding institutions like Lyons tea houses. Yet such regional and class variations should not be over-amplified as much rested on the decisive factor: local political will. Colourful and eccentric actors also did much to ensure local success. Naturally, however, much also rested on central government. In the First World War, the lofty goals of civilizational improvement held by social and food reformers failed to resonate with the commercial food lobby, whose yearning for a return to normality ultimately coalesced with the cost-cutting post-war objectives of Whitehall. Meanwhile, the introduction of a much more complete rationing system in the summer of 1918, coupled with the major public health crisis of 'Spanish' influenza, dented the appeal of social eating.

The introduction of early and comprehensive rationing in the Second World War ensured that public-feeding schemes functioned as a complement to the ration more than they had in the previous conflict. As Ina Zweiniger

Bargielowska points out, British Restaurants helped to overcome some of the shortcomings in the ration affecting certain demographic and occupational groups, for instance, men working in heavy industry. The conflict also witnessed a marked expansion in the number of social eating schemes, including feeding measures geared towards absolute emergency that provided respite to bombed-out communities. While communal dining seems not to have resonated very effectively with middle-class housewives, overall most were not hostile and the majority of Mass Observation responses were broadly favourable towards social eating, which again proved most popular with middle-class clerical workers but also gained an important working-class constituency.[14] In the Second World War, the recruitment of private retail expertise, coupled with the expanded resources and interventionist role of the state – not least its improved capacity for propaganda – did much to secure the survival of the British Restaurant further into peacetime than its First World War predecessor, the National Kitchen.

Both conflicts would prove that conventional left/right political divisions over the desirability of public feeding were dissolved by patriotic priorities, enabling social eating to become a British national institution, albeit one short-lived and rapidly forgotten as the post-war welfare state became more encompassing. In detailing the complex operation and debate around Britain's wartime public-feeding schemes, this book has sought to overcome some of the jingoism, hagiography and nostalgia which are popularly attached to the world wars by concentrating on the dynamics of food rather than the well-worn tales of Great Men. In doing so, it seeks to supplement four decades of historiography on the home fronts in both wars that has been predominantly focused on everyday experience, social change and gender. It has also sought to restore the importance of public feeding by challenging an established historiographical narrative around wartime food supply in which rationing dominates, to the detriment of other methods of ensuring the population was fed. In doing so, the book has also provided historical context to twenty-first-century debates around public feeding. The last word, though, ought to belong to a woman, for the story of emergency public feeding in twentieth-century Britain is essentially a story of female initiative. Flora Solomon, whose involvement with communal dining started with Marks and Spencer's canteens, was to be made a Member of the Order of the British Empire (MBE) for her wartime efforts in the field. She was later to reflect how, many years later, when the Beatles were similarly honoured, some previous recipients of the accolade returned their decorations in resentment against the association of the venerable award with pop musicians. 'Personally', she wrote, 'I was delighted; after all, I had received mine for feeding the masses, so why shouldn't they be recognised for entertaining the masses?'[15] As this history has demonstrated, feeding and entertaining the masses were in fact often the same thing and the success of emergency public feeding, in the final analysis, rested on the essential ingredient that makes any meal enjoyable and yet remains hard for the historian to capture: entertainment and fun.

Notes

Introduction

1 William Beveridge, *British Food Control* (London: Stationery Office, 1928); R.J. Hammond, *Food: The Growth of Policy* (London: Stationery Office, 1951); R.J. Hammond, *Food Volume II: Studies in Administration and Control* (London: Stationery Office, 1956). These works are summarized in Ina Zweiniger-Bargielowska's *Austerity in Britain: Rationing, Controls and Consumption, 1939-1955* (Oxford: Oxford University Press, 2000).

2 Report of the All-Party Parliamentary Inquiry into Hunger in the United Kingdom, *Feeding Britain: Strategy for Zero Hunger in England, Wales, Scotland and Northern Ireland* (London: Stationery Office, 2014). See also Hannah Lumbie-Mumford, *Hungry Britain: The Rise of Food Charity* (London: Policy Press, 2017); R. Loopstra, A. Reeves, D. Taylor-Robinson, B. Barr, M. McKee, D. Stuckler 'Austerity, sanctions, and the rise of food banks in the UK', BMJ, 2015; 350:h1775.

3 The most heated, and publicly accessible, public debate around the food bank has taken place in *The Guardian* newspaper. For respective examples of debate around these questions which touches on history (while still omitting wartime schemes) see, for example, Shaista Aziz, 'In Modern Britain Hunger has become normal', 21 May 2019; Gordon Brown, 'I didn't think I'd see child poverty again in my lifetime', 14 December 2018; Mary O'Hara, 'Food poverty is the new normal in the UK: We adopted it from the States', 29 August 2017; 'Patrick Butler, 'Food Bank Jobcentres: will DWP make charity handouts part of welfare state?', 28 October 2015.

4 See Philip Carstairs, 'Soup and reform: Improving the poor and reforming immigrants through soup kitchens, 1870-1910', *Journal of Historical Archaeology*, 21, 4 (2017), 901–36; for the intersection of voluntarism, food poverty and the poor law see David Englander, *Poverty and Poor Law Reform in Nineteenth Century Britain, 1834-1914, from Chadwick to Booth* (London: Routledge, 1998).

5 Harmke Kamminga and Andrew Cunningham (eds), *The Science and Culture of Nutrition, 1840-1940* (Amsterdam: Rodopi, 1995).

6 See Report of the Interdepartmental Committee on Physical Deterioration (London: Stationery Office, 1904), accessible at https://archive.org/details/b21358916.

7 Lord Bishop of Ripon, Hansard, House of Lords Debate, 20 July 1905, vol. 149, col. 1308.

8   There are several survey works on the food situation in Second World War Britain. The definitive work on British controls on consumption in the period is Ina Zweiniger-Bargielowska's *Austerity in Britain*. Lizzie Collingham's *The Taste of War: World War Two and the battle for food* (London: Allen Lane, 2011) is useful for international comparison. See also Natacha Chevalier, *Food in Wartime Britain: Testimonies from the Kitchen Front, 1939-1945* (London: Routledge, 2020).
9   For a short overview of food in Britain in both wars see Mancur Olson's classic *The Economics of Wartime Shortage: A History of British Food Supplies in the Napoleonic Wars and in World Wars I and II* (Durham, NC: Duke University Press, 1963). Both David Edgerton's *Britain's War Machine: Weapons, Resources and Experts in the Second World War* (Oxford: Oxford University Press, 2011) and Stephen Broadberry and Peter Howlett's 'The United Kingdom during World War I: Business as usual?' in Broadberry and Mark Harrison's *The Economics of World War I* (Cambridge: Cambridge University Press, 2005), 206–34, contextualize food rationing against the management of imports, shipping space and domestic agricultural output. An earlier contextualization of food controls within the broader economic management of the war is to be found in Alan S. Milward, *War, Economy and Society 1939-1945* (Berkley: University of California Press, 1979), 281–8, while Mark Harrison's edited collection *The Economics of World War II: Six Great Powers in International Comparison* (Cambridge: Cambridge University Press, 1998) is a comparative study which covers British management of food in the conflict.
10 See Stan Cox, *Any Way you Slice It: The Past, Present and Future of Rationing* (New York: New Press, 2013).
11 See Frank Trentmann and Fleming Just, *Food and Conflict in the Age of the Two World Wars* (London: Palgrave MacMillan, 2006); James Vernon, *Hunger: A Modern History* (Cambridge, MA: Harvard University Press, 2007); Peter Scholliers, 'Restaurants Économiques a Bruxelles Pendant La Grande Guerre', in Caroline Poulaine ed., *Manger et Boire entre 1914 et 1918* (Dijon, 2014), 111–18; Hans-Jurgen Teuteberg, 'Food provisioning on the German home front 1914-1918', in Ina Zweiniger-Bargielowska, Rachel Duffett and Alain Drouard eds., *Food and War in Twentieth Century Europe* (London: Ashgate, 2011), 59–72; Alice Weinreb, *Modern Hungers: Food and Power in Twentieth-Century Germany* (Oxford: Oxford University Press, 2017), 79–80; Bertram Gordon, 'Fascism, the neo-right and gastronomy: A case in the theory of the social engineering of taste', in Tom Jaine ed., *Taste: Proceedings of the Oxford Symposium on Food and Cookery* (London, 1988), 82–97; Anna Sorokina, 'How the Soviet Union brought culinary equality to the table', *Russia Beyond*, 10 January 2018 (https://www.rbth.com/russian-kitchen/327231-soviet-union-brought-culinary-equality. See also Jeromír Balcar, 'Dem tschechischen Arbeiter das Fressen geben': Factory canteens in the protectorate of Bohemia and Moravia', in Tatjana Tönsmeyer, Peter Haslinger, and

Agnes Laba eds., *Coping with Hunger and Shortage under German Occupation in World War II* (Cham, Switzerland: Palgrave Macmillan, 2018).

12 John Burnett, *England Eats Out, 1830 – Present* (London: Pearson, 2004), 151–61.
13 Chevalier, *Food in Wartime Britain*, 12–16.
14 See Derek Oddy, *From Plan Fare to Fusion Food: British Diet from the 1890s to the 1990s* (Woodbridge: Boydell Press, 2003).
15 Winston Churchill to Frederick Woolton, cited in William Sitwell, *Eggs or Anarchy* (London: Simon and Schuster, 2016), 196.
16 Flora Solomon and Barnet Litvinoff, *Baku to Baker Street: The Memoirs of Flora Solomon* (London: Collins, 1984), 179.
17 Burnett, *England Eats Out*, preface.

Chapter 1

1 See Henry Gariepy, *Christianity in Action: The International History of the Salvation Army* (Grand Rapids, MI: Eerdmans, 2009).
2 See Peter Grant, *Philanthropy and Voluntary Action in the First World War: Mobilizing Charity* (London: Routledge, 2014).
3 Asquith, cited in James Nicholls, *The Politics of Alcohol: A History of the Drink Question in England* (Manchester: Manchester University Press, 2009).
4 See Robert Duncan, 'Panic over the pub: Drink and the First World War' (PhD thesis, University of St Andrews, 2008), 10–42.
5 *Daily Express*, 29 February 1915.
6 Nicholls, *The Politics of Alcohol*, 55–7.
7 See David Gutzke, *Pubs and Progressives: Reinventing the Public House in England, 1896-1960* (New York: Cornell University Press, 2005); John Greenaway, *Drink and British Politics since 1830: A Study in Policy Making* (London: Palgrave Macmillan, 2003); Brian Harrison, *Drink and the Victorians: The Temperance Question in England, 1815-1872* (Newcastle Under Lyme: Keele University Press, 1994).
8 See Leonore Davidoff et al., *The Family Story: Blood, Contract, and Intimacy 1830-1960* (London: Longman, 1999); Anne Digby, 'Victorian values and women in public and private', *Proceedings of the British Academy*, 78 (1990): 195–215.
9 See Angela John, *Unequal Opportunities: Women's Employment in England 1800-1918* (Oxford: Blackwell, 1996); Elizabeth Roberts, *Women's Work: 1840-1940* (Cambridge: Cambridge University Press, 1988).
10 See Eve Colpus, *Female Philanthropy in the Interwar World* (London: Bloomsbury, 2018), 77. Digby, 'Victorian', 212.
11 See Sabine Hering and Berteke Waaldijk (eds.), *History of Social Work in Europe, 1900–1960, Female Pioneers and Their Influence on the Development of International Social Organizations* (New York: Springer, 2012).

12 Colpus, *Female Philanthropy*, 13.
13 Digby, 'Victorian', 201.
14 Kathleen McCarthy (ed.), *The Lady Bountiful Revisited: Women, Philanthropy and Power* (New Brunswick: Rutgers University Press, 1990); Frank Prochashka, *Women and Philanthropy in Nineteenth Century England* (Oxford: Clarendon, 1980).
15 For criticism of this tendency in the work of Arthur Marwick see Grant, *Philanthropy and Voluntary Action*, 3; Colpus, *Female Philanthropy*, 15.
16 *The Times*, 21 March 1908.
17 Colpus, *Female Philanthropy*, 41.
18 See Sarah Jackson and Rosemary Taylor, *Voices from History: East London Suffragettes* (London: the History Press, 2014); figure of 400 customers appears in Shirley Harrison, *Sylvia Pankhurst: The Rebellious Suffragette* (London: Golden Guides, 2012), 248.
19 Barbara Winslow, *Sylvia Pankhurst: Sexual Politics and Political Activism* (London: Routledge, 1996), xix.
20 Michael Lavalette, 'Sylvia Pankhurst: Suffragette, socialist, anti-imperialist … and social worker?', *Critical and Radical Social Work*, 5, 3 (2017), 369–82.
21 Chris Jones and Michael Lavalette, 'The two souls of social work: Exploring the roots of popular social work', *Critical and Radical Social Work* 1, 2 (2013), 147–65.
22 Sylvia Pankhurst, *The Home Front: A Mirror to Life in England during the First World War* (London: Cresset, [1932], 1987), 22. Cited in Lavalette, 'Sylvia Pankhurst', 161.
23 Digby, 'Victorian', 212.
24 See Peter Scholliers and Patricia van Den Eeckhout, 'Feeding growing cities in the nineteenth and twentieth centuries: Problems, innovations, and reputations', in Anne Murcott, Warren Belasco and Peter Jackson eds., *The Handbook of Food Research*, (London: Bloomsbury Academic, 2013), 74; Chevalier, *Food in Wartime Britain*, 10.
25 Yuriko Akiyama, *Feeding the Nation: Nutrition and Health in Britain Before World War One* (London: Tauris, 2008).
26 Oddy, *From Plan Fare to Fusion Food*, 67.
27 Chevalier, *Food in Wartime Britain*, 13.
28 Nadja Durbach, *Many Mouths: The Politics of Food in Britain from the Workhouse to the Welfare State* (Cambridge: Cambridge University Press, 2020), 7–8.
29 Durbach, *Many Mouths*, 57–95.
30 See John Burnett, 'The rise and decline of school meals in Britain, 1860-1990', in Burnett and Derek Oddy eds., *The Origin and Development of Food Policies in Europe* (Leicester: Leicester University Press, 1994), 60–4.
31 Martin Pugh, 'Working class experience and state social welfare, 1908–1914: Old age pensions reconsidered', *Historical Journal*, 45 (2002), 775–96; Marc Brodie, 'You could not get any person to be trusted except the state': poorer workers' loss

of faith in voluntarism in late 19th century Britain', *Journal of Social History*, 7, 1 (2014), 1071–95.

32 Although Panikos Panayi has challenged the idea that such disturbances were 'food riots', contemporary accounts, like that of Pat O'Mara, emphasize that the pricing of food was a factor in the agitation and, as Nicoletta Gullace has argued, there were flashes of moral economy at work. See Gullace, 'Kith and kin: Interpersonal relationships and cultural practices', *Journal of Social History*, 39, 2 (2005), 345–67.

Chapter 2

1 Burnett, *England Eats Out: 1830 to Present*, preface.
2 Thomas Jones, *The Unbroken Front, Ministry of Food 1916-1944* (London: Everybody's, 1944), 40.
3 See J.M. Winter, *The Great War and the British People* (London: MacMillan, 1985), 213–45; Matthew Hilton, *Consumerism in Twentieth-Century Britain* (Cambridge: Cambridge University Press, 2003).
4 Karen Hunt's 'The politics of food and women's neighborhood activism in First World War Britain', *International Labor and Working-Class History*, 77/01 (2010), 8–26, discusses communal kitchens through the prism of gender-based activism. National Kitchens are mentioned fleetingly in P.B. Johnson's *Land Fit for Heroes: The Planning of British Reconstruction* (Chicago: University of Chicago Press, 1968).
5 L. Margaret Barnett, *British Food Policy during the First World War* (London: Routledge, 1985), 151.
6 Derek Oddy, *From Plain Fare to Fusion Food: British Diet from the 1890s to the 1990s* (Woodbridge: Boydell Press, 2003), 76.
7 Departmental Committee meeting on village canteens, 11 April 1918. National Archives (hereafter TNA), Ministry of Agriculture and Food (hereafter MAF), 60/329.
8 Barnett, *British Food Policy*, 151.
9 Ian Gazeley and Andrew Newell, 'The First World War and working-class food consumption in Britain', *European Review of Economic History* 17, 1 (2013), 72.
10 Adrian Gregory, *The Last Great War: British Society and the First World War* (Cambridge: Cambridge University Press, 2008), 192–8.
11 Minutes of the Committee on Cookery, 22 March 1917, Glasgow and West of Scotland College of Domestic Science records, Glasgow Caledonian University Archives.
12 For London's invalid kitchens see Wilfrid Blunt, *Lady Muriel: Muriel Paget, Her Husband, and Her Philanthropic Work in Central and Eastern Europe* (London: Methuen, 1962), 40–6. Comparable 'Lady Bountiful' initiatives in London are

outlined in Ellen Ross (ed.), *Slum Travelers: Ladies and London Poverty, 1860-1920* (Berkley: University of California Press, 2007).
13   *The Daily Telegraph*, 26 June 1916.
14   See William Chance, *Industrial Unrest: Reports of the Commissioners (July 1917)* (London: Stationery Office, 1917), 12–14 and 32–3.
15   Flora Solomon and Barnet Litvinoff, *Baku to Baker Street: The Memoirs of Flora Solomon* (London: Collins, 1984), 73.
16   For the wartime careers of Lord and Lady Rhondda see Angela John, *Turning the Tide: The Life of Lady Rhondda* (Cardigan: Partheon, 2014).
17   For an account of Kearley's early political career see Mary Hilson, *Political Change and the Rise of Labour in Comparative Perspective: Britain and Sweden 1980-1920* (Lund: Nordic Academic Press, 2006), 101–2. See also Kearley's autobiography *The Travelled Road: Some Memories of a Busy Life* (London: Rochester, 1935).
18   Alan Simmonds, *Britain and World War One* (London: Routledge, 2013), 205.
19   Arthur Marwick, *The Deluge: British Society and the First World War* (London: Palgrave MacMillan, 1991), 233.
20   Marwick, *The Deluge*, 240.
21   J.S. Middleton to Lord Rhondda, 15 June 1917. People's History Museum Archives (hereafter PHMA), Workers National Committee (hereafter WNC) 14/4/1/2:1. Emphasis is author's.
22   Dilwyn Porter, 'Jones, (William) Kennedy (1865–1921)', *Oxford Dictionary of National Biography* (Oxford, 2004).
23   J.S. Middleton to E. Faulkner, 22 April 1918. PHMA, WNC 14/4/1/11.
24   *Yorkshire Post*, 23 June 1917.
25   J.S. Middleton to C.F. Spencer, 2 May 1918. PHMA, WNC 14/4/2/7.
26   WNC report on communal kitchens, undated. PHMA, WNC 14/4/3/1:ii.
27   WNC report on communal kitchens, undated. PHMA, WNC 14/4/3/1:iii.
28   Arthur Peters, 'communal kitchens', Transport and General Workers' Union files (hereafter TGWU), 126/TG/RES/X/1015/3, accessed via University of Warwick Digital Collections, http://contentdm.warwick.ac.uk/cdm/ref/collection/tav/id/3532, accessed 10 November 2014.
29   Brigid Allen, 'Miles, Eustace Hamilton (1868–1948)', *Oxford Dictionary of National Biography* (Oxford, 2004).
30   Elsa Richardson, 'Sun-fired foods and nutritional science: Eustace Miles and vegetarian reform', *Food Anxieties in Twentieth-Century Britain and Ireland*, University of Ulster, Belfast, 7 April 2017.
31   Richardson, 'Sun-fired foods'.
32   R. Hippisley Cox, H.J. Bradley and Eustace Miles Cox, *Public Kitchens Handbook* (London: Stationery Office, 1918), 3.
33   J.S. Middleton to C.F. Spencer, 2 May 1918. PHMA, WNC 14/4/2/7.
34   *Manchester Guardian*, 22 June 1917.

35 J.S. Middleton to J.P. Riding, 19 January 1916. PHMA, WNC 9/2/8 i.
36 J.S. Middleton to E. Faulkner, 22 April 1918. PHMA, WNC 14/4/1/11.
37 Cox et al., *Public Kitchens*.
38 William Beveridge, *British Food Control* (Oxford: Oxford University Press, 1928), 46.
39 Spencer to Rhondda, 16 January 1918. TNA, MAF 60/310.
40 Spencer to Rhondda, 16 January 1918. TNA, MAF 60/310.
41 *Manchester Guardian*, 27 January 1918.
42 Beveridge, *British Food Control*, 164.
43 For radicalism in Britain at the time see Lucy Bland and Richard Carr (eds.), *Labour, British Radicalism, and the First World War* (Manchester: Manchester University Press, 2018).
44 Spencer to Rhondda, 16 January 1918. TNA, MAF 60/310.
45 *Manchester Guardian*, 9 February 1919.
46 *Yorkshire Post*, 26 April 1914.
47 *Liverpool Daily Post and Mercury*, 22 June 1917.
48 *Yorkshire Post*, 26 April 1914.
49 *Electrical Times*, 25 April 1918.
50 Spencer memo on the future of National Kitchens, October 1918. TNA, MAF 60/310.
51 Ministry of Food, *National Kitchens Handbook* (London: Stationery Office, 1918), 31.
52 Spencer to Rhondda, 16 January 1918. TNA, MAF 60/310.
53 J. S. Middleton to J. Moore, 31 July 1917. PHMA, WNC 14/4/1/5.
54 Ministry of Food, *National Kitchens Handbook*, 27.
55 *The Times*, 22 May 1917.
56 J.S. Middleton to Lord Rhondda, 15 June 1917. PHMA, WNC 14/4/1/2:1.
57 J. Downie to Middleton, 19 November 1917. PHMA, WNC 14/4/1/6:1.
58 War Emergency Workers' National Committee, 'Food Vigilance Committees', June 1917, TGWU 126/TG/RES/X/1015/3, accessed via University of Warwick Digital Collections, http://contentdm.warwick.ac.uk/cdm/ref/collection/tav/id/3537, accessed 16 January 2015.
59 Hunt, 'The Politics of Food', 16.
60 *Llanelli Star*, 6 April 1918.
61 *Liverpool Daily Post and Mercury*, 4 May 1917.
62 *Liverpool Daily Post and Mercury*, 18 August 1917; 9 October 1917.
63 John Stewart, John Smith and John Wheatley, 'Report on National Kitchens and restaurants in London and other towns', Glasgow Corporation Minutes, 27 September 1918.
64 See Pat Thane, '*Happy Families? History and Family Policy* (London: British Academy, 2010).

65 Harry Hendrick, *Child Welfare: England 1872-1989* (London: Routledge, 1994), 121–5; see also Kate Bradley, *Poverty, Philanthropy and the State: Charities and the Working Classes in London 1918-1979* (Manchester: Manchester University Press, 2009).
66 Kate Bradley, 'Juvenile delinquency and the evolution of the British juvenile courts, c.1900-1950', https://archives.history.ac.uk/history-in-focus/welfare/articles/bradleyk.html, accessed 9 September 2019. For more on this theme in this and the later context see Laura King, 'Hidden fathers? The significance of fatherhood in mid-twentieth-century Britain', *Contemporary British History* 26, 1 (2012), 25–46; Laura King, *Family Men: Fatherhood and Masculinity in Britain, c.1914-1960* (Oxford: Oxford University Press, 2015).
67 Spencer to Rhondda, 16 January 1918. TNA, MAF 60/310.
68 Spencer to Rhondda, 16 January 1918. TNA, MAF 60/310.
69 National Kitchens Order, 1918. TNA, MAF 60/50.
70 Ministry of Food, *National Kitchens Handbook*, 17.
71 Pankhurst, quoted in Lavalette, 'Sylvia Pankhurst', 373.
72 Cox et al., *Public Kitchens*, 14.
73 Ministry of Food, *National Kitchens Handbook*, 12.
74 *Hansard*, House of Commons debate, 18 June 1918, vol. 107, col. 181.
75 *Hansard*, House of Commons debate, 17 April 1918, vol. 105, col. 397.
76 Ministry of Food, *National Kitchens Handbook*, 30.
77 Spencer to Rhondda, 16 January 1918. TNA, MAF 60/310.
78 Cox et al., *Public Kitchens*, 3.
79 Cox et al., *Public Kitchens*, 13.
80 Ministry of Food, *National Kitchens Handbook*, 23.
81 Ministry of Food, *National Kitchens Handbook*, 17.
82 Spencer to Rhondda, 16 January 1918. TNA, MAF 60/310.
83 Spencer memo on the future of National Kitchens, October 1918. TNA, MAF 60/310.
84 Spencer to Rhondda, 16 January 1918. TNA, MAF 60/310.

Chapter 3

1 Local Authorities Food Control Order (no. 2), 25 February 1918. PHMA, WNC 14/4/4/1i.
2 Hunt, 'The Politics of Food', 10. See also June Hannam and Karen Hunt, *Socialist Women: Britain 1880s to 1920s* (London: Routledge, 2002), 134–65.
3 For example, Glasgow's FCC was expanded in September and October 1917 to welcome representatives from the Glasgow Union of Women Workers,

the Women's Labour League, and the Women's Suffrage Society. See Glasgow Corporation Minutes, Minutes of Committee on Food Control, 4 September 1917 and 26 October 1917.
4 Ministry of Food, National Kitchens Order, March 1918. PHMA, WNC 14/4/4/31.
5 Spencer to Rhondda, 16 January 1918. TNA, MAF 60/310.
6 *Manchester Guardian*, 9 May 1918.
7 *Manchester Guardian*, 17 January 1918.
8 *Liverpool Daily Post and Mercury*, 30 June 1917.
9 Ministry of Food, *National Kitchens Handbook*, 23.
10 *Manchester Guardian*, 10 September 1918.
11 Ministry of Food, *National Kitchens Handbook*, 31.
12 Stewart, Smith and Wheatley, 'Report on National Kitchens and restaurants in London and other towns'.
13 *Western Times*, 22 March 1918.
14 Julia Neville, 'The National Kitchens Movement in Devon', University of Hertfordshire Everyday Lives in War blog, https://everydaylivesinwar.herts.ac.uk, 4 February 1916.
15 Middleton to E.R. Simmons, 15 April 1918. PHMA, WNC 14/4/1/9.
16 J.S. Middleton to C.F. Spencer, 2 May 1918. PHMA, WNC 14/4/2/7.
17 Spencer to Rhondda, 16 January 1918. TNA, MAF 60/310.
18 Ministry of Food, National Kitchens Order, March 1918. PHMA, WNC 14/4/4/3ii.
19 For the school feeding campaign in this period see Carolyn Steedman, *Childhood, Culture, and Class in Britain: Margaret McMillan, 1860-1931* (London: Virago, 1990).
20 Workers' National Committee memorandum on Feeding School children (undated), PHMA, WNC 9/2/69.
21 Board of Education, National Kitchens and the Provision of Meals for School Children, 11 March 1918. PHMA, WNC 14/4/4/6i.
22 *Cambrian and Merionethshire Standard*, 30 August 1918.
23 Brian Harrison, 'Phillips, Marion (1881–1932)', *Oxford Dictionary of National Biography* (Oxford, 2004); see also *Marian Goronwy Roberts, Marion Phillips* MP (Wrexham, 2000).
24 Marion Phillips, Undated Memorandum on National Kitchens, PHMA, WNC 14/4/3/1i.
25 Marion Phillips, Undated Memorandum on National Kitchens, PHMA, WNC 14/4/3/1iii.
26 *Daily Mirror*, 10 April 1918. Florence Horsburgh papers, Churchill College Cambridge, HSBR 2/1.
27 *Tatler*, 10 April 1918.
28 *Evening News*, 8 July 1918. Horsburgh papers, HSBR 2/1.

29 *Yorkshire Observer*, 3 July 1918. Horsburgh papers, HSBR 2/1.
30 *Evening News*, 17 April 1918. Horsburgh papers, HSBR 2/1.
31 *The Bristol Times and Mirror*, 18 April 1918. Horsburgh papers, HSBR 2/1.
32 *West London Press and Chelsea News*, 13 September 1918. Horsburgh papers, HSBR 2/1.
33 *Evening Standard*, 8 August 1918. Horsburgh papers, HSBR 2/1.
34 *The Daily Graphic*, 10 August 1918. Horsburgh papers, HSBR 2/1.
35 *The Daily Mirror*, 10 April 1918 and 2 November 1918. Horsburgh papers, HSBR 2/1.
36 *Evening News*, 7 August 1918. Horsburgh papers, HSBR 2/1.
37 *Pall Mall Gazette*, 18 November 1918. Horsburgh papers, HSBR 2/1.
38 *West London Press and Chelsea News*, 10 May 1918. Horsburgh papers, HSBR 2/1.
39 Edward Wallington to Horsburgh, 30 November 1918. Horsburgh papers, HSBR 2/1.
40 *The Globe*, 4 December 1918. Horsburgh papers, HSBR 2/1.
41 Frank Trentmann, 'Coping with shortage: The problem of food security and global visions of its coordination c.1890s–1950', in Trentmann and Fleming Just (eds.) *Food and Conflict in the Age of the Two World Wars* (London: Palgrave Macmillan, 2006), 17–18.
42 Cox et al., *Public Kitchens*, 15.
43 Marianne Colloms and Dick Weindling, 'West Hampstead's tennis world champion (and food fanatic)', *West Hampstead Life*, 25 June 2014.
44 Richardson, 'Sun-fired foods'.
45 G.K. Chesterton, *Irish Impressions* (London: Collins, 1919), 5.
46 Colloms and Weindling, 'West Hampstead's tennis world champion'.
47 Cox et al., *Public Kitchens*, 15.
48 Ministry of Food, *National Kitchens Handbook*, 27.
49 Gazeley and Newell, 'The First World War and working-class food consumption in Britain', 73. For a comparison between British and German experiences of feeding see Avner Offer, *The First World War: An Agrarian Interpretation* (Oxford: Clarendon, 1989). For more on the broader socio-economic significance of margarine consumption see Alysa Levene, 'The meanings of margarine in England: Class, consumption and material culture from 1918 to 1953', *Contemporary British History* 28, 2 (2014), 145–65.
50 Cox et al., *Public Kitchens*, 18.
51 These concerns were summarized in the Report of the Interdepartmental Committee on Physical Deterioration (London, 1904), accessible in its original format at https://archive.org/details/b21358916.
52 Cox et al., *Public Kitchens*, 4.
53 Cox et al., *Public Kitchens*, 15.
54 Cox et al., *Public Kitchens*, 19.

55 Ministry of Food, *National Kitchens Handbook*, 14.
56 See John Burnett, *Liquid Pleasures: A Social History of Drinks in Modern Britain* (London: Routledge, 1999). See also Susan Zieger, *Inventing the Addict: Drugs, Race and Sexuality in Nineteenth-Century British and American Literature* (Amherst, MA: University of Massachusetts Press, 2008).
57 Maud Pember Reeves, *Round About a Pound a Week* (London: Bell and Sons, 1913)
58 Vernon, *Hunger: A Modern History*, 181.
59 C. S. Peel, *Life's Enchanted Cup: An Autobiography, 1872–1933* (London: Bodley Head, 1933), 59.
60 Conference of Teachers of Domestic Science pamphlet (undated), Glasgow and West of Scotland College of Domestic Science records, Glasgow Caledonian Archives.
61 Elizabeth Waldie, *Collection of Economical Recipes Suitable for War Cookery and Notes on Meaning of Economy as Regards Food and Fuel* (Glasgow: SN, 1917), 9–28.
62 *Glasgow Herald*, 16 October 1915. See also J. Struthers to J.A. McCallum, 9 June 1917, Minutes of the Committee on Cookery, 17 May 1917, Glasgow and West of Scotland College of Domestic Science records, Glasgow Caledonian University Archives.
63 Liverpool training school of cookery minutes, April-November 1917. John Moores University Archives, F.L. Calder collection.
64 Chalmers Wilson, memorandum on food economy campaign (Scotland), 6 April 1917, Glasgow and West of Scotland College of Domestic Science records, Glasgow Caledonian University Archives.
65 Liverpool training school of cookery minutes, May 1918. John Moores University Archives, F.L. Calder collection.
66 Liverpool training school of cookery minutes, May 1918. John Moores University Archives, F.L. Calder collection
67 Minutes of departmental committee meeting, 11 April 1918. TNA, MAF 60/310.
68 Minutes of the Committee on Cookery, 14 June 1918, Glasgow and West of Scotland College of Domestic Science records, Glasgow Caledonian University Archives.
69 *Glasgow Evening News*, 15 April 1919.
70 Liverpool training school of cookery minutes, November 1917. John Moores University Archives, F.L. Calder collection.
71 *Carmarthen Journal and South Wales Weekly Advertiser*, 12 October 1918; *Cambrian and Merionethshire Standard*, 18 April 1919; *Abergavenny Chronicle*, 5 April 1918.
72 Arnold Bennett, 'Thoughts on National Kitchens' (London, 1918), 1. University of Leeds Special Collections, Cookery A/BEN.
73 Alexandra Harris, *Romantic Moderns: English Writers, Artists and the Imagination from Virginia Woolf to John Piper* (London: Thames and Hudson, 2015), 3.

74 John Carey, *The Intellectuals and the Masses: Pride and Prejudice among the Literary Intelligentsia, 1880-1939* (London: Faber and Faber, 1992), 152.
75 Bennett, 'Thoughts on National Kitchens' 2.
76 Bennett, 'Thoughts on National Kitchens', 4.
77 Bennett, 'Thoughts on National Kitchens', 4.
78 Hansard, House of Commons debate, 27 June 1918, vol. 107, col. 1221.
79 *Abergavenny Chronicle*, 2 August 1918.
80 Glasgow Corporation Minutes, Minutes of Special Committee on National Kitchens Order 1918, 23 August 1918.
81 Glasgow Corporation Minutes, Minutes of Special Committee on National Kitchens Order 1918, 23 August 1918.
82 Burnett, *England Eats Out*, 187.
83 John Pearce, 'Be British – Play the game', undated correspondence, TNA, MAF 60/310.
84 Trentmann, 'Coping with shortage', in Trentmann and Just, *Food and Conflict*, 18–19.
85 Spencer memo on the future of National Kitchens, October 1918. TNA, MAF 60/310.
86 John Pearce, 'Be British – Play the game', undated correspondence, TNA, MAF 60/310.
87 Spencer memo on the future of National Kitchens, October 1918. TNA, MAF 60/310.
88 Spencer memo on the future of National Kitchens, October 1918. TNA, MAF 60/310.
89 *Surrey Advertiser and Surrey Comet*, 23 November 1918, cited in Michael Page, 'Fighting the Flu', www.surreyinthegreatwar.org.uk, 22 January 1918.
90 Janet Owen, 'Hornsey's National Kitchen', www.hornseyhistorical.org.uk, 9 March 2018.
91 Ministry of Food National Kitchens Branch, Kitchens Advisory Committee minutes, 17 December 1918. TNA, MAF 60/329.
92 Minutes of the Joint Meeting of the Finance and Educational Methods Committees, 14 June 1918, Glasgow and West of Scotland College of Domestic Science records, Glasgow Caledonian University Archives.
93 *Glasgow Evening News*, 25 April 1919.
94 Ministry of Food National Kitchens Branch, Kitchens Advisory Committee minutes, 26 February 1919. TNA, MAF 60/329.
95 Ministry of Food National Kitchens Branch, Kitchens Advisory Committee minutes, 3 March 1919. TNA, MAF 60/329.
96 Ministry of Food National Kitchens Branch, Kitchens Advisory Committee minutes, 12 March 1919. TNA, MAF 60/329.
97 Ministry of Food National Kitchens Branch, Kitchens Advisory Committee minutes, 29 March 1919. TNA, MAF 60/329.

98 Ministry of Food National Kitchens Branch, Kitchens Advisory Committee minutes, 19 February 1919. TNA, MAF 60/329.
99 *Manchester Guardian*, 4 January 1919.
100 Ministry of Food National Kitchens Branch, Kitchens Advisory Committee minutes, 19 February 1919. TNA, MAF 60/329; see also *Manchester Guardian*, 12 April 1919.
101 Ministry of Food National Kitchens Branch, Kitchens Advisory Committee minutes, 3 April 1919. NA, MAF 60/329.
102 *Lancashire Evening Post*, Tuesday, 18 March 1919 and email correspondence with Peter Schofield, 30 September 2017.
103 National Kitchens Division weekly news service, 25 January 1919, TNA, MAF 60/50.
104 National Kitchens Division weekly news service, 25 January 1919, TNA, MAF 60/50.
105 Ministry of Food, 'How to work a travelling kitchen', TNA, MAF 60/312.
106 Untitled memorandum, March 1919. TNA, MAF 60/50.
107 Hansard, House of Commons debate, 7 April 1919, vol. 114, col. 1667.
108 Hansard, House of Commons debate, 6 May 1919, vol. 115, col. 796.
109 Jones, *The Unbroken Front, Ministry of Food 1916-1944*, 40.
110 Ministry of Food National Kitchens Branch, Kitchens Advisory Committee minutes, 30 April 1919. TNA, MAF 60/329.
111 Ministry of Food National Kitchens Branch, Kitchens Advisory Committee minutes, 30 April 1919. TNA, MAF 60/329.
112 Kennedy Jones memo on National Kitchens, 30 September 1919. TNA, MAF 60/310.
113 Ministry of Food National Kitchens Branch, Kitchens Advisory Committee minutes, 26 May 1919. TNA, MAF 60/329.
114 Kennedy Jones memo on National Kitchens, 30 September 1919. TNA, MAF 60/310.
115 Kennedy Jones memo on National Kitchens, 30 September 1919. TNA, MAF 60/310.
116 See Brock Millman, *Managing Domestic Dissent in First World War Britain* (London: Routledge, 2000).
117 Departmental Committee meeting on village canteens, 11 April 1918. TNA, MAF 60/329.
118 C.S. Peel, *How We Lived Then, 1914-1918: A Sketch of Social and Domestic Life in England during the War* (London: John Lane, 1929), 85.
119 Spencer memo on the future of National Kitchens, October 1918. TNA, MAF 60/310.
120 Vernon, *Hunger: A Modern History*, 182.
121 Spencer memo on the future of National Kitchens, October 1918. TNA, MAF 60/310.

122 Burnett, *England Eats Out*, 172.
123 Burnett, *England Eats Out*, 187.
124 Spencer memo on the future of National Kitchens, October 1918. TNA, MAF 60/310.
125 R. H. Tawney, 'The abolition of economic controls, 1918-1921', *Economic History Review* 13, 1 (1943), 1–30.
126 Spencer to Rhondda, 16 January 1918. TNA, MAF 60/310.
127 Spencer to Rhondda, 16 January 1918. TNA, MAF 60/310.
128 Niall Johnson, *Britain and the 1918-19 Influenza Pandemic – A Dark Epilogue* (London: Routledge, 2006), 127–32.
129 Food had long been advanced as a remedy against influenza. See Tom Quinn, *Flu: A Social History of Influenza* (London: New Holland, 2008), 47.
130 See Marian Moser Jones, 'The American Red Cross and local responses to the 1918 influenza: A four-city case study', *Public Health Reports* 125, 3 (2010), 92–104.
131 Tawney, 'The abolition of economic controls', 29.

Chapter 4

1 Burnett, *England Eats Out*, 182.
2 Oddy, *From Plain Fare to Fusion Food*, 115–17; Chevalier, *Food in Wartime Britain*, 13.
3 Chevalier, *Food in Wartime Britain*, 12–15.
4 Cited in Durbach, *Many Mouths*, 153.
5 Hansard, Heward Ramsbotham, Commons debate on secondary education, 16 November 1932, vol. 270, col. 1267.
6 John Boyd Orr, *As I Recall* (London: MacGibbon and Kee, 1966), 115.
7 See Durbach, *Many Mouths*, 146–149.
8 Hansard, Commons debate on milk and meals in schools, 28 January 1937, vol. 319, col. 1060.
9 Kevin Manton, 'Sir William Beveridge, the British government, and plans for food control in time of war c. 1916-1941', *Contemporary British History* 23, 3 (2009), 363.
10 William Beveridge, *British Food Control* (London: Stationery Office, 1928), 337–8.
11 Beveridge, 'Wider aspects of food control', cited in Zweiniger-Bargielowska, *Austerity in Britain*, 16.
12 Eleanor Rathbone, in Barbara Drake, *Nutrition: A Policy of National Health* (London: Fabian Society, 1936), 2–3.

13 See Ina Zweiniger-Bargielowska, *Managing the Body: Beauty, Health and Fitness in Britain, 1880-1939* (Oxford: Oxford University Press, 2010).
14 Adel Den Hartog, 'Feeding schoolchildren in the Netherlands: Conflict between state and family responsibilities', in John Burnett and Derek Oddy eds., *The Origins and Development of Food Policies in Europe* (Leicester: Leicester University Press, 1996), 70–89.
15 Peter Atkins, 'The Milk in Schools Scheme, 1934–45: 'Nationalization and resistance', *History of Education* 34, 1 (2005), 1–21.
16 Boyd Orr, *As I Recall*, 115.
17 Boyd Orr, *As I Recall*, 114–16.
18 *Daily Mail*, 22 August 1931.
19 Hansard, Douglas Hacking, House of Commons debate on Marchers, 15 February 1934, vol. 285, col. 2070.
20 Colpus, *Female Philanthropy*, 48.
21 See Susan Pederson, *Eleanor Rathbone and the Politics of Conscience* (New Haven: Yale, 2004).
22 Colpus, *Female Philanthropy*, 44.
23 Drake, *Nutrition: A Policy of National Health*.
24 Solomon and Litvinoff, *Baku*, 161.
25 For Woolton's use of statistical experts in his management of wartime food policy, which drew on his previous retail experience, see Brian Tarran, 'Lord Woolton: The man who used statistics (and more) to feed a nation at war', *Significance* 14, 3 (2017), 24–9; Sitwell, *Eggs or Anarchy*, 21.
26 See Carol Helstosky, 'Fascist food politics: Mussolini's policy of alimentary sovereignty', *Journal of Modern Italian Studies* 9, 1 (2004), 1–26.
27 Weinreib, *Modern Hungers*, 53–5. See also Gustavo Corni and Horst Gies, *Brot, Butter, Kanonen: Die Ernährungswirtschaft in Deutschland under der Diktatur Hitlers* (Berlin: Akademie Verlag, 1997); Franz-Josef Brüggemeier, Mark Cioc, and Thomas Zeller, eds., *How Green Were the Nazis? Nature, Environment, and Nation in the Third Reich* (Athens: Ohio University Press, 2005); Jörg Melzer, *Vollwerternährung: Diätetik, Naturheilkunde, Nationalsozialismus, sozialer Anspruch* (Stuttgart: Franz Steiner Verlag, 2003); Robert Proctor, *The Nazi War on Cancer* (Princeton: Princeton University Press, 1999).
28 Gordon, 'Fascism, the neo-Right and gastronomy', 82–97.
29 Anya von Bremzen, *Mastering the Art of Soviet Cooking* (London: Transworld, 2014), 39.
30 von Bremzen, *Mastering the Art of Soviet Cooking*, 61–162.
31 Anna Sorokina, 'What was it like eating out during the Soviet Union?', *Russian Kitchen*, 11 December 2018, https://www.rbth.com/russian-kitchen/329657-public-catering-soviet-canteens, accessed 19 July 2021.

32 Jared Spears, 'Spain through Orwell's Eyes', *Jacobin*, 5 January 2017, https://www.jacobinmag.com/2017/05/george-orwell-spain-barcelona-may-days, accessed 9 April 2019.
33 Anthony Beevor, *The Battle for Spain: The Spanish Civil War 1936-1939* (London: Weidenfield and Nicolson, 2007), 58; see also Chris Ealham, 'The myth of the maddened crowd: Class, culture and space in the revolutionary urbanist project in Barcelona, 1936-1937', in Chris Ealham and Michael Richards eds., *The Splintering of Spain: Cultural History and the Spanish Civil War, 1936–1939* (Cambridge: Cambridge University Press, 2005), 111–32; Danny Evans, *Revolution and the State: Anarchism in the Spanish Civil War, 1936–1939* (Chico, CA: AK Press, 2018).
34 Gabriel Pretus, 'Humanitarian relief in the Spanish Civil War: The independent and non-partisan agencies', unpublished MPhil. Thesis, Royal Holloway University of London (2013).
35 Adam Chandler, 'How the Great Depression still shapes the way Americans eat', *The Atlantic*, 22 December 2016.
36 Anne Ewbank, 'During the Great Depression "Penny Restaurants" fed the unemployed', *Atlas Obscura*, 15 June 2018.
37 Jane Ziegelman and Andrew Coe, *A Square Meal: A Culinary History of the Great Depression* (New York: Harper, 2016), 45.
38 Ziegelman and Coe, *A Square Meal*, 181–95.

Chapter 5

1 Solomon and Litvinoff, *Baku*, 179. Relevant material also gathered from Mark and Spencer archives (café material) and correspondence with archivists. My thanks to staff.
2 Solomon and Litvinoff, *Baku*, 150, 182.
3 Peter J. Atkins, 'Communal feeding in war time: British restaurants 1940–47', in Alain Drouard, Rachel Duffett and Ina Zweiniger-Bargielowska eds., *Food and War in Twentieth Century Europe* (Farnham: Ashgate, 2011), 141. Official statistics indicate that there were 2,160 British Restaurants at their 1943 peak.
4 Whereas Hammond's *Food Volume II* highlights the success of British restaurants, James Vernon in *Hunger* claims that initial enthusiasm for the scheme quickly evaporated (190) and Zweiniger-Bargielowska, *Austerity in Britain*, points to the fact that the majority of food was still home-consumed (33).
5 Atkins' 'Communal feeding in war time' is a pioneering appraisal of British Restaurants, yet is London-centric and brief. Nadja Durbach's *Many Mouths* contains a short chapter on the 'Communal feeding experiment during World War II'.

6   Manton, 'Sir William Beveridge, the British Government, and plans for food control', 379.
7   R.J. Hammond, *Food Volume II*, 51.
8   Sitwell, *Eggs or Anarchy*, 39, 71.
9   For more biographical detail on Woolton, see his memoir – Frederick James Marquis, *The Memoirs of the Right Honourable the Earl of Woolton* (London: Cassell, 1959); this citation from Sitwell, *Eggs or Anarchy*, 81.
10 See Bryce Evans, 'The National Kitchen in Britain, 1917-1919', *Journal of War and Culture Studies* 10, 2 (2017), 115–29.
11 MAF 99/1797, 'Ministry of Food, the Communal Restaurant: An Experiment', October 1940. Cited in Atkins, 'Communal feeding', 140.
12 Hammond, *Food Volume II*, 351.
13 Hammond, *Food: The Growth of Policy*, 384.
14 These themes are explored in greater depth in Paul Addison's *The Road to 1945: British Politics and the Second World War* (second edition; London: Pimlico, 1994) and Nicholas Timmins, *The Five Giants: A Biography of the Welfare State* (London: Collins, 2017).
15 Solomon and Litvinoff, *Baku*, 180.
16 Solomon and Litvinoff, *Baku*, 181.
17 For an overview of the importance of the grocer see Derek J. Oddy, 'From corner shop to supermarket: The revolution in food retailing in Britain, 1932-1992' in Adel Den Hartog ed., *Food Technology, Science and Marketing: European Diet in the Twentieth Century* (East Linton: Tuckwell, 1995); for contemporary views on rationing and retail see Dexter Keezer, 'Observations on rationing and price control in Great Britain', *American Economic Review* 33, 2 (1943), 264–82; Hermann Levy, *The Shops of Britain: A Study of Retail Distribution* (Oxford: Oxford University Press, 1948). See also Katherine Knight, *Rationing in the Second World War: Spuds, Spam and Eating for Victory* (London: History Press, 2007); see also Zweiniger-Bargielowska, *Austerity in Britain*.
18 Hammond, *Food Volume II*, 320.
19 Solomon and Litvinoff, *Baku*, 185.
20 'The Communal Restaurant: An Experiment', October 1940, TNA, MAF, 99/1797; Atkins, 'Communal feeding', 140.
21 Atkins, 'Communal feeding', 141.
22 Hansard, House of Commons Debate, 13 November 1940, vol. 365, col. 1706.
23 Hammond, *Food Volume II*, 355.
24 Hammond, *Food Volume II*, 327.
25 Hammond, *Food Volume II*, 387.
26 Memo on Establishment of British Restaurants, September 1943. TNA, MAF 99/759,

27 Ministry of Food, 'Memorandum on British Restaurants', 1941. TNA, MAF 99/1589,
28 See G.E. Wood and F. Capie, 'The anatomy of wartime inflation: Britain 1939-45', in Geofrey T. Mills and Hugh Rockoff eds., *The Sinews of War: Essays on the Economic History of World War II* (Ames: Iowa State University Press, 1993), 21–42.
29 Boyd Orr, *As I Recall*, 117.
30 Sitwell, *Eggs or Anarchy*, 305–16.
31 John Boyd Orr, *'Nutrition in War' tract 251*, 5 (London: Fabian Society, 1940).
32 Boyd Orr, *As I Recall*, 120.
33 *The Times*, 12 October 1941.
34 Boyd Orr 'Nutrition in War', 4.
35 Drummond, 'Memorandum on meals for Collective Feeding', August 1940. TNA, MAF 156/282.
36 Meeting of Scientists at Ministry of Food, 17 June 1942. TNA, MAF 83/382.
37 Hammond, *Food: The Growth of Policy*, 94.
38 See Tom Jaine's introduction to Jack Drummond, *The Englishman's Food: A History of Five Centuries of English Diet* (London: Pimlico, 1939, new edition 1994).
39 Drummond, 'Memorandum on meals for Collective Feeding', August 1940. TNA, MAF 156/282.
40 Drummond, 'Memorandum on meals for Collective Feeding', August 1940. TNA, MAF 156/282. Original emphasis.
41 James Hinton, *Nine Wartime Lives: Mass Observation and the Making of the Modern Self* (Oxford: Oxford University Press, 2010), 43.
42 See Brian Glover, *Brewing for Victory: Brewers, Beers and Pubs in World War II* (London: Lutterworth, 1995).
43 Durbach, *Many Mouths*, 203.
44 See W.M. Menzies memo, 1 January 1941. TNA, MAF 99/1796.
45 Hammond, *Food Volume II*, 370.
46 Woolton to food officers, 24 July 1942, TNA, MAF 99/1797. For 'Potato Pete' and the Ministry's cinematic propaganda see Richard Farmer, *The Food Companions: Cinema and Consumption in Wartime Britain, 1939-45* (Manchester: Manchester University Press, 2011).
47 Scientific Advisers Division, Review of canteen meals memo, 6 August 1942. TNA, MAF 83/382.
48 Scientific Advisers Division, Review of canteen meals memo, 6 August 1942. TNA, MAF 83/382.
49 Hammond, *Food: The Growth of Policy*, 369.
50 British Restaurants trading results, 19 May 1944. TNA, MAF 99/1797.
51 W.J.M. Menzies to divisional food officers, 24 May 1941. TNA, MAF 99/1797.
52 Community Feeding Division memo, 8 March 1941. TNA, MAF 99/1796.

53 Wartime Meals Division newsletter, 23 August 1944. TNA, MAF 152/55.
54 British Restaurants Equipment memo, 28 January 1942. TNA, MAF 99/1797.
55 Memo accompanying model kitchen layout (undated). MAF 99/1797.
56 Deborah Sugg Ryan, 'The curious history of government-funded British Restaurants in World War 2', https://www.findmypast.co.uk/blog/history/british-restaurants, accessed 22 June 2020. My thanks to Deborah for her help in sourcing certain of the British Restaurant images reproduced here.
57 Hammond, *Food Volume II*, 404. The murals accompanying British Restaurants are overlooked in Brian Foss's otherwise comprehensive survey *War Paint: Art, War, State and Identity in Britain, 1939-1945* (New Haven: Yale University Press, 2007).
58 See Charlie Batchelor, *Tea and a Slice of Art: the Lyons Lithographs 1946-1955* (London: Artmonsky Arts, 2007).
59 Wartime Meals Division memo, October 1941. TNA, MAF 99/1796.
60 British Restaurants trading results, 19 May 1944. TNA, MAF 99/1797.
61 Ministry memo on training courses, May 1942. TNA, MAF 99/1796.
62 Ministry memo on training courses, 30 January 1942. MAF 99/1796.
63 *The Times*, 22 August 1942.
64 Ministry of Food, Public Relations Division, Information Branch, 'British Restaurants', 3 September 1943. TNA, MAF 74/49. See also TNA, MAF 83/382 Wartime Meals Arrangements memo, 9 September 1941.
65 Wartime Meals Arrangements memo, 9 September 1941. TNA, MAF 83/382.
66 Mass Observation reports cited in Dominic Spowart, 'Beyond simplicity: Day-to-day feeding in British restaurants and emergencycommunal feeding during the Second World War' (unpublished MA thesis, Liverpool Hope University, 2018), 30.
67 Zweiniger-Bargielowska, 'Austerity', 114.
68 See the following Mass Observation Archive (hereafter MOA) diarists' entries on British Restaurants (listed chronologically): MOA/D/5132, July 1941; MOA/D/5236, January 1942; MOA/D/5192, May, 1942; MOA/D/5410, September 1942; MOA/D/5446, January 1943; MOA/D/5176, April 1943.
69 See MOA/D/5318, March 1942. See also MOA/D/5427, December 1941 and MOA/D/5239, December 1940. MOA/D/5390, May 1942.
70 Cited in Chevalier, *Food in Wartime Britain*, 116.
71 H.L. French to Local Authorities, 15 November 1940. TNA, MAF 156/282.
72 Memo by Mr Harwood, 27 October 1941. TNA, MAF 99/1716.
73 Wartime Meals Division monthly report to Cabinet, August 1941. TNA, MAF 156/282.
74 Wartime Meals Division monthly report to Cabinet, August 1941. TNA, MAF 156/282.
75 Hammond, *Food Volume II*, 411.
76 Memo on Equipment in British Restaurants (undated). TNA, MAF 99/1797.

77 Hammond, *Food Volume II*, 273–80
78 Hammond, *Food Volume II*, 281–92.
79 Hammond, *Food Volume II*, 338.
80 Hansard, House of Commons Debate, 9 July 1941, vol. 373, col. 175.
81 Notes on the preparation and cooking of vegetables (undated). TNA, MAF 99/1797.
82 Atkins, 'Communal feeding', 150.
83 MAF 83/382, Memo by Brian O'Brien, 20 August 1942.
84 Hammond, *Food Volume II*, 390.
85 'The nutritive value of Communal Meals', 15 February 1943. TNA, MAF 256/197.
86 Wartime Meals Division monthly report to Cabinet, May 1941. MAF 156/282.
87 Untitled memo, 15 November 1941. TNA, MAF 99/1797.
88 *The Daily Mail*, 26 July 1940.
89 *The Times*, 22 February 1947.
90 Memorandum citing Raymond Daniell, *New York Times*, 15 March 1942. TNA, MAF 83/382.
91 Mark Roodhouse, *Black Market Britain, 1939-1955* (Oxford: Oxford University Press, 2013), 65.
92 *Daily Express*, 4 July 1940.
93 See Matthew Sweet, *The West End Front: The Wartime Secrets of London's Grand Hotels* (London: Faber and Faber, 2011).
94 Atkins, *Communal Feeding*, 142–6.
95 Menzies memo on Community Feeding (undated). TNA, MAF 99/1797.
96 Hammond, *Food*, 158.
97 Hammond, *Food Volume II*, 393.
98 Ellen Leopold, 'LCC Restaurants and the decline of municipal enterprise', in Andrew Saint ed., *Politics and the People of London: The London County Council, 1889-1965* (London: Hambledon, 1989), 200–13.
99 See Durbach, *Many Mouths*, 178–210. This quote is from page 179.
100 Norman Longmate, *How We Lived then: Everyday Life during the Second World War* (London: Pimlico, 2002), 207.
101 For a comprehensive account of this see Zweiniger-Bargielowska, *Austerity in Britain*.
102 P.G. Scott to L.V. Murphy, 1 August 1941. TNA, MAF 99/1618.
103 Divisional Food Officers Conference, 22–3 November 1940. This is cited in Durbach's *Many Mouths,* 185 and 196 which, oddly, comes to the opposite conclusion about the intentions of the central state.
104 Churchill memo to Woolton, 21 March 1941, cited in Atkins, *Communal Feeding*, 141.
105 Edward Blishen, *A Cackhanded War* (London: Thames and Hudson, 1972), 184.

106 Bell quoted in Farmer, *Food Companions*, 104.
107 Frances Partridge, quoted in Sitwell, *Eggs or Anarchy*, 198.
108 Catering American Newsletter no. 4, 20 August 1942. TNA, MAF 83/382.
109 *Daily Mail*, 28 November 1940.
110 Cited in Sonya O. Rose, *Which People's War? National Identity and Citizenship in Wartime Britain 1939–1945* (Oxford: Oxford University Press), 146.
111 Untitled memo, 23 November 1942. TNA, MAF 99/1759.
112 'Brakes on production: Deficiencies in transport and organisation needs of women in industry', *The Times*, 3 January 1942, cited in Spowart, 'Beyond Simplicity', 7.
113 See Ministry of Information, Home Intelligence Reports, summaries of daily reports, INF 1/264, 1940–1941, http://www.moidigital.ac.uk/reports/home-intelligence-reports/morale-summaries-of-daily-reports-part-b-inf-1264/, accessed 13 June 2018.
114 Panikos Panayi, 'Anti German riots in London during the First World War', *German History* 7, 2 (1989), 184–203. Cited in Richard van Emden and Steve Humphries, *All Quiet on the Home Front: An Oral History of the First World War* (Barnsley: Pen and Sword, 2017), 45.
115 Wendy Webster, *Mixing It: Diversity in World War Two Britain* (Oxford: Oxford University Press, 2018), 47; see also Wendy Ugolini, *Experiencing War as the Enemy 'Other': Italian Scottish Experience in World War II* (Manchester: Manchester University Press, 2011).
116 Atkins, *Communal Feeding*, 144.
117 Mabane memo, 2 October 1942. TNA, MAF 99/1759.
118 W.M. Menzies Circular, 19 March 1941. TNA, MAF 99/1796. Chevalier provides evidence of women who felt guilty for eating in places they thought were reserved for essential war workers. See *Food in Wartime Britain*, 116.
119 Hardman memo, 4 January 1944. TNA, MAF 99/1626.
120 Atkins, *Communal Feeding*, 144.
121 Woolton, quoted in Farmer, *Food Companions*, 104; *The Times*, 26 March 1941.
122 Durbach (187) cites the American edition of Solomon's memoir, *A Woman's Way*, in which this quote appears. It does not appear in *Baku to Baker Street* and content is likely to have been amended for a North American audience.
123 Woolton memo, 4 October 1942. TNA, MAF 99/1759.
124 Notes for divisional food officers, 21 November 1940. TNA, MAF 99/1797.
125 Priestley cited in Farmer, *Food Companions*, 104.
126 See Nina Rogers, 'Her Father's Daughter? The role of early influence on Margaret Thatcher' (unpublished PhD dissertation, Liverpool Hope University, 2020).
127 *Daily Mail*, 17 January 1941.
128 Hammond, *Food Volume II*, 382.

129 Hammond, *Food Volume II*, 395.
130 Untitled memo, 23 November 1942. TNA, MAF 99/1759.
131 Barbara Drake, *Community Feeding in Wartime* (London: Fabian Society, 1942).
132 Charles Smith, *Food in Wartime* (London: Fabian Society, 1940)
133 Boyd Orr 'Nutrition in War', 13.
134 *Daily Telegraph*, 1 May 1941.
135 *Sunday Pictorial* editorial cited in Rose, *Which People's War?*, 35.
136 Wheeldon memo, 24 September 1943. MAF 99/759.
137 Boyd Orr 'Nutrition in War', 5.
138 Drummond, *The Englishman's Food*, introduction.
139 Frederick Le Gros Clark, *The Communal Restaurant: A Study of the Place of Civic Restaurants in the Life of the Community* (London: Council of Social Service, 1943), 24.
140 Solomon and Litvinoff, *Baku*, 183.
141 Wartime Meals Division monthly report to Cabinet, August 1941. TNA, MAF 156/282.
142 'Summary of recommendations of the Committee on Catering Establishments', 20 September 1941. TNA, MAF 83/382.
143 Hammond, *Food Volume II*, 399.

Chapter 6

1 Hammond, *Food: The Growth of Policy*, 157.
2 D. Heron to Ministry of Food, 6 June 1941. TNA, MAF 156/282.
3 Wartime Meals Division monthly report to Cabinet, April 1941. As usual, air raid feeding facilities were better developed in London than in provincial towns and cities. TNA, MAF 156/282.
4 Wartime Meals Division monthly report to Cabinet, September 1941. TNA, MAF 156/282.
5 Memorandum on Communal Feeding, November 1941. TNA, MAF 83/382.
6 Wartime Meals Division monthly report to Cabinet, September 1941. TNA, MAF 156/282.
7 Angus Calder, *The People's War: Britain 1939-1945* (London: Pimlico, 1992), 191.
8 For the bureaucratic divisions operative within the Ministry of Food and the appointment of Horder see *British Food Journal*, 1 October 1942, 44 (10), 91–100.
9 Memorandum by Menzies, Harwood, Jones and Bowley, March 1941; see also monthly report to the War Cabinet, 15 March 1941. TNA, MAF 156/282.
10 Ministry of Food memorandum on condensed milk, 27 September 1941. TNA, MAF 83/382.

11 Solomon and Litvinoff, *Baku*, 185.
12 Memorandum by Menzies, Harwood, Jones and Bowley, March 1941; see also monthly report to the War Cabinet, 15 March 1941. TNA, MAF 156/282.
13 J.C. Drummond to C.J. Bromhead, 7 July 1941. TNA, MAF 152/55.
14 Wartime Meals Arrangements memo, 9 September 1941. TNA, MAF 83/382.
15 Hammond, *Food Volume II*, 355.
16 Shelter Feeding memo, 12 November 1941. TNA, MAF 99/1598.
17 Ministry Circular to Town Clerks, 29 November 1940. TNA, MAF 99/1598.
18 'Shelter Snacks and Sandwiches' pamphlet. TNA, MAF 99/1598.
19 Wartime Meals Division monthly report to Cabinet, December 1940. TNA, MAF 156/282.
20 Wartime Meals Division monthly report to Cabinet, December 1940. TNA, MAF 156/282. The theft of crockery and cutlery would recur in British Restaurants, as discussed in Spowart, 'Beyond simplicity', 29–36. See also Roodhouse, *Black Market Britain*, 72.
21 Wartime Meals Division monthly report to Cabinet, August 1941.
22 Hammond, *Food Volume II*, 319. TNA, MAF 156/282.
23 Shelter Feeding memo, 12 November 1941. TNA, MAF 99/1598.
24 Development and Work of the Shelter Feeding Branch, October 1940 to February 1941. TNA, MAF 99/1598.
25 O'Brien to L.F. van Zwanenberg, 16 September 1942. Soon after this despatch, O'Brien would be muzzled by his embarrassed superiors. TNA, MAF 83/382.
26 Wiltshire County Council memo, undated. TNA, MAF 152/55.
27 Untitled memo, 28 July 1941. TNA, MAF 152/55.
28 Memorandum on Communal Feeding, November 1941. TNA, MAF 83/382.
29 Memorandum on the provision of British Restaurants and Emergency Feeding Centres, 11 June 1941. TNA, MAF 99/1618.
30 Scottish divisional officer to G.R. Oake, 8 August 1941. TNA, MAF 152/55.
31 Emergency Feeding Arrangements memo, undated. TNA, MAF 152/55.
32 See for example County of Southampton to Ministry, 29 September 1941, County of Leicester to Ministry, 25 September 1941. TNA, MAF 99/1618.
33 W.J.M. Menzies to Austin Chadwick, 2 July 1941. TNA, MAF 99/1618.
34 Memo to local education authorities, 24 June 1941. TNA, MAF 99/1618.
35 Memorandum on Communal Feeding, November 1941. TNA, MAF 83/382.
36 Memorandum on Communal Feeding, November 1941. TNA, MAF 83/382.
37 Woolton memo, 5 November 1940. TNA, MAF 99/1797.
38 Baptist Union of Great Britain and Ireland to Woolton, 11 October 1941. TNA, MAF 99/1714.
39 Wartime Meals Division monthly report to Cabinet, May 1941. TNA, MAF 156/282.

40 Hammond, *Food Volume II*, 384.
41 Wartime Meals Division monthly report to Cabinet, February 1941. TNA, MAF 156/282.
42 Wartime Meals Division monthly report to Cabinet, August 1941. TNA, MAF 156/282.
43 Durbach, *Many Mouths*, 190.
44 See Atkins, 'Communal Feeding', 151.
45 See Chevalier, *Food in Wartime Britain*, 116.
46 Wartime Meals Division monthly report to Cabinet, February 1941. TNA, MAF 156/282.
47 Wartime Meals Division monthly report to Cabinet, December 1941. TNA, MAF 156/282.
48 Hansard, House of Commons Debate, 9 July 1941, vol. 373, col. 176.
49 Hansard, House of Commons Debate, 26 June 1941, vol. 372, col. 1088.
50 Hammond, *Food Volume II*, 380.
51 Amanda Herbert-Davies, *Children in the Second World War: Memories from the Home Front* (Barnsley: Pen and Sword, 2017), 78.
52 Herbert-Davies, *Children in the Second World War*; see also MOA/D/5390, May 1942.
53 Mass Observation file report 990, Public Feeling about Wartime Reforms, cited in Durbach, *Many Mouths*, 201.
54 W.M. Menzies, Ford Emergency Vans Circular, 17 March 1942. TNA, MAF 99/1796.
55 Hammond, *Food Volume II*, 346.
56 Influenza epidemic memo, 8 December 1943. TNA, MAF 99/1797.
57 Hammond, *Food Volume II*, 392.
58 Sitwell, *Eggs or Anarchy*, 110–12.
59 Hammond, *Food Volume II*, 366.
60 *The Daily Telegraph*, 12 October 1940.
61 Cited in Chevalier, *Food in Wartime Britain*, 53.
62 For the communal paradigm in British wartime cinema see James Chapman, *The British at War: Cinema, State and Propaganda, 1939-1945* (London: I.B. Tauris, 1998). See also Farmer, *Food Companions*, 99–104.
63 Ministry of Information, *Eating Out with Tommy Trinder*, 1941.
64 Barbara Cartland Obituary, *The Daily Telegraph*, 22 May 2000.
65 *The Daily Telegraph*, 24 September 1941.
66 For the broader significance of the housewife to wartime consumption see Amy Bentley, *Eating for Victory: Food Rationing and the Politics of Domesticity* (Urbana, IL: University of Illinois Press, 1998); Ina Zweiniger-Bargielowska, 'Housewifery'

in Ina Zweiniger-Bargielowska ed., *Women in Twentieth-Century Britain* (Harlow: Longman, 2001), 149–64.
67 Chevalier, *Food in Wartime Britain*, 116.
68 Zweiniger-Bargielowska, *Austerity in Britain*, 114; Atkins, 'Communal Feeding', 151.
69 Longmate, *How We Lived then*, 155.
70 *The Times*, 26 April 1941.
71 Sitwell, *Eggs or Anarchy*, 223.
72 *The Daily Telegraph*, 11 February 1943.
73 Wartime Meals Division memo on British Restaurants, January 1943. TNA, MAF 152/55.
74 Hansard, House of Commons Debate, 19 April 1944, vol. 339, col. 197.
75 See Mabane memo, 2 October 1942. TNA, MAF 99/1759. For an account of social and economic conditions in rural Britain at this time including rationing and food distribution see Brian Short, *The Battle of the Fields: Rural Community and Authority in Britain during the Second World War* (Woodbridge: Boydell, 2014); Sadie Ward, *War in the Countryside: 1939-45* (London: Cameron, 1988).
76 Memo on Establishment of British Restaurants, September 1943. TNA, MAF 99/759.
77 See W.M. Menzies memo, 1 January 1941. TNA, MAF 99/1796.
78 Memo on Establishment of British Restaurants, September 1943. TNA, MAF 99/759.
79 *The Daily Telegraph*, 27 August 1942.
80 D. Watson to Opray, 1 July 1941. TNA, MAF 99/1618.
81 J.J, Opray to W.J.M. Menzies, 30 June 1941. TNA, MAF 1618/4300.
82 S.E.G. Taylor memo, 23 August 1943. TNA, MAF 99/1626.
83 Minister's Standing Committee minutes, 16 September 1943. TNA, MAF 99/759.
84 British Restaurants and the Catering Industry memo, 9 February 1942. TNA, MAF 99/1797.
85 Ministry of Food Bulletin 100, 22 August 1941. TNA, MAF 152/55.
86 British Restaurants trading results, 19 May 1944. TNA, MAF 99/1797.
87 Ministry of Food Circular, 20 September 1943. TNA, MAF 99/1626.
88 Solomon and Litvinoff, *Baku*, 183.
89 Memo on Establishment of British Restaurants, September 1943. TNA, MAF 99/759.
90 Ministry Statement on British Restaurants, 10 April 1945. TNA, MAF 152/55.
91 British Restaurants trading results, 19 May 1944. TNA, MAF 99/1797.
92 Ministry of Food Circular, September 1943. TNA, MAF 99/759. See also Ministry of Food, *How Britain Was Fed in Wartime: Food Control 1939-1945* (London: Stationery Office, 1946).

93 Hammond, *Food Volume II*, 381.
94 Hammond, *Food Volume II*, 388.
95 C.S. Bishop to Murrie, 14 May 1946. TNA, MAF 99/1760. See also Hammond, *Food Volume II*, 401.
96 Jack Drummond, 'War time nutrition and its lessons for the future', *British Food Journal* 1 April 1944, 45, 11 (1943), 31–40.
97 'Brief for the Minister', 21 May 1946. TNA, MAF 99/137.
98 Hammond, *Food Volume II*, 392–9.
99 Atkins, *Communal Feeding*, 145.
100 Hammond, *Food Volume II*, 388.
101 See Zweiniger-Bargielowska, *Austerity*, 114.
102 Hammond, *Food Volume II*, 399.
103 Memorandum on the nutritional significance of meals consumed off ration in Britain, 13 March 1942. TNA, MAF 83/382.
104 Mass Observation, *People in Production: An Enquiry into British War Production* (London: John Murray, 1942), 273.
105 Robert Mackay, *Half the Battle: Civilian Morale in Britain during the Second World War* (Manchester: Manchester University Press, 2002), 200.
106 Chevalier, *Food in Wartime Britain*, 114–16.
107 Durbach, *Many Mouths*, 178.
108 Farmer, *Food Companions*, 3.
109 Churchill, Cabinet minutes, 14 May 1945, TNA, CAB 65/50/24.

Conclusion

1 *Daily Mail*, 18 November 1965.
2 Peter Simple, 'The well-planned Life', *Daily Telegraph*, 20 April 1960.
3 Peter Simple, 'Euphemism', *Daily Telegraph*, 15 September 1960.
4 *Daily Mail*, 30 August 1951.
5 *Daily Telegraph*, 10 March 1979.
6 Email correspondence with John McDonnell MP, 11–13 September 2021.
7 Lord Sumption, 'Government by decree: Covid-19 and the Constitution', 2020 Cambridge Freshfields Lecture, 27 October 2020, https://resources.law.cam.ac.uk/privatelaw/Freshfields_Lecture_2020_Government_by_Decree.pdf. accessed 29 October 2020.
8 For the most important recent iteration of Karl Marx's remark in the 'Eighteenth Brumaire of Louis Napoleon' *Die Revolution* (New York, 1852) see Slavoj Žižek, *First as Tragedy, then as Farce* (London: Verso, 2009).
9 *The Times*, 4 September 2020.

10 See Boris Johnson, *The Churchill Factor: How One Man Made History* (London: Hodder, 2015).
11 These divisions are themselves telling of the division between 'idealism and non-idealism' identified in John Offer's *An Intellectual History of British Social Policy* (Bristol: Policy Press, 2006).
12 Hannah Lambie-Mumford, 'Feeding hungry children: The growth in charitable breakfast clubs and holiday hunger projects in the UK', *Children and Society*, 32, 3 (2018), 244–54; see also Food Foundation, 'A year of children's food: A progress review of policy on children's food and nutrition across the four UK nations 2019-2020', https://foodfoundation.org.uk/wp-content/uploads/2020/07/CR2F_ProgressBriefing_DIGITAL-1.pdf, accessed 3 October 2020.
13 Marina Hyde, 'Only the government could miss the open goal of free school meals', *The Guardian*, 27 October 2020. For the breadth of public support for food-based anti-poverty initiatives see, for example, Elizabeth Clery and Jane Perry, 'The public opinion case', in Hannah Lambie-Mumford and Rachel Loopstra eds., *Why end UK Hunger? The case for ending hunger in the UK* (Salford: Church Action on Poverty, 2019), 17.
14 Zweiniger-Bargielowska, *Austerity in Britain*, 74.
15 Solomon and Litvinoff, *Baku*, 200.

Bibliography

Archival collections

Blair Castle, Perthshire
    Castle and Estate Archives
British Library, London
    Listener Historical Archive
Churchill Archives Centre, Churchill College Cambridge
    Florence Horsburgh papers
    Winston Churchill papers
Glasgow Caledonian University Archives
    Glasgow and West of Scotland College of Domestic Science records
Glasgow Corporation Records
    Corporation Minutes
    Food Control Committee minutes
Liverpool John Moores University Archives
    F.L. Calder collection
Marks and Spencer Archive, Leeds
    M&S Cafés material
Mass Observation Archive, University of Sussex
    Diaries
    File reports
Ministry of Information
    Daily reports 1940–1
The National Archives
    Board of Trade files (BT)
    Cabinet files (CAB)
    Ministry of Food (MAF)
    Prime Minister's Office (PREM)
National Library of Wales
    Welsh Newspapers collection
People's History Museum Archives, Manchester
    Workers National Committee files
University of Leeds Special Collections
    Cookery collection
University of Warwick Digital Collections
    Transport and General Workers' Union files

Official publications, broadcasts

All-Party Parliamentary Inquiry into Hunger in the United Kingdom, *Feeding Britain: A Strategy for Zero Hunger in England, Wales, Scotland and Northern Ireland* (London: Stationery Office, 2014).
Annual Abstract of Statistics.
Board of Trade, *Report of the Retail Trade Committee* (London: Stationery Office, 1943).
Hansard, House of Commons and House of Lords debates.
Hippisley Cox, R., H.J. Bradley and Eustace Miles Cox, *Public Kitchens Handbook* (London: Stationery Office, 1918).
Industrial Unrest: Reports of the Commissioners (London: Stationery Office, 1917).
Mass Observation, *People in Production: An enquiry into British War Production* (London: John Murray, 1942).
Ministry of Food, *Canteen Catering* (London: Stationery Office, 1941).
Ministry of Food, *How Britain Was Fed in Wartime: Food Control 1939-1945* (London: Stationery Office, 1946).
Ministry of Food, 'Kitchen Front' broadcasts (various).
Ministry of Food, *National Kitchens Handbook* (London: Stationery Office, 1918).
Ministry of Information, *Eating Out with Tommy Trinder*, 1941.
Report of the Interdepartmental Committee on Physical Deterioration (London: Stationery Office, 1904).

Newspapers, periodicals, reference

Abergavenny Chronicle
Bristol Times and Mirror
British Food Journal
British Medical Journal
Cambrian News and Merionethshire Standard
Carmarthen Journal and South Wales Weekly Advertiser
Daily Express
Daily Graphic
Daily Mail
Daily Mirror
Daily Telegraph
Economist
Electrical Times
Evening News
Glasgow Evening News
Glasgow Herald

The Globe
Guardian
The Lady
Lancashire Evening Post
Liverpool Daily Post and Mercury
Llanelli Star
Manchester Guardian
New Statesman
Oxford Dictionary of National Biography
Pall Mall Gazette
Sunday Pictorial
Surrey Advertiser and Surrey Comet
Tatler
The Times
Yorkshire Post
West London Press and Chelsea News
Western Times

Books, articles, pamphlets

Addison, Paul. *Now the War Is Over: A Social History of Britain, 1945-51* (London: Jonathan Cape, 1985).

Addison, Paul. *The Road to 1945: British Politics and the Second World War* (second edition; London: Pimlico, 1994).

Atkins, Peter J. 'Communal Feeding in War Time: British Restaurants 1940-47', in Alain Drouard, Rachel Duffett and Ina Zweiniger-Bargielowska eds., *Food and War in Twentieth Century Europe* (Farnham: Ashgate, 2011).

Atkins, Peter J. 'The Milk in Schools Scheme, 1934-45: 'Nationalization and resistance', *History of Education*, 34, 1 (2005), 1–21.

Barnett, Margaret. *British Food Policy during the First World War* (London: Routledge, 1985).

Beevor, Anthony. *The Battle for Spain: The Spanish Civil War 1936-1939* (London: Weidenfield and Nicolson, 2007).

Beveridge, William. *British Food Control* (Oxford: Oxford University Press, 1928).

Bland, Lucy and Carr, Richard (eds.). *Labour, British Radicalism, and the First World War* (Manchester: Manchester University Press, 2018).

Blishen, Edward. *A Cackhanded War* (London: Thames and Hudson, 1972).

Blunt, Wilfrid. *Lady Muriel: Muriel Paget, Her Husband, and Her Philanthropic Work in Central and Eastern Europe* (London: Methuen, 1962).

Boyd Orr, John. *As I Recall* (London: MacGibbon and Kee, 1966).

Boyd Orr, John. *'Nutrition in War' tract 251*, 5 (London: Fabian Society, 1940).

Broadberry, Stephen and Harrison, Mark. *The Economics of World War I* (Cambridge: Cambridge University Press, 2005).

Burnett, John. *England Eats Out, 1830 – Present* (London: Pearson, 2004).

Burnett, John. *Liquid Pleasures: A Social History of Drinks in Modern Britain* (London: Routledge, 1999).

Burnett, John, and Oddy, Derek. *The Origins and Development of Food Policies in Europe* (Leicester: Leicester University Press, 1996).

Calder, Angus. *The People's War: Britain 1939-1945* (London: Pimlico, 1992).

Carey, John. *The Intellectuals and the Masses: Pride and Prejudice among the Literary Intelligentsia, 1880-1939* (London: Faber and Faber, 1992).

Chapman, James. *The British at War: Cinema, State and Propaganda, 1939-1945* (London: I.B. Tauris, 1998).

Chester, D.N. *Lessons of the British War Economy* (Cambridge: Cambridge University Press, 1951).

Chesterton, G.K. *Irish Impressions* (London: Collins, 1919).

Chevalier, Natacha. *Food in Wartime Britain: Testimonies from the Kitchen Front, 1939-1945* (London: Routledge, 2020).

Collingham, Lizzie. *The Taste of War: World War Two and the Battle for Food* (London: Allen Lane, 2011).

Colquhoun, Kate. *Taste: The Story of Britain through Its Cooking* (London: Bloomsbury, 2007).

Cox, Stan. *Any Way You Slice It: The Past, Present and Future of Rationing* (New York: New Press, 2013).

Den Hartog, Adel (ed.). *Food Technology, Science and Marketing: European Diet in the Twentieth Century* (East Linton: Tuckwell, 1995).

Digby, Anne. 'Victorian Values and Women in Public and Private', *Proceedings of the British Academy*, 78 (1990), 195–215.

Drake, Barbara. *Community Feeding in Wartime* (London: Fabian Society, 1942).

Drake, Barbara. *Nutrition: A Policy of National Health* (London: Fabian Society, 1936).

Drummond, Jack. *The Englishman's Food: A History of Five Centuries of English Diet* (London: Pimlico, 1939, new edition 1994).

Drummond, Jack. 'War Time Nutrition and Its Lessons for the Future', *British Food Journal* 1 April 1944, 45, 11 (1943), 31–40.

Durbach, Nadia. *Many Mouths: the Politics of Food in Britain from the Workhouse to the Welfare State* (Cambridge: Cambridge University Press, 2020).

Ealham, Chris. and Richards, Michael. *The Splintering of Spain: Cultural History and the Spanish Civil War, 1936-1939* (Cambridge: Cambridge University Press, 2005).

Edgerton, David. *Britain's War Machine: Weapons, Resources and Experts in the Second World War* (Oxford: Oxford University Press, 2011).

Evans, Bryce. 'The National Kitchen in Britain, 1917-1919', *Journal of War and Culture Studies* 10, 2 (2017), 115–29.

Evans, Danny. *Revolution and the State: Anarchism in the Spanish Civil War, 1936-1939* (Chico, CA: AK Press, 2018).

Englander, David. *Poverty and Poor Law Reform in Nineteenth Century Britain, 1834-1914, from Chadwick to Booth* (London: Routledge, 1998).

Farmer, Richard. *The Food Companions: Cinema and Consumption in Wartime Britain, 1939-45* (Manchester: Manchester University Press, 2011).

Foss, Brian. *War Paint: Art, War, State and Identity in Britain, 1939-1945* (New Haven: Yale University Press, 2007).

Francis, Martin. 'A Flight from Commitment? Domesticity, Adventure and the Masculine Imaginary in Britain after the Second World War', *Gender & History*, 19, 1 (2007), 163–85.

Gazeley, Ian. *Poverty in Britain, 1900-1965* (New York: Palgrave Macmillan, 2003).

Gazeley, Ian, and Newell, Andrew, 'The First World War and Working-class Food Consumption in Britain', *European Review of Economic History*, 17/1 (2013), 71–94.

Giles, Judy. *Women, Identity, and Private Life in Britain, 1900-50* (New York: St. Martin's Press, 1995).

Glover, Brian. *Brewing for Victory: Brewers, Beers and Pubs in World War II* (London: Lutterworth, 1995).

Gregory, Adrian. *The Last Great War: British Society and the First World War* (Cambridge: Cambridge University Press, 2008).

Hammond, R.J. *Food: The Growth of Policy* (London: Stationery Office, 1951).

Hammond, R.J. *Food Volume II: Studies in Administration and Control* (London: Stationery Office, 1956).

Hannam, June and Hunt, Karen. *Socialist Women: Britain 1880s to 1920s* (London: Routledge, 2002).

Harris, Alexandra. *Romantic Moderns: English Writers, Artists and the Imagination from Virginia Woolf to John Piper* (London: Thames and Hudson, 2015).

Harrison, Mark. *The Economics of World War II: Six Great Powers in International Comparison* (Cambridge: Cambridge University Press, 1998).

Hennessy, Peter. *Never Again: Britain 1945-51* (London: Jonathan Cape, 1992).

Herbert-Davies, Amanda. *Children in the Second World War: Memories from the Home Front* (Barnsley: Pen and Sword, 2017).

Hilson, Mary. *Political Change and the Rise of Labour in Comparative Perspective: Britain and Sweden 1980-1920* (Lund: Nordic Academic Press, 2006).

Hilton, Matthew. *Consumerism in Twentieth-Century Britain* (Cambridge: Cambridge University Press, 2003).

Hinton, James. *Nine Wartime Lives: Mass Observation and the Making of the Modern Self* (Oxford: Oxford University Press, 2010).

Hunt, Karen. 'The Politics of Food and Women's Neighborhood Activism in First World War Britain', *International Labor and Working-Class History*, 77/01 (2010), 8–26.

John, Angela. *Turning the Tide: The Life of Lady Rhondda* (Cardigan: Partheon, 2014).

Johnson, Niall. *Britain and the 1918-19 Influenza Pandemic – A Dark Epilogue* (London: Routledge, 2006).

Johnson, P.B. *Land Fit for Heroes: The Planning of British Reconstruction* (Chicago: University of Chicago Press, 1968).

Jones, Thomas. *The Unbroken Front, Ministry of Food 1916-1944* (London: Everybody's, 1944).

Kamminga, Harmke and Cunningham, Andrew (eds.). *The Science and Culture of Nutrition, 1840-1940* (Amsterdam: Rodopi, 1995).

Kearley, Hudson. *The Travelled Road: Some Memories of a Busy Life* (London: Rochester, 1935).

Keezer, Dexter. 'Observations on Rationing and Price Control in Great Britain', *American Economic Review*, 33, 2 (1943), 264–82.

King, Laura. *Family Men: Fatherhood and Masculinity in Britain, c.1914-1960* (Oxford: Oxford University Press, 2015).

King, Laura. 'Hidden Fathers? The Significance of Fatherhood in Mid-Twentieth-Century Britain', *Contemporary British History*, 26, 1 (2012), 25–46.

Knight, Katherine. *Rationing in the Second World War: Spuds, Spam and Eating for Victory* (London: History Press, 2007).

Lavalette, Michael. 'Sylvia Pankhurst: Suffragette, Socialist, Anti-imperialist ... and Social Worker?', *Critical and Radical Social Work*, 5, 3 (2017), 369–82.

Le Gros Clark, Frederick. *The Communal Restaurant: A Study of the Place of Civic Restaurants in the Life of the Community* (London: Council of Social Service, 1943).

Leopold, Ellen. 'LCC Restaurants and the Decline of Municipal Enterprise', in Andrew Saint ed., *Politics and the People of London: The London County Council, 1889-1965* (London: Hambledon, 1989).

Levene, Alysa. 'The Meanings of Margarine in England: Class, Consumption and Material Culture from 1918 to 1953', *Contemporary British History*, 28, 2 (2014), 145–65.

Levy, Hermann. *The Shops of Britain: A Study of Retail Distribution* (Oxford: Oxford University Press, 1948).

Longmate, Norman. *How We Lived then: Everyday Life during the Second World War* (London: Pimlico, 2002).

Lumbie-Mumford, Hannah. *Hungry Britain: The Rise of Food Charity* (London: Policy Press, 2017).

Mackay, Robert. *Half the Battle: Civilian Morale in Britain during the Second World War* (Manchester: Manchester University Press, 2002).

Manton, Kevin. 'Sir William Beveridge, the British Government, and Plans for Food Control in Time of War c. 1916-1941', *Contemporary British History*, 23, 3 (2009), 363–85.

Marquis, Frederick James. *The Memoirs of the Right Honourable the Earl of Woolton* (London: Cassell, 1959).

Marwick, Arthur. *The Deluge: British Society and the First World War* (London: Palgrave MacMillan, 1991).

Mennell, Stephen. *All Manners of Food: Eating and Taste in England and France from the Middle Ages to the Present* (Oxford: Blackwell, 1985).

Millman, Brock. *Managing Domestic Dissent in First World War Britain* (London: Routledge, 2000).

Mills, Geofrey T. and Rockoff, Hugh (eds.). *The Sinews of War: Essays on the Economic History of World War II* (Ames: Iowa State University Press, 1993).

Milward, Alan S. *War, Economy and Society 1939-1945* (Berkley: University of California Press, 1979).

Minns, Raynes. *Bombers and Mash: The Domestic Front 1939-45* (London: Virago, 1980).

Moser Jones, Marian. 'The American Red Cross and Local Responses to the 1918 Influenza: A Four-city Case Study', *Public Health Reports*, 125, 3 (2010), 92–104.

Oddy, Derek. *From Plan Fare to Fusion Food: British Diet from the 1890s to the 1990s* (Woodbridge: Boydell Press, 2003).

Olsen, Mancur S. *The Economics of Wartime Shortage: A History of British Food Supplies in the Napoleonic Wars and in World Wars I and II* (Durham, NC: Duke University Press, 1963).

Panayi, Panikos. 'Anti German Riots in London during the First World War', *German History*, 7, 2 (1989), 184–203.

Peel, C.S. *How We Lived then, 1914-1918: A Sketch of Social and Domestic Life in England during the War* (London: John Lane, 1929).

Peel, C.S. *Life's Enchanted Cup: An Autobiography, 1872-1933* (London: Bodley Head, 1933).

Quinn, Tom. *Flu: A Social History of Influenza* (London: New Holland, 2008).

Reeves, Maud Pember. *Round about a Pound a Week* (London: Bell and Sons, 1913).

Roodhouse, Mark. *Black Market Britain, 1939-1955* (Oxford: Oxford University Press, 2013).

Rose, Sonya O. *Which People's War? National Identity and Citizenship in Wartime Britain 1939-1945* (Oxford: Oxford University Press).

Ross, Ellen (ed.). *Slum Travelers: Ladies and London Poverty, 1860-1920* (Berkley: University of California Press, 2007).

Scholliers, Peter. 'Restaurants Économiques a Bruxelles Pendant La Grande Guerre', in Caroline Poulaine ed., *Manger et Boire entre 1914 et 1918* (Dijon, 2014), 111–18.

Scholliers, Peter and van Den Eeckhout, Patricia. 'Feeding Growing Cities in the Nineteenth and Twentieth Centuries: Problems, Innovations, and Reputations', in Anne Murcott, Warren Belasco and Peter Jackson eds., *The Handbook of Food Research* (London: Bloomsbury Academic, 2013), 69–81.

Short, Brian. *The Battle of the Fields: Rural Community and Authority in Britain during the Second World War* (Woodbridge: Boydell, 2014).

Simmonds, Alan. *Britain and World War One* (London: Routledge, 2013).

Sitwell, William. *Eggs or Anarchy* (London: Simon and Schuster, 2016).

Smith, Charles. *Food in Wartime* (London: Fabian Society, 1940).

Solomon, Flora and Litvinoff, Barnet. *Baku to Baker Street: The Memoirs of Flora Solomon* (London: Collins, 1984).

Steedman, Carolyn. *Childhood, Culture, and Class in Britain: Margaret McMillan, 1860-1931* (London: Virago, 1990).

Sweet, Matthew. *The West End Front: The Wartime Secrets of London's Grand Hotels* (London: Faber and Faber, 2011).

Tarran, Brian. 'Lord Woolton: The Man Who Used Statistics (and More) to Feed a Nation at War', *Significance*, 14, 3 (2017), 24–9.

Tawney, R. H. 'The Abolition of Economic Controls, 1918-1921', *Economic History Review* 13, 1 (1943), 1–30.

Trentmann, Frank, and Just, Fleming. *Food and Conflict in the Age of the Two World Wars* (London: Palgrave MacMillan, 2006).

Tönsmeyer, Tatjana, Haslinger, Peter and Laba, Agnes (eds.). *Coping with Hunger and Shortage under German Occupation in World War II* (Cham, Switzerland: Palgrave Macmillan, 2018).

Ugolini, Wendy. *Experiencing War as the Enemy 'Other': Italian Scottish Experience in World War II* (Manchester: Manchester University Press, 2011).

Van Emden, Richard and Humphries, Steve. *All Quiet on the Home Front: An Oral History of the First World War* (Barnsley: Pen and Sword, 2017).

Vernon, James. *Hunger: A Modern History* (Cambridge, MA: Harvard University Press, 2007).

Von Bremzen, Anya. *Mastering the Art of Soviet Cooking* (London: Transworld, 2014).

Waldie, Elizabeth. *Collection of Economical Recipes Suitable for War Cookery and Notes on Meaning of Economy as Regards Food and Fuel* (Glasgow: SN, 1917).

Ward, Sadie. *War in the Countryside: 1939-45* (London: Cameron, 1988).

Webster, Wendy. *Mixing It: Diversity in World War Two Britain* (Oxford: Oxford University Press, 2018).

Weinreb, Alice. *Modern Hungers: Food and Power in Twentieth-Century Germany* (Oxford: Oxford University Press, 2017).

Winter, J.M. *The Great War and the British People* (London: MacMillan, 1985).

Ziegelman, Jane and Coe, Andrew. *A Square Meal: A Culinary History of the Great Depression* (New York: Harper, 2016).

Zweiniger-Bargielowska, Ina. *Austerity in Britain: Rationing, Controls and Consumption, 1939-1955* (Oxford: Oxford University Press, 2000).

Zweiniger-Bargielowska, Ina, Duffett, Rachel, and Drouard, Alain (eds.). *Food and War in Twentieth Century Europe* (London: Ashgate, 2011).

Index

Boldface locators indicate figures; locators followed by 'n.' indicate endnotes

aerial bombardment, feeding 86, 111, 113, 120
Air Raid Canteens 4, 120
air raid shelters
   catering, private traders 109
   emergency public feeding ventures 3, 114
   field kitchens and mobile canteens 112–13
   food demand 109, 115–16
Anglo-Boer war (1899–1902) 5, 52
anti-suffragism 14
Armistice 23
Asquith, Herbert Henry
   New Liberalism 12
   'Wait and See' administration 23
Atkins, Peter 120, 126
   'Communal Feeding in War Time' 157 n.5
'Aunt Sammy' 80–1

Barnett, Margaret 22–3
Beatty, Ethyl 49
Beevor, Anthony, 'Gastronomic Unit No. 1' 79
Bell, William 104
Benenson, Flora. *See* Solomon (Benenson), Flora
Bennett, Arnold 69, 124
   vs. Chesterton 56–9
   'distinctions of class' 59
   on national kitchens (opinions) 57–9
   'quasi paternal' institutions 59
Beveridge, William 2–3, 26, 74–5, 87, 109
   military terminology 74
   'Wider Aspects of Food Control' (1936) 74, 86, 111
Bevin, Ernest 105–6
Birmingham central kitchen 43
Blishen, Edward 104
   A Cackhanded War 107

'Blood Purifiers and Bone Formers' (food group) 55
Booth, Catherine 11–12
Booth, Evangeline 76
Booth, William 11
Boyd Orr, John 73, 75, 90–1, 108–9, 114
Bradley, H.J. 27–8, 30, 50, 54. *See also Public Kitchens Handbook* (Cox, Bradley and Miles)
'Brains on Toast' (recipe) 55
Brave New World (public feeding) 1, 8, 30, 32, 92
Brighton, national kitchen 43
British Food Journal 131
British Medical Association, 'minimum cost' 90, 114
British Restaurant 3–4, 6, 23, 81, 84–9, 92, 106, 113, 119, 121, 128, 132, 140
   and catering trade 129, 131
   celebrity endorsement 125
   cheap prices 105
   decoration 94, **95**, 96
   'fair shares' 94, 99, 110
   fare 93
   financial assistance 98
   in Grantham and Lincolnshire 107
   in Hackney 126
   local authorities and 94–103, 129–30
   Mass Observation (survey) 97–8, 126
   misconception 102
   'mutual assistance pacts' 98
   potatoes feature 93
   price structure 96
   profits 129–30
   public dining function 99–100
   pudding course 99
   regional disparities and anomalies 118
   sampling meals from 93
   staffs and wages 96
   state's role in 109–10, 133
   statistics 120, 157 n.3

Swindon's 104
training courses 96
'vegetable supply statistics' 93
The British Women's Total Abstinence Society 92
bulk purchasing, system 61, 107–8
Burnett, John 9
   England Eats Out 7, 21–2

Calder, Angus 133
Canteen Catering 99
Capell, Iris 125
Cartland, Barbara 3, 9, 125–6
'Cash and Carry' Centres 120
'cash and carry' feeding 119, 132
Chamberlain, Neville 85
charitable feeding ventures 23–4
charity, food 4, 12, 73, 113
   avoiding taint of 16, 34–9, 107
   re-emergence of 7
   taint of 44
Chelsea National Kitchen 47–9, 101
Chesterton, G. K. 51, 104
   Bennett *vs.* 56–9
Chevalier, Natacha 120, 126, 133, 162 n.118
Children Act (1908) 35
Churchill, Winston 3, 9, 22–3, 30–1, 84–6, 90, 100, 103, 133, 136
   left/right political divisions 103–10
   'wartime leadership' 137
'Citizens' Kitchen (London) **103**
Civic Restaurants Act (1946) 131
civilizational value 56–9
Clark, Bill 109
Clark, Elizabeth 95
class kitchens 36
clerical workers (community restaurants) 106
comedores populares (popular dining rooms) 79
communal dining 1, 5, 26–7, 29, 35, 53, 62, 68–9, 97, 104, 119, 121, 123, 130, 132, 140. *See also* British Restaurant
   with authoritarianism 77
   'enormous public demand' 65
   features of 79
   growth of 65
   'Londoners' Meal Service' 88

modernism and 57
as 'national kitchens' 105
programme 125
radical threat of 29–33
schemes 6, 127
state's commitment to 110
ventures 65
communal eating 2, 8, 29, 35, 75, 104, 126, 131, 133, 135
   patriotic rebranding 85
   wartime 22
communal feeding 25, 29, 36, 104, 133, 136
   centre 3, 9, 85, 125, 127
   as communism 75–7
   critics 107
   development of 131, 135
   initiatives 67
   as National Kitchen 16
   schemes 24, 26, 127
   utility of 127–30
communalist gastronomic paradigm 133
communal kitchens 7, 35, 41, 51, 55, 66, 76
   bottom-up female voluntarism 39
   critics 44
   FCCs to 42
   gender-based activism 146 n.4
   of Newcastle-upon-Tyne 88
   origins of 30
   soup kitchens to 23–9
   state's adoption of 29
   voluntary 26, 37
   WNC's recommendations 26
communal restaurant 71, 79, 83, 87, 99, 106, 111
communism
   communal feeding as 75–7
   and workhouse 3, 9, 85
communitarianism and anti-epicurianism 78
community feeding 106, 111, 118, 129
Community Feeding Centres 88, 120
community kitchens 7, 29, 31, 34, 69, 97, 106, 120
comprehensive rationing system 21, 26, 139
consumption (food) 5–7, 9, 32, 52, 59, 86, 93, 114, 143 n.8, 151 n.49
   of alcohol 54
   'alien' cultures of 50

communal (Brave New World) 1, 8
  egalitarianism 126
  'the failure of voluntary restraint' 16
  faith and 11–13
  Home Front propaganda 123
  regional differentiation 92
  scientific approach to 17
  in Soviet Union 78
convoys of food 113, 122
cookery schools 17, 55–6
Cooperative Party 108
Cornish pasties 43, 64, 120
Coronavirus pandemic (2020) 1, 137
  food banks and emergency feeding 4, 7
  measures 1, 136, 138
council-run kitchens 64
Coventry Evening Telegraph 104
Cox, R. Hippisley 27–8, 30, 50, 54. *See also Public Kitchens Handbook* (Cox, Bradley and Miles)
Croydon Communal Kitchen 26–7, 30, 88

Daily Express 100
Daily Mail 54, 75, 100, 104, 107
Daily News 57
Daily Telegraph 125, 136
Davies, J. G. 135
Defence of the Realm Act 31
deficiency diseases 17, 90
Dickens, Charles 137
  A Christmas Carol 137
  Oliver Twist 137
Dock Canteens 120
Drake, Barbara 76, 108
  Nutrition: A Policy of National Health 76
Drummond, Jack 90, 92, 109, 115, 131–2
  The Englishman's Food: A History of Five Centuries of English Diet 91
  Oslo breakfast 91, 99, 114
Durbach, Nadia 18, 102
  Many Mouths 101, 157 n.5
  'pickup spot' 92

East London Federation of Suffragettes (ELFS) 15
eating out 2, 7–8, 22, 67, 72, 101, 123, 132
  history of 21
  in private restaurants (restrictions) 100
  as public endeavour 9
  at restaurant 21–2
  in Whitehall, London **112**
Eating Out with Tommy Trinder 122–7
'Eat Out to Help Out' scheme 1, 137
economics by human laws 74
Edinburgh School of Cookery 55
Education (Provision of Meals) Acts 45
egalitarian eating 55, 64, 66
egalitarianism (public dining) 22, 126
Eintopf (one pot) meal 78
Electrical Times 32
emergency feeding centres 14, 113, 116–18, 121
emergency feeding/public feeding 1–4, 9, 19, 56, 101, 110, 113, 120, 131, 138, 140–1
  of Coronavirus crisis 4, 7
  disappearance 75
  of First World War 56
  nutritional standards 114
  re-establishment 3
  schemes 103, 111–12, 138
  'soup and salvation' model 76
  state-supported 16
  take-away model of 33, 37
  and temporary feeding 118
emergency food 112–14, 117
Emergency Food Kitchens 120
emergency food parcels 1, 4, 7
Emergency Meals Centres 120, 129
emergency measures 8–9, 67, 136, 138
emergency shopping centres 129
English Settlement Movement 15
Escoffier, Georges Auguste 7
Eustace Miles Restaurant Company Ltd 28
evacuee-feeding centres 99–100, 119–20
Evening Standard 48
Exeter Penny Dinner Society 44

'fair play' 44, 61, 68, 105, 107, 109, 127
Falangist forces of Francisco Franco 79
fascist dictatorships (Europe) 77–8
February Revolution 24
female. *See also* working class women
  egalitarian eating 66
  leadership in public feeding 46–50
  national kitchens and 34–9
  voluntarism, class and gender 13–16, 87, 97

First World War (1914–1918) 1, 6, 73, 81, 101, 110, 139
  diet change during 52
  dietetics, notion 17
  eating out 8
  emergency public feeding in 2–3, 19, 56, 69, 85, 92, 113
  local authorities 98
  national kitchen 2–3, 21, 77, 84, 86–7, 94, 100, 102, 105, 140
  National Kitchens Division 119
  nutritional improvement 116
  Salvation Army's approach 11
  social eating 75, 99
  statist measures of 12
  working-class women 79
'Flesh Formers' (food group) 55
Fletcher, Horace 54
Fletcherizing 54
food banks 4, 7, 31, 113, 142 n.3
Food Control Committees (FCCs) 41–6, 108–9
food controls 31, 100, 143 n.9
Food (Defence Plans) Department 73
food deficiency 73, 75
Food Economy Campaign, meatless cooking 55
'Food, Health and Income' report 75
food policy 21, 74, 90, 107, 139
  'basal' diet 90–1
  and foodways 22
  New Poor Law (1834) 137
  scientific advisory committee 90, 93, 122
  wartime 22–3, 87, 156 n.25
food poverty 139, 142 n.3
  charity 113
  and poor law 142 n.4
food preservation techniques 16
food pricing 19, 27, 67, 88, 146 n.32
food rationing 6, 41, 59, 87, 102, 108, 132–3, 139–40, 143 n.9
  demands for 69
  and distribution 166 n.75
  extension of 41, 44, 46, 68
  and price controls 21–2, 25, 109
'food riots' 19, 146 n.32
food shortages 19, 21, 42, 54, 79
food supply 41, 87, 108, 122, 140
  history of 93, 107
  and nutritional standards 45

  and price inflation 2
  as remedy 69
'Food Train' (London) 113
food vigilance committees 34, 36, 42
Ford Motor Company 121–2
Freedman, Barnett 96
free trade 50, 61
French, Henry 129
full rationing 16, 23, 25, 62, 68–9

Gardiner, Clive 94–5
The Gaylord 79
Glasgow Corporation 43, 61, 149 n.3
Glasgow District Restaurateurs' 60
Grant, Peter 15
Greater London Council (GLC) 136
Great Irish Famine 18
grocery store, obliteration 87
The Guardian 138, 142 n.3
Gullace, Nicoletta 146 n.32

Halifax National Kitchen **32**
Hammersmith's central kitchen 43
Hammond, Richard J. 2
  Food Volume II 157 n.4, 160 n.57
haute cuisine 7
'Hay diet' 91–2
health food products (Miles)
  'bean-based' image problem 54
  'Emprote' 51
  nutritional instruction 52
  'Plasmon' 51
  and vegetarianism 27–8, 51
'Heat and Energy Producers' (food group) 55
Hemingway, Ernest, *For Whom the Bell Tolls* 79
'Home Front' wartime, food and 1, 6, 123
Hoover, Herbert 80
Horder, Thomas Jeeves 113, 115, 163 n.8
  Scotch Sprout 115–16
  Woolton sandwich 115–16
Horsburgh, Florence 46–7, **48**, 50, 83, 101
  Chelsea's national kitchen 47–8
  enthusiastic embrace of public feeding 49
  'queer queues' 48
  received advice 47
  reporters and 48–9
Hotel Keepers' Association 60

Howard League 35
Hull's central national kitchen 38
humanitarianism 18–20, 76, 80

'idealism and non-idealism' 168 n.11
individualism 6, 29, 107
   and class distinctions 105
   and consumerism 135
industrial canteens 13, 102
   government-run 24
   for manual workers 106
infectious diseases 90
Interdepartmental Committee on Physical Deterioration Report (1904) 54
interwar period, British food/feeding 71, 81
   communal feeding as communism 75–7
   cultural Americanization 72
   decline 71
   international comparisons 77–80
   'leisure time' 74
   middle classes 72
   Milk in Schools Scheme 71–2, 74
   'National Fitness Campaign' 74
   nutrition 73–5
   'Oslo Breakfast' 74
   society changes 71–3
   totalitarianism 76
   unemployment 71–2
'invalid kitchens' 14, 23

John Bull 105
Johnson, Boris 137–8
Jones, Kennedy 26–8, 30, 63, 67
   catering in royal parks 66
   'Do-it-now' political ethic 45

Kearley (Viscount Devonport), Hudson 24–5
Keeling, Edward 127
kitchen(s) 18–19, 63, 65. *See also* national kitchens
   factories 79
   soup to communal 23–9
   subsidiary 43
'Kitchen for All' 27, 30, 34, 38
'Kitchen Front' propaganda 114

'Lady Bountiful' 2, 14, 22–4, 29, 36, 39, 83–4, 86, 146 n.12
League of Nations, 'optimum diet' 90
Leeson, Cecil 35
Lewis's 77, 108
Liverpool cookery school 56
Llewellin, J. J. 127
Lloyd George, David 13, 24, 88
   'excessively puritan' 12
   'Push and Go' approach 23–4
Lloyd-George, Gwilym 88
Local Education Authority 45, 73
London County Council 88
London Meals Service 120
London Passenger Transport Board 120
London Vegetarian Society (1888) 28
The Lusitania, sinking 19, 105

malnutrition 73–5, 90
Manchester Guardian 31, 64
Manley, Kate 54
Marks and Spencer 77, 83, 87, 108–9, 114, 140
Marks, Simon 77, 83
Marquis (Lord Woolton), Frederick 3, 77, 81, 84–8, 93, 97–8, 100, 106, 108, 113–14, 116, 119, 126–7, **128**, 129–30
   egalitarian nutritional mission 90
   national nutritional standards 90
   urban anti-poverty programmes 86
   wartime food policy 156 n.25
Marx, Karl 137, 167 n.8
Mary, Queen 14, 22, 29–30, 36, 50
Mass Observation survey 97–8, 121, 123, 125–6, 133, 140, 160 n.66
McCurdy, Charles 64
McFadden, Bernarr 80
McKinlay, Adam 108
McMillan, Margaret 18
'meatless days' control 24
Mickey the Midget 130
Middleton, J. M. 26, 29, 44–5
Miles, Eustace 2, 27–31, 33, 47, 50–1, **53**, 53–4, 58, 74–5, 80, 91. *See also* health food products (Miles); Public Kitchens Handbook (Cox, Bradley and Miles)
   red-meat masculinity 28
   'second wave' of vegetarianism 28

Millions Like Us (1943) 123
Ministry of Food 2, 4, 12, 23, 26–7, 29–30, 33, 36, 42–3, 46, 54, 61, 63, 67, 81, 83, 86, 97–9, 101, 106, 110–11, 121, 131–2, 139, 163 n.8
   catering firms, deputation 60
   celebrities to promote public feeding 122–7
   'communal feeding centre' 3
   Communal Feeding Division 88
   domestic economy schools 55–6
   Economy section 45
   'Emergency Feeding Centres' 116–17
   feeding programme 84
   financial assistance 42–3, 88, 98
   milk supply scheme 119
   National Kitchens Handbook 36–7
   post-war downsizing 63–4, 69, 131
   Shelter Feeding Division 113
   Wartime Meals Division 112
Ministry of Health 86, 114, 121
Ministry of Information 58, 105, 123
Ministry of Labour 99, 106, 118
mobile 'agitprop' (travelling kitchen) 33
mobile canteens 32, 85, 87–8, 112, 119, 122
mobile distribution of food 2–3, 122, 132
mobile feeding centres 113
mobile snack-in-hand model 111
Montagu, John 115
Morrison, W.S. 85
municipal kitchens (Hamburg and London) 59
'municipal restaurant' 87
Muspratt, Max 35

'national disgrace' 50
'National Fitness Campaign' 74
National Health 81
National Health Service 1
national kitchens 2–3, 6, 13, 17, 21, 29–31, 33, 36, 57, 69, 80, 86, 88, 100–1, 132, 139
   advisory committee 54, 63–4, 66
   in Barrow-in-Furness (1919) 64
   in Bow, London (1918) **60**
   as businesses 37
   campaign of resistance 60
   communal dining as 105
   eating out at 67
   emergency commensality and 16
   expansion 39, 45
   government's sponsorship of 29
   'Ladies of the Ladel' role 2, 83
   London **34**
   'National Kitchens Order' (1918) 42
   in Newcastle, Liverpool and Llanelli 35
   organization of new 34–9
   'pauperism' 73
   'permanent national institution' 23
   post-war 59, 65
   sample menu 38
   scheme 15
   standardization of 42
   top-down 66
   in urban centres 64
   values of 45
   woman's domestic role, removing 35
National Kitchens Division 37, 66, 119
national restaurants 46, 60–1, 63–4, 69
national school canteens 46
The National Training School of Cookery (London) 17, 56
National Unemployed Workers' Movement 76
New Bridge restaurant (London) 43, 62–4
New Liberalism 12, 18–20
New Poor Law (1834) 102, 137–8
New York Times 100
Nissen hut restaurant 94
'NK movement' 64–5
nutrition
   body and national health 73–5
   diet and 71, 75, 81
   instruction and egalitarian eating 50–6
   poor (*see* poor nutrition)
   and public health 45
   in Soviet Union 78
nutritional chemistry 5
nutritional knowledge 91
nutritional reform/reformers 2, 28, 54, 80, 90–3
   national food policy 90
   scientific advance and 16–17, 20
   vs. sausage roll 112–18

O'Brien, Brian 115–16
Oddy, Derek 22
   'the failure of voluntary restraint' 16

Oliver, Jamie 138
O'Mara, Pat 146 n.32
Orwell, George, *Homage to Catalonia* (1938) 79
Oslo breakfast 74, 91, 99, 114
'ostentatious eating' 100

Paget, Muriel 14–16, 23, 76. *See also* 'invalid kitchens'
Panayi, Panikos 146 n.32
Pankhurst, Sylvia 15–16, 22, 24, 36
Partridge, Frances 104
Patriotic Food League 23
Pearce, John 61–2
Peel, Constance 54, 67
    The Daily Mail 54
    economical use of food 54
    The Lady 54
    The Queen 54
peripatetic piewoman (case study) 46–50, 83, 101. *See also* Horsburgh, Florence
Phillips, Marion 45–6
    national restaurants 46
    post-war housing projects 63
    principle of community dining 46
    Round about a pound a week 54
'pie scheme' 116
Pit Head Canteens 120
Pitt Club 102
Poor Law Amendment Act (1834) 19
Poor Law era 101, 110
'Poor Man's Goose' (recipe) 55
poor nutrition 52
    and health 71
    and overcrowding 5
    and poverty 76
'Potato Pete' 93
poverty 45, 54, 85, 129, 136, 139, 142 n.3
    diets 91
    poor nutrition and 76
price-capped dining 16, 89
price inflation 2, 6, 15, 19, 21, 23–5, 67
Priestley, J. B. 9, 107, 109
private catering trade 67
private faith-based charity 20
private restaurants, restrictions on 25, 105
private retail trade 3, 62–3, 77, 87
Provision of School Meals Act 18

public artwork (public dining spaces) 96
public feeding 2, 4–6, 11, 13, 18, 23, 64, 69, 83, 87, 91, 120–1, 125, 127, 131, 135, 140. *See also* emergency feeding/public feeding
    Brave New World version 1, 8, 30, 32, 92
    on Clydeside (bombing raid) **89**
    and communism 76–7
    economies of scale 62, 110
    fair shares 113
    FCCs and 41–6
    female leadership in (case study) 46–50
    goal of 54
    history of 139
    limps on as British society changes 71–3
    nutritional improvement 92
    schemes 1–2, 4, 8–9, 22, 34, 78, 84, 99, 101, 110, 112–13, 120–1, 123, 132, 137, 139–40
    utility 127–30
    in Victorian period 5, 138
public health crisis 23, 139
'public kitchens' 30
Public Kitchens Handbook (Cox, Bradley and Miles) 28, 30, 50–2, 54, 57, 99, 123, 135
    patriotism, food culture and diet 52–3
    public 'suspicion' 51

Queen's Messenger Service 122

Rashford, Marcus 137–8
Rathbone, Eleanor 19, 74, 76
Reeves, Maud Pember 54, 66–7
restaurant dining, features 21
Rest Centres 118, 120
Ritz Hotel (Barcelona) 79
Roberts, Alf 3, 107
Roberts, George 65
Ronay, Egon 135
Roosevelt, Franklin 80
Runciman, Walter 15
Russian October Revolution 31

Sailors Three 123
Salvation Army 11, 23, 73, 119
    female initiative 11–12
    'soup and salvation' model 76
    volunteers of 12

Savoy 126
Scarborough Post 38
Schiøtz, Carl 91
school dinners 45, 91
school feeding 72–3
school meals 18–19, 73–4, 76, 91, 137–8
   canteens 73, 99–100, 129
   in England and Wales 73
   feeding centres 73
Second World War (1939-1945) 1, 4, 6, 77, 81, 96, 136–7
   British Restaurant of 110
   communal restaurants 9, 83
   emergency public feeding in 2, 32–3, 84, 87, 111–13, 121, 123, 132
   moments of crisis 136
   private retail expertise, recruitment 140
   rationing 132, 139
   survey works on food situation 143 n.8
   voluntary female initiative 87
   Welfare Food Service 101
Shaw, George Bernard 28
slum kitchen (Exe Island) 44
Smith, Charles 109
   Food in Wartime 108
Smith, Montague 107
social and food reformers 17, 20, 27, 30, 33, 41, 50–6, 58, 72, 75–6, 91–2, 99, 115, 131, 139. *See also specific food reformers*
social class 22, 126, 133
social eating 1, 5, 13, 46, 59, 75–6, 78–80, 131, 133, 139
   bottom-up 79
   during Depression 80
   interwar Europe 71
   municipality of 99
   private retailers in wartime 102
   schemes 140
   state-funded 86
   stolovayas 78–9
socialism 11, 18–20, 30, 36
   system of war 31
social reform and universalism 19
Solomon (Benenson), Flora 3, 9, 24, 77, 83–4, **84**, 87, 106, 108–9, 114, 130, 140

soup kitchens 5, 12, 39, 51, 80
   'bean-based dishes' 51
   communal feeding model of 11
   to communal kitchens 23–9
   national kitchens and 38, 67
Spanish Civil War (1936–39) 79
'Spanish flu' 62–3, 69, 139
'special kitchens' 37, 120
Spencer, Charles 2, 30, 36–8, 45, 56, 61–3, 67–9, 98, 106, 113
   anti-socialism 31
   'distribution centres' 42
   food vigilance committees 36
   home-grown radicalism 31
   national kitchens division 30–1, 33, 42, 45, 55, 67
   'The National Restaurant' 63
   post-war 'reconstruction' 62, 65
   public relations mechanism 36
   'special kitchens' 120
   'special water-jacketed carrier' 33
   state-subsidized communal dining (memorandum) 62
   travelling kitchens 32–3
state feeding 101, 133
state-run canteens 78
state's role 5–7, 20, 24, 35, 105, 138
   plethora of schemes 111, 118–22
   providing sustenance 75
   in spreading British Restaurants 109
state-subsidized communal dining 1, 6, 61–2, 84, 137
stock market crash (1929) 72
stolovayas 78–9
'Sugars and Starches' (food group) 55
Sunak, Rishi 137

'taint of institutionalism' 59
take-away model 31, 33, 37, 45, 50, 119, 132
targeted feeding 14, 18–19, 72, 138
Tatler magazine 47
Taunton's national kitchen 44
Tawney, R. H. 69
Telegraph 127
Thatcher, Margaret 3, 107, 136
Thomas (Lord Rhondda), D.A. 24–5, **25**, 29–31, 33, 36–7, 41, 45, 57–8, 65, **68**, 68–9, 106
   anti-socialism 31

'Do-it-now party' 26
voluntarism over statism 26
wartime anti-individualism 29
The Times 96, 100, 105, 126
travelling kitchen 32, 47
    as mobile 'agitprop' 33
Trinder, Tommy 123, 126. *See also Eating Out with Tommy Trinder*
    public eating propaganda 123
    time-saving gadgetry 124
Trussell Trust 113
tube shelter canteen (London) **117**

U-boat campaign 24
unemployment 19, 62, 69, 71–2, 76
universalism
    and purchasing power of supermarkets 58
    social reform and 19
universal national feeding programme (schools) 45
The US-based British Food Mission 104
US Bureau of Home Economics 80
utility (public feeding) 127–31

'VC Restaurant' 71
vegetarianism 27–8, 51
Vegetarian Society, 'a many-sided liberalism' 28. *See also* London Vegetarian Society (1888)
Vernon, James, *Hunger: A Modern History* 157 n.4
'Very Economical Plum Pudding' (recipe) 55
village canteens 43, 146 n.7
voluntarism 19, 146 n.31
    female 13–16, 39, 87, 97
    over statism 26
voluntary communal kitchens 26, 37

Waldie, Elizabeth 55–6, 63
    Economical Recipes suitable for War Cookery 55
War Emergency Workers National Committee (WNC) 26–9, 31, 44–5
wartime economics 67, 113, 143 n.9
    efficiency and 55
wartime food policy 22–3, 87, 156 n.25
Wartime Meals Division 112, 120–1
wartime nutrition (Waldie) 55
Webb, Beatrice 46
Welfare Food Service 101
Western Times 44
Westminster Bridge canteen 29–30, 33
Wharton, Michael 135
'Wider Aspects of Food Control' (1936, Beveridge) 74, 86, 111
Women's Voluntary Service (WVS) 97, 122, 125
Workers National Committee 88
working-class communities 21, 34–5, 87
Working Class Cost of Living (Sumner) Committee (1918) 52
working class diet (surveys) 17
working class women 16, 22–3, 36, 127, 135
    communal kitchens (Liverpool) 42
    female leadership in public feeding 46–50
    during First World War 79
    at organizational level 45
    Patriotic Food League 23
    'permanent relief' 75–7
    voluntary communal kitchens 37
    wartime communal eating 22

Zweiniger-Bargielowska, Ina 126, 139–40
    Austerity in Britain 157 n.4

Printed in Dunstable, United Kingdom

65232524R00112